REVIVAL

Also by Richard Wolffe

The Victim's Fortune (with John Authers)

Renegade

REVIVAL

THE STRUGGLE FOR SURVIVAL
INSIDE THE OBAMA WHITE HOUSE

RICHARD WOLFFE

Broadway Paperbacks
NEW YORK

For Paula, Ilana, Ben, and Max

CONTENTS

PROLOGUE

The day after he signed health care reform into law, and into the history books, Barack Obama was walking the hallways of the West Wing in unusually high spirits. He had just endured the most desperate struggle for political survival since his presidential campaign. Two months earlier, on the anniversary of his extraordinary inauguration, his presidency was pronounced dead, his political capital spent, his party in disarray. His domestic agenda was lost, along with the Senate seat held by the late Ted Kennedy, who had loudly championed both health care and Obama's election.

But today he paced through his aides' offices in his shirtsleeves, with an energy that had been absent from those hallways for the last several weeks. "We're fired up and ready to go!" he said as he burst out of the office of his press secretary and longtime aide Robert Gibbs. The next day he would return to Iowa City, for a rally with the students of the University of Iowa, where he had promised to deliver health care reform three years earlier. The young voters of Iowa had believed in him and his candidacy at a time when his campaign was flatlining and even he harbored doubts about his prospects. Yet Iowa had proved the pundits wrong about the renegade candidate, and health care had done the same for the ambitious new president.

The last two months seemed to mirror the long campaign, with its huge pendulum swings from failure to triumph and back again. Looking back through the prism of his ultimate victory, Obama seemed destined to win. But that was not the reality of the campaign in real time. He was an ingénue until he won in Iowa; then he was an overnight phenomenon. His defeat in New Hampshire turned him into just another flash in the pan; then victory in South Carolina turned him into a postracial healer. He was on a winning streak for a month of primaries; then he was a loser who could not close the deal for several months. He united a confident party with Joe Biden and Hillary Clinton in Denver; then he watched his party promptly lose its head for the next several weeks over Sarah Palin.

His presidency followed the same trajectory: from the historic unity of his inauguration to the determined opposition of congressional Republicans; from the quick passage of the vast Recovery Act to the slow death of health care and the defeat in Massachusetts. Now the pendulum had swung back toward triumph with his signing of health care reform, and he was savoring the moment of delivering on a big campaign promise.

"Hey, what are you doing here?" he asked me, as he glimpsed me sitting in the corner outside Gibbs's office, waiting to interview one of his aides. "How did you get one of those big fancy passes?" he asked, pointing to the red press pass around my neck.

"Stand up," one of his staffers whispered to me as she jumped to attention. I looked at her, and looked at him. The president rolled his eyes, and I rolled mine. "Yeah, sorry," I said, standing up slowly. I asked how it felt to have just made history with health care.

"I'm good," he said. "This is a big day."

They were all big days at this stage of his presidency. When he wasn't confronting Republicans, negotiating with members of Congress, or rallying Democrats, he was confronting the Iranian regime, negotiating with the Israeli prime minister, and rallying allies. All presidents need to balance their domestic and international policies, and they all bounce between the planned events of their agenda and the chaos of the latest crisis. But he was emerging from a series of crises with a spirit of revival and a sense of humor.

"Gibbs, do you know Wolffe is here? Have you all checked the thumb drives?"

This book is the result of more than two months of intensive, daily reporting from the White House, and several more months of extensive interviews with every senior West Wing official from the president and vice president on down. While Obama's aides did not share their thumb drives, they did share memos, PowerPoints, notes, and many hours of real-time and rearview observations.

The initial idea was to paint a portrait of a White House at work, as it pivoted from governing to campaigning in the midterm elections and beyond. The traditional notion of the first year (or the first one hundred days) seemed totally arbitrary; you could only tell the full story of a presidency after four or eight years. So this book was intended as a picture of a work in progress, covering thirty days of action from the economy to national security. Gibbs identified mid-January to mid-February 2010 as a good month to start the stopwatch, "because health care will be over by then," he assured me two months earlier. He could not have been more wrong. Health care, along with the presidency, moved from the disaster of the Massachusetts defeat to the realization of a Democratic dream. In a two-month span, around the first anniversary of Obama's inauguration, you could trace the arc of this presidency. On the journey from near death to rebirth, you could see the near-fatal flaws and the dogged defense, the internal rifts and the instincts that led to recovery.

More than capturing the behind-the-scenes drama of the West Wing, one of my goals was to examine the core question of this new presidency: how did the president and his staff transition from campaigning to governing? The Obama White House faced a unique version of this age-old challenge. Obama had spent twenty-one months campaigning to be president, far longer than any of his recent predecessors. The campaign was more than just the formative experience of his aides: it was their shared identity. Not until the midterm elections of 2010 had they spent the same length of time inside the White House as on the campaign trail. For a president who had managed nothing of size until his own campaign, this was more than just a question of counting months. His adaptation from electioneering to governing—finding a balance between his campaign spirit and his presidential persona—was the essential challenge inside the Obama White House. Could he bring Change to Washington without Washington changing him?

When you witness how quickly presidents age in office, it is hard to believe they can pass through the Oval Office unchanged. Obama's fresh candidate face had rapidly grown as scored and worn as his temples had grown gray. Perhaps a president's core principles survive intact even as he shifts his positions on policies. But even Obama's closest aides conceded there were changes, if only in his style of decision making. "It's like watching kids grow. If you're there every day you don't really see it," said David Axelrod, Obama's senior adviser and chief strategist. "The remarkable thing about him was how natural governing was from the beginning. He looked comfortable in there on the first day. I'm too close to know how he's changed. When you have to make the kind of decisions he's made you become wiser. I think the decision-making process becomes easier. You know what you need to make decisions and you know what you need to get there."

If Axelrod did not know how Obama had changed, other aides confessed they shared the outside world's incomprehension of Obama's true feelings. There was an inscrutable quality to his steadiness, which could make him seem calm in a crisis and clinical in a catastrophe. Did he ever enjoy the office of the presidency, which he had worked so long and hard to win? "I would love to know the answer to that question," said one long-standing aide. "Does he enjoy being president? He doesn't show it. Other than getting gray hair, there seems no difference to me. He still has a sense of humor. But he's an amazingly steady guy."

Others witnessed something other than steadiness: a steeliness when shutting down even close aides, and a soft touch when opening up to others. Senior staff spoke privately of policy discussions that ended with a piercing presidential stare and an icy, abrupt command from Obama: "Next!"

That brusque manner was a stark contrast to the personal attention he paid to those who needed help. He encouraged overweight staffers to shed pounds. He gave one aide a salad for lunch, then listened to him protest that he could take care of his own health. "I love you, man," Obama said. "I want you to look after yourself. Eat the salad."

He sympathized with staffers when the media came after them, as they came after him on a regular basis. Axelrod felt miserable when a *New York Times* profile criticized his own performance after the Massachusetts defeat. Later that day, Obama walked into Axelrod's office and slumped into his sofa. "It's just Washington nonsense," he said. "Don't worry about it." Axelrod was surprised that his boss took the time to lift his mood. "He's not cold and detached," he said. "He's the first person to be concerned if you're having a bad day. He's attuned to people's moods in ways you don't expect."

For all his self-discipline and steadiness, Obama found it hard to dismiss the Washington nonsense quite so easily himself. Despite his advice to Axelrod, he seemed obsessed by the media coverage and consumed it voraciously. "He reads everything," said one close aide. "And I mean *everything*. Every news story, every column. It's driving everyone crazy."

As their political fortunes declined around the anniversary of the inauguration, Obama's aides started to miss the old campaign days of constant travel and uncertainty. "I told the president I long for the carefree days of simply getting him elected to this office," said Gibbs in the middle of the health care debate. "Everything that comes to me is hard and it hasn't been solved because it's hard. Then I understand why the days are so long here. I look at my schedule every morning and there aren't a lot of things going great. You go to the Situation Room and everything isn't going great. You feel it at the end of the week."

The solution for Gibbs and other campaign veterans was to revive the campaign spirit inside the White House. If they did not return to the mood of the 2008 election, they would be facing far more people like Scott Brown, the Republican candidate who won Ted Kennedy's Senate seat in one of the safest Democratic states in the country. "I think in many ways what drove people to vote for Barack Obama in '08 is the same thing that drove people to vote for Scott Brown in '10," Gibbs said. "They're frustrated with what is happening in this country. People also understand this isn't going to happen overnight. It's going to take two years to dig out of this hole. I think people have seen recently somebody who is willing to challenge both sides to get a solution. We have to keep reminding them that the Barack Obama [who] is president of the United States is the same guy who ran. He has the same cares and concerns."

Perhaps that was true of his politics. But the pressures of the presidency—the constant scrutiny and security—seemed to turn his focus inward once he entered the black gates of the White House. Obama's circle of friends and confidants shrank rather than expanded. "Our conversations are a little more intimate now because there are very few people he can really talk freely with, without them misreading something into it," said Obama's close friend Marty Nesbitt. "He's more inclined to think out loud when I'm around."

How and why Obama grew detached from Change—even as he was enacting big changes—is one of the stories at the heart of his White House. It is the paradox of a president who wanted to effect change while seeming unchanged, who entered office on a wave of public emotion while appearing unmoved by it all, who campaigned as an outsider and governed as an insider. In this defining period of his presidency, he was forced to reexamine himself and his team. From the depths of a brutal winter inside the Oval Office to the beginnings of spring in the Rose Garden, this is a tale of despair and discovery, of survival and revival.

ONE

DESTINATION

Behind the tall front doors of the White House, the Executive Mansion is normally empty most mornings. The brooding portrait of John F. Kennedy watches over the pink marble floors, bloodred carpet, and gilded chairs. The only sound tends to come from the cramped usher's office that is tucked away in a corner of the entrance hall, on what they call the State Floor.

Not today. A Marine pianist jauntily taps out "The Entertainer" on the White House Steinway. Al Franken, the comedian-turned-senator, lingers in the hallway to chat with a group of his new peers, while other Democratic grandees rush up the stairs from the visitors' foyer.

Most are desperate to grab a prominent seat inside the expansive East Room. The front rows are already full of self-satisfied lawmakers. The new arrivals look confused about where to locate themselves, not least Arlen Specter, the Republican senator from Pennsylvania who only recently switched parties in an attempt to save his political career. A frail Frank Lautenberg, the octogenarian New Jersey Democrat, shuffles along the front row, his hair cropped short as he endures treatment for stomach cancer.

The atmosphere is something between an office party and a tourist attraction. When they are not thumbing their BlackBerrys, the guests are snapping photos of each other. Representative Sheila Jackson Lee from Texas has a small digital camera, while Senator Patrick Leahy from Vermont shoots with his full-blown professional SLR. Others are taking shots with their BlackBerrys. At the back of the opulent room, close to the portraits and crystal lights, is a compressed pack of photographers, TV cameras, and reporters. Some members of Congress can resist everything but the temptation of the media. New York's Anthony Weiner, one of the loudest liberal voices, grants another radio interview at the back of the room. The chatter from members of Congress almost drowns out the music. A few weeks ago, many of the politicians in this room were rushing to abandon the president's agenda and to question his leadership abilities. Now they are squeezing into the White House to see him sign a piece of paper. "It's a shit show in there," says one young White House staffer, pushed out of the East Room doors by the congressional crush.

White House staffers look even less certain about where to sit. Zeke Emanuel, a health policy adviser in the budget office and older brother to Obama's chief of staff, spots a seat in the fourth row. Chief economic adviser Larry Summers finds an empty space in the same section, close to Susan Sher, the First Lady's chief of staff. Press secretary Robert Gibbs walks in as the room reaches full capacity. "I'm very happy, very happy," he says. "But probably not as happy as the people who did the legislative drafting." Still, he is far happier than the staffers trying to enter the room behind him. A Secret Service agent blocks the doorway to political director Patrick Gaspard. "We're not letting staff in right now," the agent tells Gaspard, who can only smile at his bad luck. Gaspard is shooed back into the stairway leading down to the ground floor, along with Treasury adviser Gene Sperling, a veteran of the Clinton White House. Another White House staffer insists on clearing a path for the congressional leaders who have yet to arrive. "Can I just hang out here?" Gibbs asks, pressing himself close to a fireplace. "I'm just happy to be here," he explains.

Suddenly the room hushes as Joe Reinstein, the East Wing's deputy social secretary, makes an announcement: please refrain from holding cameras in the air as the president signs the bill; otherwise the media will not have a clear shot of the historic moment. "What did you say? What? What?" barks out Roland Burris, the new Illinois senator, whose reputation has never recovered from his questionable appointment by the state's scandal-plagued governor. Burris is simultaneously speaking on his cell phone as he challenges the White House aide, and the rest of his colleagues join in to jeer at the new rules. "If they want to see it, the entire press corps is here to film it for them," complains the East Wing staffer. "They don't need to get their own YouTube video."

The amateur photography does not stop. Even Bobby Rush, the Illinois representative who defeated Obama in his first run for Congress in 2000, is playing nice. Rush, a former Black Panther, can barely hide his disdain for Obama in front of the media. But now he is taking photos of David Axelrod and Susan Sher. A cheer goes up as several women senators walk in. "Rowdy animals," says Reinstein, growing ever more troubled by the unruly scene. Eighty-three-year-old John Dingell hobbles into the room on crutches, ahead of a procession of Democratic leaders from Capitol Hill. Dingell first won his seat in Congress in 1955, after the untimely death of his father, who had helped create Social Security and started work on national health care. At the beginning of every session of Congress since 1957, Dingell reintroduced his father's health care bill, in a vain gesture toward the priorities and principles of another era. Now he hauls himself to witness the realization of what remains.

Standing alone by the fireplace, with a raincoat draped over his arm, is Patrick Kennedy, the younger son of Ted Kennedy. It is nearly seven months since the death of his father, the most influential early supporter of the Obama campaign and the chief advocate of health care reform. And it is barely a month since Patrick himself declared he would not run for reelection as a congressman for Rhode Island. A year from now, there will be no Kennedys in Congress for the first time in almost half a century. Struggling with the death of his father, Kennedy explained that he wanted to continue to work with people who, not unlike himself, were suffering from depression and drug addiction. He smiles wanly as staffers walk up to offer their congratulations and looks on from a distance as his stepmother, Vicki Kennedy, embraces David Axelrod.

In his hand is an oversized card with some scribbled handwriting in blue Sharpie. It is a facsimile of a Senate bill numbered 4297, introduced by his father in 1970, called the Health Security Act. That bill was a long way from today's legislation: a single-payer government-run system covering the entire country at no direct cost to the patient and financed through payroll taxes. But written at the bottom, Patrick suggested that Obama had inherited the Kennedy spirit. "President Obama, My father carried on his brothers' legacy of social justice in health care," he wrote. "You not only have completed it, but you renewed our faith in the possible and made us once again proud to call you our president." He signed off, as if writing to a cousin, "Love, Patrick."

Patrick Kennedy had been there onstage, alongside his father and his cousin Caroline, when the family endorsed Obama in the midst of the epic primary contest against Hillary Clinton. Little more than two years ago, Ted Kennedy drew a direct line from his own brother John to the freshman senator who had burst onto the scene. "With Barack Obama, we will break the old gridlock and finally make health care what it should be in America—a fundamental right for all, not just an expensive privilege for the few," he promised a raucous crowd of students at American University in Washington, D.C. Now was the time to reject what he called "the counsels of doubt and calculation." Kennedy cited the plea for unity, for an end to petty quarrels, echoing a speech that his brother had planned to deliver to Democrats in Austin, Texas, on the day of his assassination: "When John Kennedy thought of going to the moon, he didn't say no, it was too far, maybe we couldn't get there and shouldn't even try. I am convinced we can reach our goals only if we are 'not petty when our cause is so great'—only if we find a way past the stale ideas and stalemate of our times—only if we replace the politics of fear with the politics of hope—and only if we have the courage to choose change." The hyperbole was rarely, surprisingly, too much for Obama: a moment when his extreme self-control cracked. "It was the first time I got emotional," he told me later. "I actually choked up. It wasn't just the endorsement. It was the young people out there. You could see that it was something similar to what had happened all those years ago."

Yet the stalemate of our times had stubbornly endured. The politics of hope had struggled with the politics of fear for a year, and only just emerged victorious by the narrowest of margins. Politics had been petty, and the Democrats had quarreled, even when the cause was great. In place of hope-filled students, there was a giddy room full of career politicians, including many of those "counsels of doubt and calculation." And there was a copy of a 1970 bill that had languished for four decades, undergoing several reincarnations, before this day of resurrection. Across the top of the facsimile, Patrick's older brother, Edward, wrote the date, March 23, 2010, adding, "The day, Mr. President, when you completed what my Dad called the great unfinished business of our country."

At precisely 11:30, Barack Obama and Joe Biden walk into the East Room to cheers, whistles, and a standing ovation. The Air Force aides working at the White House—normally the most stiff and formal of figures who control the crowds of visitors—jam their way through the doors to capture their own photos of the moment.

"Fired Up! Ready to Go!" chant the members of Congress, turning the White House into one of the rallies that pushed Obama to victory sixteen months earlier.

"Fired Up! Ready to Go!" They shout faster and louder, as Obama tries to quiet them.

"Fired Up! Ready to Go!" Just like the little woman in Greenwood, South Carolina, who revived the candidate on a dismal day when his campaign was struggling to survive.

"They're ready. Let them celebrate a little bit," Biden tells Obama as an aside.

"Mr. President, I think we got a happy room here," he says out loud, to laughter, as the lawmakers settle down. "Ladies and gentlemen, to state the obvious, this is a historic day." Few speakers like to state the obvious quite so much as Joe Biden, but self-awareness rarely constrains him. He launches into an extended soliloquy on his boss's place in history.

"History is not merely what is printed in textbooks. It doesn't begin or end with the stroke of a pen. History is *made*. History is made when men and women decide that there is a greater risk in accepting a situation that we cannot bear than in steeling our spine and embracing the promise of change. That's when history is made."

The steel in Obama's spine had long fascinated Joe Biden. A month before the election, he told campaign donors that the world would test Obama in the first six months in office. "They're going to want to test him, just like they did young John Kennedy," he warned. "And they're going to find out this guy's got steel in his spine."

Only today, the steel begins to buckle.

"History is made when a leader steps up, stays true to his values, and charts a fundamentally different course for the country," Biden gushes. "History is made when a leader's passion—*passion*—is matched with principle to set a new course. Well, ladies and gentlemen, Mr. President, you are that leader."

Unnoticed by the many reporters in front of him, Obama struggles to keep his tears in check. He purses his lips and presses his cheeks into his jaw. He attempts a feeble smile but keeps his jaw firmly clenched. As the room stands and applauds, Biden turns to Obama. "You deserve it, man," he says quietly. "You deserve it."

Turning back to the cameras, Biden heaps hyperbole on top of excess emotion. "Mr. President, your fierce advocacy, the clarity of purpose that you showed, your perseverance—these are in fact, it is not hyperbole to say—these are the reasons why we're assembled in this room together, today," Biden pours forth. Obama begins to breathe deeply and swallow hard. "But for those attributes, we would not be here. Many, many men and women are going to feel the pride that I feel in watching you shortly, watching you sign this bill, knowing that their work—their work has helped make this day possible. But, Mr. President, you're the guy that made it happen."

Obama clasps his hands tightly and hangs his head. There was only one other time when he lost his composure in public like this: on the eve of election day, when he told a crowd in Charlotte,

North Carolina, how his grandmother—the last living person to raise him through childhood—had just died. Then he managed to delay his tears just long enough to launch into his stump speech. Now it's not clear if he can make it through his vice president's introduction.

"Mr. President, I've gotten to know you well enough. You want me to stop because I'm embarrassing you," Biden says as the room breaks into laughter. Obama manages to crack a feeble smile and mouths the word *yes*. But he looks less embarrassed than pained.

With his head pressed down in front of the cameras, Obama is digging up some of the most emotional moments of his political career and his personal life. "I was thinking about . . . all the people I'd met over the course of the years, dating back to when I was a state legislator, who had told me heartbreaking stories about trying to get their kids insurance, trying to get their spouses insurance, losing their homes, struggling to pay medical bills," he tells me later.

He casts his mind back to a year earlier, when he first began to push for health care reform. Alongside him that day, in the same room, was the man who had worked so hard, and yet failed so many times, in the same quest: Ted Kennedy. Undergoing treatment for brain cancer in Florida, Kennedy had not traveled to Washington in a month. The only thing that could raise him from his bed, in what would be one of his last public appearances, was Obama's drive for health care reform. Kennedy insisted that now was the time for action; that the industry's competing interest groups were all on board; that much work had already been done in the Senate. "I'm looking forward to being a foot soldier in this undertaking," he signed off. "And this time, we will not fail."

They did fail at first, before they finally staggered their way to the point of success. And the memory of Ted Kennedy, the foot soldier they had sorely missed in the Senate, pushes Obama close to tears. "I thought about Ted Kennedy and how in that same room

I had escorted him out at one of his last public appearances, when he was so determined to get this done," he recalls.

When Biden finally hands the podium over to Obama, he leans into the president's left ear to leave him with an immortal statement of the obvious. For the last two weeks, it was beginning to dawn on Biden just how important health care reform would be for Obama and for their agenda. "I hadn't really focused on this," he would tell his staff, "but when this passes, it's going to be a big deal. It's going to be a game changer." Now, with the game changing before them, Biden can't resist a little more hype: "This is a big fucking deal."

Even more than the history, Obama wants to savor the moment: a moment when he can finally wrest control of the health care story from his opponents and turn a narrative of disappointment and defeat into one of hope and victory. "Today, after almost a century of trying; today, after over a year of debate; today, after all the votes have been tallied"—he pauses for a little drama—"health insurance reform becomes law in the United States of America. Today." Each time he says the word *today*, he pinches his finger and thumb together and pins the moment onto an imaginary board.

As the applause dies down, and the lawmakers sit down, he concedes that he—and they—are only just emerging from a long, discontented winter. "It is fitting that Congress passed this historic legislation this week," he says. "For as we mark the turning of spring, we also mark a new season in America. In a few moments, when I sign this bill, all of the overheated rhetoric over reform will finally confront the reality of reform." He acknowledges that Congress had taken its lumps over health care. ("Yes we did!" quips Gary Ackerman, a Long Island Democrat.) So he salutes the leadership of House Speaker Nancy Pelosi. ("Nancy! Nancy! Nancy!" chants her caucus.) And he praises Senate leader Harry Reid (to a polite round of applause). There were no Republicans to salute or praise.

These Democrats had taken tough votes, under enormous pressure. They had broken through the messy politics and the public attacks to vote with their conscience. And he admired them for that. "You felt like politics and democracy worked the way it should," he says later. "Not that it should be easy. Not that it should be smooth. But that a lot of hard work had paid off."

There is one more ghost in the East Room. The woman who struggled with her insurance as she fought against her cancer. The woman who drove his own hard work and his idealism. The woman who passed away before she saw him as a senator, a candidate, and a president. Her experience and his fraught memory of her final days were among the biggest reasons that he gambled his presidency on health care reform. "Yeah, I thought about my mom," he tells me later, in a subdued and somber tone, "and what she had to go through."

Before he recounts some of the most powerful stories he has told about health care—before signing the bill for the regular voters he met along the epic journey of the last year—he says that the bill is for the first patient whose insurance struggles outraged him.

Early in his presidential campaign, Obama was reluctant to tell the story of what happened to his mother. The story was too personal, and he professed to dislike politicians who exploited their personal lives. But for someone who had mined his own life story in his books and speeches, that position seemed untenable, and he was soon taping ads about his mother's experience and weaving her story into his stump speech. "I don't accept the idea that we don't have a decent health care system. And part of the reason I don't is because I remember my mother," he told an outdoor rally in Santa Barbara, California, two and a half years earlier.

> She was fifty-two years old when she died of ovarian cancer. And
> you know what she was thinking about in the last months of her

life? She wasn't thinking about getting well. She wasn't thinking about coming to terms with her own mortality. She had been diagnosed just as she was transitioning between jobs. And she wasn't sure whether insurance was going to cover her medical expenses because they might consider this a pre-existing condition. And I remember just being heartbroken, seeing her struggling through the paperwork and the medical bills and the insurance forms. So I have seen what it's like when somebody you love is suffering because of a broken health care system.

He was heartbroken by her insurance struggles, and stricken by her loss. Stanley Ann Dunham succumbed rapidly to uterine and ovarian cancer, which was initially misdiagnosed. It was 1995, the same year Obama published his memoir, nominally about another, absent parent, *Dreams from My Father*. In September he announced his first run for elected office, for an Illinois state senate seat. Less than two months later, his mother passed away in Hawaii. His sister Maya arrived from New York on the day Ann died; Obama did not make it until the day after. The sorrow of missing her final hours weighed on him even as his presidential campaign drew to a close, when his maternal grandmother, Madelyn Dunham, suddenly neared her end. Just two weeks before election day, he was determined to say good-bye in person and stole away to Hawaii to see her for the last time.

As president, he could do so much more than watch as a bystander while others endured struggles like his mother's. His searing memories of her suffering made similar stories from regular Americans more personal. They gave him a reason to endure a year of attacks, widespread predictions of his political demise, and the near death of the entire effort. "This is something very personal for me," he told one town hall audience in July 2009, before launching into his mother's story early in the health care debate.

His mother's insurer ultimately relented; Obama didn't. "Today, I'm signing this reform bill into law on behalf of my mother," he says eight months later, as he raises his head and straightens his back, "who argued with insurance companies even as she battled cancer in her final days."

Now, in the public splendor of the East Room, he reaches for some redemption. He talks about America rewriting its destiny, overcoming all the odds and all the doubts to fashion a more hopeful future:

> Our presence here today is remarkable and improbable. With all the punditry, all of the lobbying, all of the game-playing that passes for governing in Washington, it's been easy at times to doubt our ability to do such a big thing, such a complicated thing; to wonder if there are limits to what we, as a people, can still achieve. It's easy to succumb to the sense of cynicism about what's possible in this country.
>
> But today, we are affirming that essential truth—a truth every generation is called to rediscover for itself—that we are not a nation that scales back its aspirations. We are not a nation that falls prey to doubt or mistrust. We don't fall prey to fear. We are not a nation that does what's easy. That's not who we are. That's not how we got here.

He may be talking about the country, but his words apply just as well to himself: a new president who overcame the cynics to rewrite his own legacy; a new senator, with no money or machine, who beat the biggest names in politics to win the presidency; a rootless young man, with little family support, who found purpose and drive in his books and his politics. Now he could write another chapter of the American story, weaving together his experience with the nation's—no matter how unusual and unique his identity was. It was a perspective, and a political device, that had succeeded since he rose to fame onstage at the Democratic convention six years ago. And it still had the power to sound optimistic, patriotic, and uplifting after months of petty Washington squabbling, backstabbing, and name-calling.

As the president is speaking, Patrick Kennedy steps forward to kiss Nancy Pelosi and his stepmother, Vicki. Obama's senior advisers David Axelrod and Robert Gibbs pose for more photos. And soon the room is on its feet, with cameras aloft, no matter what the East Wing aide had requested.

Obama walks across the stage, sits down at a small desk, and signs into law the Patient Protection and Affordable Care Act. The long-awaited Democratic dream of health care reform takes a little longer to be signed: Obama uses twenty-two pens to write his name, dividing each letter into partial strokes. He gives away nineteen pens as mementos, keeps one for himself, and donates two to the archives. "I've got to use every pen, so it's going to take a really long time," he explains. "I didn't practice."

He stands up, shakes hands, and turns out of the room to his motorcade. His staffers scramble to their vans. "Suck it up," one junior staffer shouts into his cell phone as he negotiates a logistical road bump. "We're changing the world today." Outside, the South Lawn is alive with cherry blossoms on an overcast spring morning. The armored presidential limo rumbles past the golden Victory statue on top of the column honoring the U.S. Army's First Division. It picks up speed close to a group of tourists perched atop Segways. Then it stops at the austere Depression-era Department of the Interior less than a minute after leaving the White House.

Inside a darkened auditorium, a giant golden eagle spreads its wings over an old-fashioned stage, whose proscenium arch is framed by stone reliefs. Six flags stand in front of a deep blue backdrop and behind the presidential podium flanked by teleprompters. From the neat rows of seats—filled with administration officials, political friends, and former campaign staffers—comes the chant that carried him through his first major defeat in New Hampshire: "Yes We Can." The stage fills with the faces that helped humanize the health care debate. Marcelas Owens, an eleven-year-old boy who lost his uninsured mother. The sister of Natoma Canfield, an Ohio mother who ditched her insurance and is now battling leukemia. Vicki Kennedy, whose husband never witnessed the final victory for the cause of his life, joins in the chant. "Yes We Can."

"Yes he did!" says a beaming Joe Biden.

Obama's words circle around the aspirations and themes of twenty-one months on the campaign trail. He talks of the power of organizing people, of faith and hope overcoming fear and failure. "After a century of striving, after a year of debate, after a historic vote, health care reform is no longer an unmet promise," he says to sustained applause. "It is the law of the land."

In fact, the entire Obama project—the notion that Change can overcome the vested interests and professional skeptics that populate the nation's capital—is no longer an unmet promise. Throughout his campaign, candidate Obama galvanized his volunteers and voters by insisting that their mission was not about him—even as he was its organizing principle. Now he speaks about their combined effort, even though this victory had far less to do with their resilience than with his. "Although it may be my signature that's affixed to the bottom of this bill, it was your work, your commitment, your unyielding hope that made this victory possible," he said. "And when the opposition said this just wasn't the right time, you didn't want to wait another year, or another decade, or another generation for reform. You felt the fierce urgency of now."

"The fierce urgency of now" was his rallying cry in the fall of 2007, when he took the fight to Hillary Clinton before the primary season began. It was a phrase he used at Howard University in D.C., borrowing from Martin Luther King Jr. Now was the time, he argued, to build on the history of the civil rights movement. "I am not just running to make history," he told students at the historically black college. "I'm running because I believe that together, we can change history's course. It's not enough just to look back in wonder of how far we've come—I want us to look ahead with a fierce urgency at how far we have left to go." King spoke of the fierce urgency of now at New York's Riverside Church, the year before he was gunned down. He was opposing the war in Vietnam, pushing his movement toward action in a new direction. "We are now faced with the fact, my friends, that tomorrow is today," King said. "We are confronted with the fierce urgency of now. In this unfolding conundrum of life and history, there is such a thing as being too late. Procrastination is still the thief of time."

Obama idolized the movement, lying awake at night and dreaming of civil rights and Dr. King. He knew he was too late, and too young. Still, he deployed the language and techniques of the movement, the idealism and impatience, to help propel his presidential campaign. But it rang hollow—or worse, presumptuous and self-absorbed—to demand the fierce urgency of his own election. King had tried to change the nation, and succeeded.

Now, after two years of campaigning and a year of the presidency, Obama casts himself as the leader of another movement that changed history's course. He and his followers did not face down billy clubs and police dogs, but more abstract foes. "You met the lies with truth. You met cynicism with conviction," he says. "Most of all, you met fear with a force that's a lot more powerful—and that is faith in America. So this victory is not mine—it is your victory. It's a victory for the United States of America."

In February 2007, Obama had warned of the smallness of our politics on a frigid day in Springfield, Illinois, when he launched his presidential campaign—what he called his improbable journey. In contrast to what he called petty and trivial distractions, he played the role of the grand narrator of a sweeping American story. To build his campaign, he combined his young ambition to be a novelist with the techniques of a community organizer, weaving together the stories of the people he met along the way.

The movement and his spirits have been sustained by stories. The stories of people like Marcelas and Natoma. And especially the story of a young campaign volunteer named Ashley Baia, who is sitting in the auditorium today. Baia had become a totem of the campaign. He told her story in Atlanta at King's church, Ebenezer, and again in Philadelphia, during his speech on race, as he tried to quash the controversy surrounding his own pastor, the Reverend Jeremiah Wright. A twenty-three-year-old white woman, Ashley was organizing mostly African Americans in Florence, South Carolina. She started a discussion by telling her own story: how, when she was nine, her mother got cancer and lost her job. To save money to pay medical bills, Ashley ate mustard and relish sandwiches for a year. She told how she joined the campaign to help millions of children like her, whose families had no health care. Then she asked everyone to share their stories, before she came to an elderly black man who had been sitting silently. When Ashley asked why he was there, he didn't say for health care, or the economy, or to see the first African American president. He said, "I am here because of Ashley. I am here because of this young girl, and the fact that she's willing to fight for what she believes in. And that reminds me that I still have some fight left in me, and I'm going to stand up for what I believe in."

Now Ashley's story reminds Obama why he has been fighting. He seeks her out in the auditorium to help explain why he risked everything in the last few months. "Where's Ashley? She's around here somewhere. I know she is." He looks out into the darkness.

"There she is, right in front. She just doesn't like waving. Ashley decided to get involved with our campaign a couple of years ago because her own mother lost her job, and with it, her health insurance when she got sick. And they had to file bankruptcy. And so Ashley worked tirelessly, not to get me elected, but to solve a problem that millions of families across the country were facing.

"Each of these Americans made their voices heard. It's because of them, and so many others, so many of you, that real, meaningful change is coming to the United States of America. It is because of you that we did not quit. It's because of you that Congress did not quit. It's because of you that I did not quit. It's because of you."

He rubs his eye as the emotion rises and subsides. "Now," he says, the steel returning to his spine, "let me tell you what change looks like."

For the twenty-one months of his presidential campaign, Barack Obama had promised to bring Change to Washington—Change you could believe in, as his backdrop promised at every event through the primary contests. But for most of the first twelve months of his presidency, it looked like Washington had changed him. He wanted to find common ground with Republicans, but compromise only seemed to take place on the small stuff, like credit card reform, where the public mostly couldn't see it. He campaigned as an outsider who could battle the nation's vested interests and the tired old political class. Yet he seemed to govern as an insider who would cut deals with those same vested interests and who was beholden to the same political class. The sense of authenticity in his candidacy gave way to the conventional tokens of the presidency: a round seal stuck to a stocky podium, precooked remarks on a teleprompter, a motorcade led by two limos with darkened windows.

His presidency began with a flurry of Change. There was a

monumentally large economic stimulus bill, designed to save an economy in free fall, at a cost of $814 billion, which equaled his predecessor's spending on the wars in Afghanistan and Iraq. There was outreach to foreign capitals that were either disillusioned with or downright hostile to the United States. And there were sweeping changes to the so-called war on terror: a promise to close the toxic prison at Guantánamo Bay, and the release of the Bush administration's secret memos justifying torture.

Yet those changes seemed to rest on shifting sands. The Recovery Act stopped the free fall but failed to halt the sharp rise in unemployment for many months. The outreach to Tehran was ultimately met with disdain, and the administration reverted to the pursuit of sanctions to stop Iran's nuclear programs. Guantánamo Bay could not be closed within the self-imposed deadline of one year. The president who once taught constitutional law had halted torture but was now considering the indefinite detention of terrorist suspects.

Were these real changes in Obama's politics and personality, or misconceptions based on faulty first impressions? Was he adapting to new realities or showing his true, hidden colors? What Change did *he* believe in?

A year before his inauguration, flying through the night on his campaign plane from Omaha to Seattle as the primaries dragged on beyond Super Tuesday, candidate Obama tried to spell out what he wanted to change. "It has been a running theme in my political career—the notion that there's something about our democracy that is broken that prevents us from solving real problems," he told me. "I think throughout my career I have tried to describe that, about what in our broken political process needs to be fixed. Divisions based more on ideological or racial or religious constructs than they're based on deeply rooted beliefs—that's part of the change I've talked about. The dominance of special interests and money in politics—

that's part of the change I've talked about. The lack of participation and involvement in decision making—that's part of the change I've talked about. The need to cut through the spin and PR and to be able to present things honestly to the American people—that's part of the change I've talked about."

Long before he started work on health care legislation, Obama wanted to change the national political debate to bring about Change. "There's a need to recognize what we have in common, a sense of empathy with each other in order to come to some basic agreements," he continued. "I would include in that list a need to engage in some long-term thinking. Our politics isn't designed to think about the next generation. The biggest challenge of our campaign isn't that people necessarily disagree with my analysis of what needs to be changed. I think those who prefer Senator Clinton over me may be more skeptical about the possibilities of change and there might be some correlation with older voters thinking, 'You know what? The system can't be fixed and so the best we can do is to find somebody who can work the system.'

"I don't believe we can counteract the power of special interests and lobbyists in the health care debate unless the American people are engaged in that process, and are not going to be persuaded that serious health care reform is going to make them worse off. So ensuring that the American people trust what their government says, that they are part of an honest debate, that money isn't completely skewing the process, all these things are necessary to deliver on better housing, better schools, better health care, affordable college education."

Two years later, the debate about his approach was no less intense. Was he naive about the system, about winning over Republicans, about beating down the lobbyists? Or was he just the opposite? Was he using the language of reform to reach out to independents, while still holding on to his base and passing big legislation through Congress? Was he writing new political rules or mastering the same old ones?

The conundrum was a familiar one to the enigmatic and contradictory character now known as the president of the United States. Obama campaigned most effectively as a renegade (his Secret Service code name). He didn't wait his turn to run for president; instead he leapfrogged over the party's most established, better-funded, and more connected names. He galvanized his supporters by challenging conventional politics: encouraging Republicans and independents to vote in Democratic primaries; refusing lobbyists' cash and seeking small donations on the Internet; questioning short-term political gimmicks to deal with rising gas prices. He took his campaign overseas with a full press plane, staged his acceptance speech outdoors, and refused public financing in the general election.

Yet for all the rule breaking and history making, he was also deeply cautious, hesitant, second-guessing and indecisive. He pandered to interest groups or labor unions as well as any other politician. He lavished attention on the party insiders who would decide his nomination as superdelegates. His policy framework was conventionally Democratic, from health care to the economy and foreign policy.

Finding a balance between the renegade rule breaker and the conventional rule follower was never clear, easy, or predictable. He eschewed personal-attack politics and called out his campaign staff when they engaged in the usual slash-and-burn electioneering. But when he needed to prove himself and rescue his candidacy—at the latest possible stage—he could tear down his rivals in a way that belied his previous reluctance. He questioned Hillary Clinton's credibility and courage; he challenged John McCain for being erratic, uncertain, and confused. He was, as his friends liked to call him, a clutch fourth-quarter player.

On the first anniversary of his inauguration, he was already in the fourth quarter. He had spent the best part of the year negotiating a health care package in a protracted struggle that prompted dismay among progressives and reenergized opposition among conservatives. While the economy continued to shed jobs, he was spending billions of taxpayers' dollars to save the banks and carmakers. Then, on the verge of a historic deal over health care reform, the bottom fell out.

What followed was a personal, defining test of this president: of his character, his mission, and his style of politics; of who he is and who he wants to be. The Massachusetts defeat shocked him out of his complacency and stagnation, forcing him to change course but not his destination. For his predecessor, the terrorist attacks of 9/11 were the touchstone moment that would attest to his character and define his mission. Barack Obama's trial by fire was less violent and yet harder to pass. There was no immediate public rallying behind his position as leader. Indeed, the conventional wisdom from elected politicians and pundits was that he should drop his plans, scale back his ambitions, and retool his White House.

Obama had faced such gloomy turning points before: after losing his first race for Congress in 2000, as his campaign flatlined in 2007, and after successive primary defeats the following year. But there was one early challenge that foreshadowed his current situation. This was a test of purpose and willpower, of identity and self-belief. After Obama spent just one year working on the South Side of Chicago as an ill-defined and poorly paid community organizer, his boss decided to quit, and he thought Obama should go, too. The scale of the problems—the local politics and racial divisions—was too great for his mentor Jerry Kellman (named "Marty" in Obama's memoir). If Obama stayed, he was bound to fail. If he wasn't really trying to change things, he might as well forget it.

"Ah, yes. *Real* change," Obama wrote a decade later about his work at the Altgeld Gardens housing project. "It had seemed like such an attainable goal back in college, an extension of my personal will and my mother's faith, like boosting my grade point average or giving up liquor: a matter of taking and assigning responsibility. Only now, after a year of organizing, nothing seemed simple. Who was responsible for a place like Altgeld? I found myself asking. There were no cigar-chomping crackers like Bull Connor out there, no club-wielding Pinkerton thugs. Just a small band of older black men and women, a group characterized less by malice or calculation than by fear and small greeds."

Without an obviously evil enemy, and with downtrodden and lackluster allies, Obama was left with himself: with his abilities and discipline, his expectations and ambitions. "I did feel that there was something to prove—to the people of Altgeld, to Marty, to my father, to myself," he explained about his reasons for staying. "That what I did counted for something. That I wasn't a fool chasing pipe dreams."

This is the story of how President Obama tried to prove that he wasn't a fool chasing pipe dreams.

Just two days before the Democrats' loss of the Massachusetts Senate race, the Obama family drove a few minutes north of the White House to Sunday services at a redbrick church capped by a tall steeple. Founded by seven freed slaves, the Vermont Avenue Baptist Church was ready to celebrate the birthday of Martin Luther King Jr. As the Obamas entered through a side door, the choir fired up the gospel classic "We'll Understand It Better By and By," an up-tempo affirmation of endurance in hard times: "Temptations, hidden snares / Often take us unawares / And our hearts are made to bleed / For a thoughtless word or deed / And we wonder why the test / When we try to do our best / But we'll understand it better by and by." The church's nervous pastor, Cornelius Wheeler, stepped up to the podium. "In case you haven't noticed, some important stuff is happening here today," he said, before boasting about the birth of his granddaughter. "Oh, by the way, President Obama is here," he added, to laughter, before explaining how proud the church felt about Obama's inauguration a year ago, almost to the day. What he couldn't figure out were Obama's many foes. "I don't know about the political correctness of this next statement, but it took eight years for them to mess everything up," the reverend told the president. "I don't know why they don't have a little more patience while you fix it."

The Sunday before Martin Luther King Day was a special moment on the Obama calendar. On the same day two years ago, Obama was speaking at King's church in Atlanta as he fought for survival in the early stages of the presidential primaries. He had just lost in New Hampshire and Nevada, and desperately needed the overwhelming support of African Americans in the next contest in South Carolina. Today he was on the verge of defeat in Massachusetts, the economy was stubbornly slow to recover, and his domestic agenda seemed doomed to failure.

On the cover of the church program was a photo of Martin Luther King Jr., who had preached at the same Washington church a half century earlier, in far more desperate times. When he spoke there, King had just won the Supreme Court order to stop segregation on Montgomery's buses after a historic, yearlong boycott. Yet there was little confidence to believe that this court ruling would end Jim Crow any faster than *Brown v. Board of Education* had changed the South's schools two years earlier. In short, there was little confidence in Change.

Not for the first time, Obama drew a direct line between the trials of the civil rights movement and his own plight today:

It's not hard for us, then, to imagine that moment. We can imagine folks coming to this church, happy about the boycott being over. We can also imagine them, though, coming here concerned about their future, sometimes second-guessing strategy, maybe fighting off some creeping doubts, perhaps despairing about whether the movement in which they had placed so many of their hopes—a movement in which they believed so deeply—could actually deliver on its promise.

Reverend Wheeler mentioned the inauguration, last year's election. You know, on the heels of that victory over a year ago, there were some who suggested that somehow we had entered into a post-racial America, all those problems would be solved. There were those who argued that because I had spoke of a need for unity in this country that our nation was somehow entering into a period of post-partisanship. That didn't work out so well. There was a hope shared by many that life would be better from the moment that I swore that oath.

Of course, as we meet here today, one year later, we know the promise of that moment has not yet been fully fulfilled.

High unemployment, two wars, rising poverty, poor health care, bankruptcy: the litany was bleak. "Bruised, battered, many people are legitimately feeling doubt, even despair, about the future. Like those who came to this church on that Thursday in 1956, folks are wondering, where do we go from here?" he asked.

"So, yes, we're passing through a hard winter. It's the hardest in some time. But let's always remember that, as a people, the American people, we've weathered some hard winters before."

How had previous generations, especially King's, survived all those winters? They were firm in their resolve and they believed in the power of government to do good. They took small steps and compromised when large steps weren't possible. And they appealed to the conscience, to a shared sense of equality and justice. Above all, King overcame his challenges because he refused to be diverted.

> He remained strategically focused on gaining ground—his eyes on the prize constantly—understanding that change would not be easy, understanding that change wouldn't come overnight, understanding that there would be setbacks and false starts along the way, but understanding, as he said in 1956, that "we can walk and never get weary, because we know there is a great camp meeting in the promised land of freedom and justice."

For all the tough talk, the historical references, and the inspirational rhetoric, Obama wasn't just talking about something abstract. The trial, the disappointment, the harsh winter were also acutely personal. He, too, was facing failure. Even as he presumptuously likened his position to that of one of the most consequential African American leaders in history, he was conceding his frailties, his temper, his impatience, and his thin skin.

"You know, folks ask me sometimes why I look so calm," he said as the congregation chuckled. "They say, all this stuff coming at you, how come you just seem calm? And I have a confession to make here. There are times where I'm not so calm. Reggie Love knows. My wife knows. There are times when progress seems too slow. There are times when the words that are spoken about me hurt. There are times when the barbs sting. There are times when it feels like all these efforts are for naught, and change is so painfully slow in coming, and I have to confront my own doubts."

What helped him to overcome his doubts? He called it faith, as he stood in church. But it sounded like something more than that: there was a trust in God but also the power of self-belief, stubborn optimism, sheer determination, and a sense of community.

"But let me tell you, during those times it's faith that keeps me calm," he continued to applause.

> It's faith that gives me peace. The same faith that leads a single mother to work two jobs to put a roof over her head when she has doubts. The same faith that keeps an unemployed father to keep on submitting job applications even after he's been rejected a hundred times. The same faith that says to a teacher even if the first nine children she's teaching she can't reach, that that tenth one she's going to be able to reach. The same faith that breaks the silence of an earthquake's wake with the sound of prayers and hymns sung by a Haitian community. A faith in things not seen, in better days ahead, in Him who holds the future in the hollow of His hand. A faith that lets us mount up on wings like eagles; lets us run and not be weary; lets us walk and not faint.
>
> So let us hold fast to that faith, as Joshua held fast to the faith of his fathers, and together, we shall overcome the challenges of a new age. Together, we shall seize the promise of this moment. Together, we shall make a way through winter, and we're going to welcome the spring.

King and the civil rights movement had always been something much more than a source of inspiration to Obama. When he thought of the movement, he recalled images that his mother had described to him as a child, and the images grew into a source of faith and community for him. "Such images became a form of prayer for me, bolstering my spirits, channeling my emotions in a way that words never could," he later wrote. "They told me (although even this much understanding may have come later, is also a construct, containing its own falsehoods) that I wasn't alone in my particular struggles, and that communities had never been a given in this country, at least not for blacks. Communities had to be created, fought for, tended like gardens. They expanded or contracted with the dreams of men—and in the civil rights movement those dreams had been large." Politics and community organizing were his ways of finding a home, an identity, a purpose. "It was," he said, "a promise of redemption."

Faith, community, redemption: he spoke of the same themes when he sat down in the Oval Office a few days before Martin Luther King Day to sketch out the speech with his writer Adam Frankel and Josh DuBois, a young Pentecostal minister who runs the White House Office of Faith-based and Neighborhood Partnerships. Frankel had talked with the King historian Taylor Branch and explained the context of King's speech to the president. That prompted Obama to expand on how the lessons of the movement were relevant to today's struggles. He wanted to end the speech by talking about his own doubts and how he overcame them. As they walked out of the Oval, Frankel and DuBois turned to each other with the same reaction: they were struck by the rare window he had opened into his personal feelings. For these two tired staffers, who were true believers from the campaign, it was an inspiring moment in itself.

Looking back from the safety and power of the Oval Office three months later, Obama tried to play down his public expression of self-doubt. "Look, I mean, we were grinding out health care at that point," he told me, appearing ground down by fatigue even then. "And I thought it was important to acknowledge that these were some heavy lifts; that the key to America's better history has been a willingness to keep your shoulder against the wheel even when it's hard, even when you're tired, even when the news is discouraging.

"So, you know, in some ways I was just whining. I just wanted to share with the congregation, as we were talking about Dr. King and the civil rights struggle, the fact that that struggle to make America a better place continues, and that it was never easy. It wasn't easy then. It's not easy now."

As he spoke inside the Oval Office, the bust of Martin Luther King was looking over his right shoulder. But King was no throwaway reference on a special day inside a black church. He was a constant presence in Obama's career, from his days as a community organizer to his brief time in the Senate, to the White House itself. King's sculpture now sat on a small table, taking the place of a bust of the British wartime leader Winston Churchill, whom George W. Bush had seen as his role model after the terrorist attacks of September 2001. The symbolism was not subtle for either president.

The day after speaking at the Baptist church, Obama hung a new frame above King's bust. It held an original copy of the Emancipation Proclamation signed by his other inspiration: Abraham Lincoln, whose bust sat on the other side of the Oval Office fireplace. When Obama was deciding whether to run for president, his best friend, Marty Nesbitt, suggested that his election would have the biggest impact on African American children since the signing of the Emancipation Proclamation. Now here he was, a year into his presidency, with a copy of the proclamation in his own office.

King and Lincoln represented a historic conversation about his presidency, his ambition, and his self-image. They faced him when he sat at the president's iconic desk, which had been carved from the timbers of the HMS *Resolute*. And they found their meeting point on the Oval Office bookshelf next to Lincoln's portrait. Inside a small black picture frame sits a program from the 1963 March on

Washington for Jobs and Freedom. The Lincoln Memorial program once hung on Obama's so-called wall of heroes in his Senate office, alongside photos of Gandhi, Kennedy, and Lincoln himself. The bottom of the program simply says "We Shall Overcome."

Was he really just whining when he invoked King's suffering and strategy? The self-pity might have been superficial. But the comparisons, the rhetorical echoes, and the self-modeling were so often repeated as to seem entirely intentional. His original stump speech as a candidate for senator and for president ended with a story that concluded with one of King's most famous lines: "The arc of the moral universe is long but it bends toward justice." That arc could bend if people reached out to put their hands on it, he promised. On election night in Chicago's Grant Park, little more than a year earlier, he had praised the voters for deciding to "put their hands on the arc of history and bend it once more toward the hope of a better day." King had borrowed the phrase from the abolitionist Theodore Parker; Obama borrowed it again and had it woven into the rug on the floor of his Oval Office, alongside the words of Lincoln. If he wasn't talking to the portraits and busts inside the Oval Office, he was at least having a running conversation with their spirit and legacy.

Comparisons of living presidents with historic figures always seem far-fetched. But there are times when, despite a degree of White House humility, the outside world insists on sizing up the present against the past. Early in the morning of October 9, 2009, less than a year into his presidency, Obama woke to one of those times with a startling phone call. "Mr. President," said his press secretary, Robert Gibbs, "you just won the Nobel Peace Prize."

"Are you shitting me?" the president asked.

"If I was, do you think I'd do it like this?" Gibbs shot back.

What followed between the president and his senior staff veered between headless panic and historic pondering. At the end of his daily national security briefing, Obama chatted briefly with his senior foreign policy aides Ben Rhodes and Denis McDonough to share some more eloquent thoughts to spin into a press statement in the Rose Garden. Obama's chief speechwriter, Jon Favreau, was already huddled over his computer, with senior adviser David Axelrod in his office in the West Wing basement, close to the Situation Room. Early that morning, Favreau hadn't checked his BlackBerry before he stepped into the shower; moments later, he found forty e-mails screaming at him. His first reaction: "Who died?" Axelrod's reaction was more wistful than shocked. "This is one of the first times since the campaign that we've had to work like this," he said of the frenetic pace. "We used to do this every day."

For the next two hours, the team tried to craft a response to two awkward questions. How could Obama, at this early stage of his presidency, follow in the footsteps of the great Nobel laureates before him? And how could he legitimately win a peace prize as a commander in chief at war on two or more battlefields? He was barely a month into an intensive review of the struggling military strategy in Afghanistan and already feeling intense pressure—not least because of documents leaked to the *Washington Post*—to deploy thousands more soldiers. Later that same day, he would be listening to General Stanley McChrystal, the top commander in Afghanistan, spell out options for up to eighty thousand additional troops.

"To be honest, I do not feel that I deserve to be in the company of so many of the transformative figures who've been honored by this prize," Obama told reporters in the Rose Garden later that morning. "Men and women who've inspired me and inspired the entire world through their courageous pursuit of peace. But I also know that this prize reflects the kind of world that those men and women, and all Americans, want to build—a world that gives life to the promise of our founding documents."

The Nobel Peace Prize represented more than just a flattering challenge for a world leader who had only recently taken power. It posed a fundamental question about Obama's identity and politics, and whether they had shifted inside the Oval Office. As a presidential candidate he had wowed the Left with his early opposition to what he called the dumb war that was the invasion of Iraq; without it, he may never have won the support of the party's base. But the same base chose to ignore his hawkish position on Afghanistan and his refusal to agree to a full withdrawal from Iraq by a date certain. If anything, he had grown more hawkish inside the White House. He ramped up the use of Predator drones to strike at al Qaeda and Taliban targets in Afghanistan and Pakistan. Now he was considering more ground troops there, even as he was moving ahead with withdrawal from Iraq.

Obama approached the Nobel conundrum as if it were a familiar argument from his community organizing days: how to reconcile the world as it should be with the world as it is. The civil rights movement led by King had changed the world with idealism as well as action: they strived for a world as it should be. Community organizers, guided by the firebrand Saul Alinsky, were supposed to be far more hardheaded about the exercise of power and the futility of idealism. They were trained to deal with power—wielded by government and corporations—in the world as it is. From day one, Obama approached the Nobel as an extension of that debate between those two worlds. Obama had built his career on an uneven mixture of the two: hope-filled rhetoric and a coldly pragmatic set of compromises. Now that he was joining the wall of heroes, he needed to talk about the grim reality of his job as president and at the same time about the dreams that made it more than just a job.

"Even as we strive to seek a world in which conflicts are resolved peacefully and prosperity is widely shared, we have to confront the world as we know it today," he explained. "I am the Commander-in-Chief of a country that's responsible for ending a war and working in another theater to confront a ruthless adversary that directly threatens the American people and our allies. I'm also aware that we are dealing with the impact of a global economic crisis that has left millions of Americans looking for work. These are concerns that I confront every day on behalf of the American people."

A month later, on a long flight to Tokyo at the start of an Asian tour, Obama took an unusual step. He asked his speechwriters Rhodes and Favreau to join him at the front of Air Force One to begin work on his Nobel Prize speech. Normally they were the ones who prodded him for input as the speech deadline neared. "I'm thinking about this peace prize speech," he told them. "I'd like to write some of it myself. And this is one I'd actually like to have you guys do some research for me so that I can start thinking about it. So if you could put together stuff: everything from past presidents who won the peace prize. But also in a couple of weeks I'll be making a decision on Afghanistan. When I make that decision, the fact that I'm getting a peace prize a week or two after that has been weighing heavily on my mind. I want this speech to be about war and peace. So if you could gather me research about war and peace. And I'm talking everything from past presidents and generals, to philosophers and theologians talking about just-war theory, like Niebuhr. Just get me as much as you can. Also include King, Gandhi, George Marshall."

What emerged was a three-hundred-page binder that comprised a sweep of civilized thought on war and peace. There was Truman's August 1945 statement hailing the detonation of the first atomic bomb at Hiroshima and the scientific endeavor that led to its creation.

Beside Truman's celebration was Gandhi's condemnation of the diabolical science of the atom bomb.

Obama's reading was delayed by his own speech on the war in Afghanistan, when he announced another round of troop increases in front of the cadets at West Point. His critics were dismayed by his refusal to rally the troops at West Point, but that was entirely intentional. He wanted to restore a sense of gravity to war, in place of what he saw as the flag-waving and fearmongering of the Bush years.

By the time he focused on the binder, there was one week left before he accepted the peace prize. Cramming through the material over a weekend, Obama emerged with a pile of scribbles on small White House notepaper. He sketched out three outlines of a speech on the back of some of the briefing papers. What stood out was the work of the liberal theologian Reinhold Niebuhr on the concept of the "just war." Obama wanted to argue for the necessity of some kinds of war while at the same time expressing the tragic nature of all war.

His writers turned those scribbles into a draft, but the serious work of the speech was delayed by the season's festivities. Before he could return to the peace prize speech, Obama attended the Kennedy Center Honors for stars including Bruce Springsteen, Robert De Niro, and Mel Brooks. He was already in heavy demand at the back-to-back Christmas parties in the Executive Mansion. So he finally buckled down to a late night of scrawling on a yellow legal pad after a brief appearance at a White House party for his own staff. The next morning—the day of his departure for Oslo—he sat down with his speechwriters to hand over his notes. They were full of the lines from the original draft, studiously copied out in longhand and interspersed with his own additions.

"So here's what I got," he began. "I'm pretty happy now with the first two or three pages, but it became four in the morning.

Here's how I want to see it ending, but I'm not even sure yet. I didn't have time to write it out. So you guys need to do a new draft for me today and give it to me this afternoon before we leave tonight for Oslo."

For the rest of the day, a handful of Obama staffers huddled down in the basement closet space that passed for Ben Rhodes's office. To enter the windowless room, you had to pass through the office of the health reform director, Nancy-Ann DeParle, and that of the chief speechwriter, Jon Favreau. There, Rhodes and Favreau worked intensively on a new draft with help from Obama's foreign policy aide and Pulitzer Prize–winning author Samantha Power. "All right, we're getting closer, but we're really going to need to do some work on this on the plane," the president said as he reviewed their latest draft. Besides finishing the work, the team also had to get their words cleared by the combined teams of the director of National Intelligence and the National Security Council. Ahead lay a seven-hour overnight flight to Oslo, Norway. "I don't know how we're going to get this done," Favreau told Rhodes.

On board Air Force One there were more than just the regular crew of fatigued aides. On this journey, Obama was joined by his best friends from Chicago—Marty Nesbitt and Eric Whitaker—as well as his wife and daughters, his sister Maya, and his brother-in-law Konrad. The plane's conference room was a peace prize war room, a Nobel combat zone, with versions of the speech passed around on paper and computer flash drives. Rhodes paced to and from Obama's office at the front of the plane, carrying the president's latest scribbles on paper. "Good luck, guys," said Robert Gibbs wearily. "Let me know how it works out."

Three hours before landing, Obama called his team into his office. "Okay, I actually have to give this speech at some point," he said. "So I'm trying to figure out what I should do here."

"You should sleep," said Rhodes. "Go sleep for three hours. We'll continue to refine and cut down and finish up the ending. When you wake up you can do another round of edits before you get off the plane." Obama continued to edit and slept for barely one hour. When Air Force One arrived in Oslo, there was a lengthy delay as Obama reviewed the latest draft that was written while he slept. On a long bus ride to their Oslo hotel, the speechwriters worked on scraps of paper, before delivering a final version to the president in his hotel. Obama returned his final edits on the elevator down to his motorcade, as he prepared to head to the speech. The doors opened at the staff floor inside the hotel and the president thrust the sheets through the gap.

"The rhythm in the last line still isn't right," he told Favreau. "Just put it in and I'll give it."

Obama traveled with his wife to the Nobel Institute to sign the guest book, thanking the Nobel committee for the prize, for its work on peace, and for giving voice to the voiceless and oppressed. He and Michelle stopped to admire the wall of past winners and lingered over the photo of Martin Luther King. "When Dr. King won his prize, it had a galvanizing effect around the world but also lifted his stature in the United States in a way that allowed him to be more effective," he told reporters a few moments later. En route to Oslo City Hall to deliver his speech, he called Favreau. "What did you figure out for that last line?" he asked. It was a grandiloquent, three-part summary of his speech: about the story of human progress, the hope of all the world, and our work here on Earth. "Yeah, yeah," he said. "That works."

For all the impossible haste, the speech was a philosophical and political road map to Obama's compromises. More than a meditation on war and peace, it was his best effort to reconcile hope and reality, principle and power, the desire for Change and the demands of the commander in chief. The conversation between King and Obama was no longer an imaginary figment; it became the central dynamic of the speech. King won the same prize in 1964, after the lynching of three civil rights workers in Mississippi, the signing of the landmark Civil Rights Act, and riots in New York and New Jersey. In his brief speech, King linked war and racism together. "I refuse to accept the view that mankind is so tragically bound to the starless night of racism and war that the bright daybreak of peace and brotherhood can never become a reality," he said in Oslo, when Obama was just three years old. Now the president who once longed to be part of King's movement needed to answer the stinging criticism of war by his fellow prizewinner.

"We must begin by acknowledging the hard truth: We will not eradicate violent conflict in our lifetimes," Obama conceded.

> There will be times when nations—acting individually or in concert—will find the use of force not only necessary but morally justified. I make this statement mindful of what Martin Luther King Jr. said in this same ceremony years ago: "Violence never brings permanent peace. It solves no social problem: it merely creates new and more complicated ones." As someone who stands here as a direct consequence of Dr. King's life work, I am living testimony to the moral force of non-violence. I know there's nothing weak, nothing passive, nothing naïve, in the creed and lives of Gandhi and King. But as a head of state sworn to protect and defend my nation, I cannot be guided by their examples alone. I face the world as it is, and cannot stand idle in the face of threats to the American people. For make no mistake: Evil does exist in the world. A non-violent movement could not have halted Hitler's armies. Negotiations cannot convince al Qaeda's leaders to lay down their arms. To say that force may sometimes be necessary is not a call to cynicism—it is a recognition of history; the imperfections of man and the limits of reason.

As the first African American president, he could only admire everything King had achieved to build the world as it should be. But as a highly political president and commander in chief, he needed to operate in the world as it is. War was necessary because men could be evil; but war could also be the result of human folly. That was why he, like all leaders, needed to live by international standards of war. Peace would come from what John F. Kennedy called "a gradual evolution in human institutions," not a sudden revolution that led to peace. It was not exactly worthy of a bumper sticker, but it distilled Obama's notion of what politics could achieve at home and overseas: a gradual evolution.

Having defended war and incrementalism, Obama ended by hanging on to hope. Having defended the world as it is, he insisted he still believed in the world as it should be. It was his most high-minded effort to reconcile his idealism with his pragmatism, the bold campaign rhetoric with the policy shifts of government, his self-image with his record.

> But we do not have to think that human nature is perfect for us to still believe that the human condition can be perfected. We do not have to live in an idealized world to still reach for those ideals that will make it a better place. The non-violence practiced by men like Gandhi and King may not have been practical or possible in every circumstance, but the love that they preached—their fundamental faith in human progress—that must always be the North Star that guides us on our journey. For if we lose that faith—if we dismiss it as silly or naïve; if we divorce it from the decisions that we make on issues of war and peace—then we lose what's best about humanity. We lose our sense of possibility. We lose our moral compass. Like generations have before us, we must reject that future. As Dr. King

said at this occasion so many years ago, "I refuse to accept despair as the final response to the ambiguities of history. I refuse to accept the idea that the 'isness' of man's present condition makes him morally incapable of reaching up for the eternal 'oughtness' that forever confronts him." Let us reach for the world that ought to be—that spark of the divine that still stirs within each of our souls.

Obama's senior staff was so impressed with the last-minute effort they joked they should fire up Air Force One every time there was a big speech in the works. Too exhausted to celebrate, Favreau went to bed satisfied that the speech was better than expected. He awoke to a phone call from his boss. "Sorry to wake you," Obama said. "I just wanted to say you guys did a great job. But we shouldn't do this again."

"That's what you said after the health care speech," Favreau replied, recalling the last mad dash to a deadline, just three months earlier.

"Well, this time I'm serious."

February was African American History Month, and the official theme of this year's celebration was nothing less than "black economic empowerment." But what kind of empowerment was Obama presiding over, as the nation's first African American president, when black unemployment was more than 50 percent higher than the general jobless rate? And what kind of celebration could you have in the White House when your political fortunes had collapsed at the one-year stage? The economy had shed jobs only slightly quicker than the president had shed his own approval ratings. His domestic agenda was stalled, his foreign policy stymied.

A giant storm had just dumped more than twenty inches of snow on the nation's capital, shutting down the federal government. And Sarah Palin had just dumped derision on the president at the first convention of the new Tea Party movement, in Nashville's Opryland resort. The former vice presidential candidate lampooned Obama's supporters for believing he would run a transparent government, as promised. "And now, a year later, I've got to ask some supporters of all that"—she smirked before wrinkling her nose—"how's that hopey, changey stuff working out for ya?"

The answer came a few days later in the gilded East Room. Only now it was transformed into an incongruous nightclub, with black metal rigs flooding red and green light across a stage at the south end of the room, where a Yamaha drum set was standing next to two candelabra. Portraits of George Washington and Teddy Roosevelt watched from stage right, while a giant flat-screen TV stood opposite the stage, at the north end. The event was the fifth in a series of White House concerts celebrating American music, but this one was more personal than most. For this concert—unlike the earlier country music gig or the classical recital—celebrated the movement the president dreamed of joining when he entered politics.

"It's been said that when Dr. King and his associates were looking for communities to organize and mobilize, they'd know which were disciplined enough and serious enough when they saw folks singing freedom songs," Obama said from a presidential podium perched in front of the band.

Dr. King himself once acknowledged that he didn't see "the real meaning of the movement" until he saw young people singing in the face of hostility. You see, it's easy to sing when you're happy. It's easy to sing when you're among friends. It's easy to sing when times are good. But it is hard to sing when times are rough. It's hard to sing in the face of taunts, and fear, and the constant threat of violence. It's hard to sing when folks are being beaten, when leaders are being jailed, when churches are being bombed.

It's hard to sing in times like that. But times like that are precisely when the power of song is most potent. Above the din of hatred; amidst the deafening silence of inaction; the hymns of the civil rights movement helped carry the cause of a people and advance the ideals of a nation.

So Barack and Michelle Obama sat down in the front row, in front of PBS cameras, and sang. They sang as gospel singer Yolanda Adams belted out Sam Cooke's "A Change Is Gonna Come," as the East Room drapes turned red with the stage lighting. And they sang with two of the aging musical leaders of a generation: Joan Baez and Bob Dylan. "One day in 1963, they joined hundreds of thousands on the National Mall and sang of a day when the time would come; when the winds would stop; when a ship would come in," Obama said. "They sang of a day when a righteous journey would reach its destination."

Baez strummed her steel-stringed guitar alone to play "We Shall Overcome," and Obama sang enthusiastically. But her righteous journey did not quite reach its destination. After singing the second verse, beginning "We'll walk hand in hand," Baez told the story behind the next verse: "One day Dr. King realized the nonviolence fight went far beyond the shores of this great country, went far across the sea to a war that was being fought by God's children on both sides of that great fight. And he knew that he had to speak out against that, and he was afraid. He was very afraid. So we all raised our voices just a little bit louder, and we said, 'We are not afraid, today.'"

In the front row, Michelle Obama sang out loud, while her husband clasped his left leg, crossed firmly over his right, and gently nodded his head to the music. It was a little more than two months since he traveled to West Point to announce that another thirty thousand troops would be deployed to Afghanistan, and a little less than two months since he traveled to Oslo to argue the need for just wars. The power of song might revive his personal spirits. But his political revival required more than walking hand in hand to overcome his fear. He needed to overcome the doubts of his friends and the discipline of his foes.

TWO

TERMINAL

It was a nauseatingly familiar feeling inside the West Wing in January 2010. The sickening sensation of imminent defeat. The sense of waste and frustration after months of long days, short nights, conference calls, and back-to-back meetings.

For the best part of a year, they had struggled and grappled with health care reform. The Democratic dream for most of the last half century was within their grasp with successful votes in both the House and the Senate. After all the painstaking negotiations with members of Congress and industry executives, after all the self-interested backroom deals and the high-minded speeches, the entire effort—and the prospects for Obama's presidency—came down to a single, doomed special election.

The irony of the location was lost on no one: Massachusetts, the seat held by Ted Kennedy for five decades since his own special election, when his brother won the presidency. The unfinished business of Kennedy's life would be undone by the contest that followed his death. The Democratic candidate, Martha Coakley, the state's attorney general, had started the race six weeks earlier with a thirty-point lead in the polls over state senator Scott Brown. By the end of December, Coakley had lost two-thirds of her advantage and Brown was airing an audacious first TV ad. It began with President Kennedy announcing tax cuts in 1962 and morphed into Brown finishing the same speech today.

Few people inside the White House noticed that Coakley was rapidly losing the race for the Kennedy seat while her rival was claiming Kennedy's mantle. There were plenty of distractions for Obama's aides: Brown's first ad aired just a week after an attempted terrorist attack on a Christmas Day flight from Amsterdam to Detroit.

A week later, Brown released a second ad featuring him driving his trusty old black pickup truck through the state to his suburban home strung with Christmas lights, where his daughter greeted him with a jaunty "Hey, Dad!" Two days later, the pollster Scott Rasmussen showed that Coakley's lead was down to nine points.

Inside the White House, there was what one senior aide called "total meltdown" as they realized it was already too late to intervene. "How could we miss this?" asked one incredulous campaign veteran. "Some of us were hearing what was going on and asking what was happening. The answer was nothing. The political shop wasn't doing anything. The DNC [Democratic National Committee] was doing nothing. They only have one race to look after. They said in December they had a 'strong single-digit lead.' That's all it was. The week after Brown went up on the air, we were all focused on the terror plot. There was only one or two of us who could see what was happening. And how *horrible* she was as a candidate." Coakley seemed to have little appetite for the public side of her campaign, focusing instead on the support of party officials. When the *Boston Globe* asked her why she seemed so passive in her campaign, Coakley fired back, "As opposed to standing outside Fenway Park? In the cold? Shaking hands?" If that wasn't enough to insult the beloved Boston Red Sox, Coakley followed up a few days later by suggesting to a local radio interviewer that Curt Schilling, the legendary Red Sox pitcher who supported her opponent, was in fact "another Yankee fan." Her campaign suggested this was a deadpan joke, but it was really just deadening. By this time, polls placed her below 50 percent and the race was effectively tied.

"She's going to be buried," said David Axelrod as he grazed his way through a bowl of chips and salsa in a downtown Washington restaurant the day before voting began in Massachusetts. "And I'm going to take a lot of arrows for it. I fully expect it."

Many of Obama's closest aides—the wayfarers who embarked on this journey in the campaign's earliest days—had felt something similar on the night before the last big primaries of 2008. After fifteen months of toil and turmoil, they were on the verge of clinching the presidential nomination with primaries in North Carolina and Indiana. Then, suddenly, their internal polls collapsed in the final twenty-four hours. They blamed a new media frenzy over Obama's pastor, Jeremiah Wright. Whatever the cause, as the voting began, Obama's inner circle believed they were headed for a crushing defeat and the end of their effort to turn a freshman senator into a presidential nominee. Instead, they won big in North Carolina and narrowly missed winning in Indiana. That marginal victory ended the public doubts about Obama's candidacy. But the near-death experience sat in a shallow grave, as painful and proximate as the earlier, real failure in New Hampshire.

Now, inside the White House, the finger-pointing and flash-backs had returned.

At the start of the presidential campaign, David Axelrod wrote a memo suggesting his candidate would not take well to the public criticism about to get dumped on his head. "At the risk of triggering the very reaction that concerns me," Axelrod wrote, "I don't know if you are Muhammad Ali or Floyd Patterson when it comes to taking a punch." Three years later, the punches were raining down from all sides. The left hook was Obama's readiness to compromise with business executives. The right jab was his belief in the role of government. He was both a traitor to the Democratic cause and a revolutionary in the socialist style. "This is hard stuff. It's difficult stuff," said Axelrod. "But he's as resilient as anyone I have known. What happened is that he became tougher. I didn't know if he was going to be Muhammad Ali or Floyd Patterson. He turned out to be Muhammad Ali."

But even Muhammad Ali was on the ropes, as the pressures inside the first family were taking their toll on the president and his inner circle. Unsettled by three gate-crashers at their first state dinner two months earlier, Michelle Obama was herself a vocal critic of her husband and his team. "Michelle is really giving him a hard time," said one White House confidant on the day of the Massachusetts election. "She's worried after the gate-crashers about his security, and the girls and the family as a whole. She feels he isn't being served well by the message. That the economic crisis wasn't his doing, that he is the one to change Washington. She isn't in a good place at all. And he's feeling that. Yesterday was the first time I really saw him angry and down about the whole situation." The First Lady's staff denied that Mrs. Obama ever felt concerned about her family's safety following the gate-crashing revelations. Other staffers believed Mrs. Obama was deeply unhappy with her husband's political plight. But they also thought the president might be exaggerating her displeasure. "He ascribes things to her, saying she's angry and what can he do," said one trusted aide. "But he's also really angry." Whatever the anger level, inside the West Wing they all felt the pressure individually and took the attacks as personal accusations of failure. "It is not a happy place right now," said another senior Obama aide. "This is like the night before Indiana."

There was at least one person in the West Wing who seemed to relish the fight. Rahm Emanuel, the hyperactive chief of staff, was even more agitated than normal when the first Rasmussen poll landed. He wanted members of Congress to curtail their Christmas break and come back to Washington early—before their scheduled return on January 12—to complete their work merging the House and Senate versions of health care reform. "You're playing with fate," he thought. "If it's tightening, we needed to finish our work, to see if we could finish it before. And without deadlines, it's very hard to get people to work." A week later, as the polls showed the Massachusetts race was tied, Emanuel believed that Brown was on a path to victory. "He was tapping into the zeitgeist, the energy," the chief of staff said. "He was a way to be basically antiestablishment. He was raw, fresh and the real deal and natural, to her kind of everything else." Emanuel wanted to impart a sense of energy and urgency to everything surrounding health care. "We've got to get going," he would say to everyone around him. "We've got to finish up. We've got to recalibrate what we're doing here."

However, other senior staffers believed that Emanuel's excess energy was a major part of the problem, one of the reasons why they were suffering this near-terminal condition. In place of the rigid discipline of the presidential campaign, instead of their no-drama style and the strategic focus, ideas ricocheted around the West Wing with each firing of Emanuel's synapses. "It's all tactics and no strategy," said one of Emanuel's close colleagues. "That's something the president feels very strongly he's missing. How do I get from here to where I want to go? It's all tactical and it's all Rahm. He has no follow-through and no management. Nobody is there to check that what was decided at the seven-thirty meeting actually happens. The problem with Rahm is that, yes, he's brilliant. But he is purely tactical, and he changes his mind based on a conversation he just had with Paul Begala. There are many times when Axe has to shout him down to drop an idea or a tactic. And his style is unbelievably bad. It's just too abusive."

It was unlikely that anyone in the White House could have made much difference in Massachusetts. But the news was no less devastating inside the West Wing. Scott Brown beat Martha Coakley by almost five points in a state where Democrats outnumber Republicans by a margin of three to one, and little more than a year after Barack Obama beat John McCain by twenty-six points on the same terrain.

The next day, Emanuel was in another of his fighting moods. "Everyone should remember *for six months* we functioned without a senator from Minnesota. So you can still function with fifty-seven plus two, okay?" he told the senior West Wing staff. "It's not impossible. You just have to calibrate what it is you're trying to achieve. Don't lose your bearings." His own bearings pointed straight at the opposition. "Run the ball *at* these guys," he said. "Because their weak spot is when they have to pick between accountability—solving the problem—and throwing bricks. We've got to make them pick, because that doesn't work for them electorally."

While Emanuel was ready to charge out of the bunker, other senior Obama aides were teaching their coworkers how to survive under fire. At his regular 9:15 morning meeting with his communications staff, Robert Gibbs shut the door to his office to deliver a rare pep talk. "We're going to have a really bad day," he told his mostly young aides. "People are going to say we're stupid and we failed and we're incompetent. We blew this and the presidency hangs in the balance. Don't ever think it was ever anything you did. There are always these ups and downs. Don't blame yourself. And don't believe it."

People were already saying they had failed by the time Gibbs tried to buck up his team. It was a rare moment of unity across the partisan divide, and across the nation's capital. Democrats and Republicans, politicians and pundits, agreed on this: health care reform was dead and buried, along with what remained of the president's political fortunes. On the left, Representative Anthony Weiner from New York determined on the day of voting that "you can make a pretty good argument that health care might be dead." Representative Barney Frank from Massachusetts, his fellow progressive Democrat, said of the old legislation and strategy, "I think that's dead."

Republican senators were in a giddy mood when they lined up to speak to reporters in the Senate radio and TV gallery inside the Capitol the next morning. "The people of Massachusetts had an opportunity to speak yesterday and they spoke rather loudly that they'd like to see the Congress go in a different direction," said Mitch McConnell, the Senate minority leader and architect of the dogged opposition to health care. "This was in many ways a national referendum, principally, on the major issue we're wrestling with here in the Congress, which is whether or not the government should take over one-sixth of our economy, slash Medicare by half a trillion dollars, raise taxes by half a trillion dollars, and drive insurance rates up for most of the rest of our country. And I think we heard a large and resounding message yesterday in one of the most, if not arguably the most liberal state in America."

The White House had finally found common ground between red and blue America, as pundits on all sides read the last rites. "It's deliberate, pre-meditated murder for health care," declared Chris Matthews on MSNBC before the race was called. "A Democratic defeat could not only put an end to health care, but it would weaken President Obama's standing nationwide, send Democrats running for cover, and provide a path to victory for other Republicans nationwide." The Fox News analyst Fred Barnes was even more definitive, writing in *The Weekly Standard*: "Oh yes. The health care bill, Obama Care, is dead with not the slightest prospect of resurrection."

It was the anniversary of an extraordinary, historic moment. A year ago to the day, the National Mall that stretched behind the White House was a reflecting pool of faces. Some 1.8 million people stood in the blustery January chill to witness the inauguration of the first African American president. The official theme was "a new birth of freedom," drawn from Lincoln's rallying cry in the Gettysburg Address, invoking the example of Obama's presidential hero on the 200th anniversary of his birth. But after a single year of the presidency, the inaugural story of unity, hope, and rebirth was replaced by a depressing slew of obituaries.

Inside the White House, there was an overwhelming sense of hopes dashed and self-image crushed. After campaigning for two years as the antiestablishment, anti-Clinton force that could transform American politics, and after a year of trying to heed the lessons of the Clinton years, they were no different after all. "For all of our hope of doing things differently, and having success where others failed, that day—just for a day—it felt like health care was dead," said communications director Dan Pfeiffer, a true believer in the spirit of the Obama campaign. "We were going to go down with the seven other presidents who tried and failed. We would end up in the same place, seventeen years later, where Clinton had been. We had won with a much broader coalition. We had 53 percent of the vote; he had 42. And after all that, it felt like we had ended up at the same place." The sadness was only intensified by the sense of helpless victimhood: if Coakley had been a better candidate, or run a competent campaign, the prospects for health care—and the presidency—would have looked so different. "It felt like cruel randomness had squashed a lot of what we hoped to do," said Pfeiffer. "We had been in bad places before. We had lost New Hampshire and Ohio. We spent 2007 being complete idiots. But it was this weird Shakespearean tragedy that health care was going to fail because a Democrat lost Ted Kennedy's seat."

That morning, Obama gathered his senior advisers in the Oval Office. His first reaction was to sympathize with the disappointment of his health reform director, Nancy-Ann DeParle. "I feel so bad for Nancy-Ann," he said. "It's so unfair. She put so much work into this." Then he rattled off a list of all they had accomplished over the last year, before adding his own pep talk. "I know this is going to be a tough time in this town right now," he began. "I'm not giving up on health care or anything else. But take a moment and recognize that for a lot of people in this country, their lives are a lot better for what we've done in the last year."

Obama wanted health care in 2009. His first year. Not in 2010, when elections would interfere with a complex debate. He would never have this many votes in Congress. "In order to get it done in the first term, we had to start it now," said David Axelrod at the year-one mark of the presidency. "If you don't do it now, when do you do it?" Through the long presidential campaign, Obama had only promised to tackle health care by the end of his first term. And after the biggest financial collapse since the Great Depression, he had good political and economic reasons to delay and defer the Democratic dream. But he wasn't interested in the political reasons for action later; only the political reasons for action now.

From his transition office in Chicago, Obama started planning his health care strategy. He created a White House Office of Health Reform, to be led by his friend and adviser Tom Daschle, the former Senate leader. Daschle would be able to leverage his friendships in Congress as well as run the sprawling Department of Health and Human Services. But Daschle's nomination died in early February 2009, after stories about two tax omissions and his earnings as a business consultant. By mid-February, without anyone of Daschle's stature in place, Obama faced a simple decision. "Once we got to the White House, the discussion became whether you talk about something comprehensive or something smaller," said Axelrod. "What size program would you try and do?"

Obama's ambition was always of supersized proportions. How else could he have staged his preposterous challenge to the Clintons for the presidential nomination? Having won the presidency—with no money machine, an alien name, and a brief political résumé—why would he limit himself now? "I'd rather be here for four years and get something done," he liked to tell his senior aides inside the West Wing, "than walk around these halls for eight years and get nothing done." Whether or not he said it out loud, Obama rejected the model of the Clinton presidency: two terms of survival was not enough. From the earliest days when he mused about running for the presidency, he believed that it took a combination of character and opportunity to achieve greatness. "What makes a great president, as opposed to a great person, is the juxtaposition of that president's personal characteristics and strengths with the needs of the American people and the country," he told his best friend, Marty Nesbitt, as he was deciding whether or not to run for the White House. "And when you are a president who happens to come into office at that juxtaposition, there's an environment for you to be a great president." He was thinking of Ronald Reagan, who had "changed the trajectory of America," as he put it.

He began by changing the trajectory of his own approach to health care, taking his campaign promises and making them more—not less—ambitious. Through the primaries, he argued fiercely against Hillary Clinton's position on mandating individuals to buy health insurance. He opposed a mandate because it meant the government was compelling individuals to buy insurance through some form of fine or tax penalty. It was perhaps the only substantive policy difference between the two bitter rivals on any issue. But once inside the Oval Office, he promptly dropped his opposition in favor of making his reforms bigger. In order to expand coverage, he needed to expand the number of people buying coverage. For instance, among the great injustices facing patients like his own mother were the constant and complex disputes over preexisting conditions. It was all too easy for insurers to exclude claims and customers by arguing that their sickness predated their policy. So to convince insurers to extend costly insurance to everyone, Obama offered them a bigger pool of healthy customers. That included younger people who chose not to buy insurance, but who would now face penalties for that choice.

Obama wanted to avoid the Clinton experience of going too big or too small. But most of his senior aides wanted to avoid another Clinton experience: total failure. The two aides leading his health care overhaul were both Clinton veterans with painful memories of 1993. As much as they believed in the dream of comprehensive health care reform, their pressing goal was to prevent comprehensive defeat.

For Rahm Emanuel, one of the top strategists behind the Clinton health care effort, avoiding failure was an obsession. Even in a resting state, his mind and moods raced, his deep-scored eyes set in a semipermanent state of shock. "Hard-charging" was a soft way to describe the chief of staff and his two brothers: Zeke, a bioethicist working inside the White House budget office, and Ari, a Hollywood superagent. "He is deeply insecure. Failure wasn't an option in the Emanuel household," said one senior Obama aide. "So he cares about every detail and keeps himself up worrying about everything."

Where Emanuel gunned for victory, his fellow Clinton veteran Nancy-Ann DeParle sought consensus. DeParle was no less determined than Emanuel, but her soft Tennessee twang and patient manner represented his polar opposite. In the early 1990s, she had served as the White House budget expert on health care, and later became the administrator of Medicare and Medicaid at the Department of Health. When Daschle's nomination collapsed, she took his place inside the White House with a clear sense of mission: to stop a repeat of 1993. "From the moment I came in to talk to Rahm about this job, we agreed we weren't coming out of this with nothing," she said. "Both of us had been through the Clinton experience together and we both felt that the Clintons got bad advice and that it might have been possible to at least have gotten children's health insurance in '94 as opposed to '97, to have come out with something. So we made a promise to each other that we weren't coming out of this with nothing." While the party's activists believed that now was the time to get everything, Obama's top aides wanted to emerge with something less than everything and more than nothing.

The balance between the two extremes was constantly shifting. Emanuel rapidly grew into the biggest advocate of a smaller, less ambitious package. While he followed Obama's orders in wanting a bigger, more comprehensive bill, his methods often took the president's staff in the opposite direction, toward a quicker hit. He often asked DeParle to look at other policy options, scoping out the prospects for an alternative route to success. "Rahm was for doing what the president wanted to do," said DeParle. "But Rahm wanted to be sure that this president didn't end up with nothing. That's how I perceived all of his ideas. He was worried. Can we get it done? And if we can't get it done, what does that do to the presidency? Rahm's job was always to make sure we were looking around the corner, at what could be coming at us, and what our plan B was." Even Obama's campaign loyalists came to see that Rahm's relentless horse-trading served a greater purpose. "Rahm wanted to do the deals and move on," said one senior Obama adviser. "It was the president who said, 'No, I actually want to reform health care and improve it for people.' Otherwise the deals would have been done and we'd have moved on. Looking back, Rahm was probably right. It was our idealistic, perfectionist president who wanted to get the best reform he could. Rahm just has a very good sense of the political mood in the House, of what needs to be done when."

There were few around him who thought health care was the right way for Obama to define his first year. David Axelrod was more interested in a big education bill. Several senators pushed for action on climate change. But Obama stuck to health care. It was what he worked on in the Illinois state senate; what he ran on to get elected to the United States Senate; what he talked about at almost every rally on the presidential campaign trail. "This was a huge issue for him and something he felt was going to be a personal measure of his success as president," said one senior aide. "And it's something the First Lady also feels very strongly about. African American leaders feel he ignores their issues, but the health disparities in this country are felt most horribly in their community. I've always felt you can't overlook that piece of it. He spent a lot of time on the South Side of Chicago with laid-off steelworkers."

Obama's idealism came from a simple source: the people he met, at seemingly every campaign stop and town hall, whose health care stories echoed his mother's. The stories wove into his own narrative as a politician who cared about something more than his own survival. But his senior advisers, who were paid to care about his survival, were not enthusiastic about his commitment to a comprehensive health care package. Five months into his presidency, he traveled to a high school in Green Bay, Wisconsin, to be introduced by a woman with terminal breast cancer and thousands of dollars in unpaid medical bills. Laura Klitzka, a young mother of two, had undergone eight rounds of chemotherapy and thirty-three rounds of radiation, as well as a double mastectomy. That treatment failed to stop the cancer from spreading to her bones. Even with her husband's insurance, Laura faced more than $12,000 in unpaid medical bills, and resorted to paying her mortgage with a credit card. She said she didn't want to waste the little time left with her children in worrying about health care bills. Yet Laura's simple smile, her matter-of-fact delivery, and her singsong upper midwestern accent gave little hint of her suffering. Obama walked to the microphone and thanked Laura for sharing her story. "It takes courage to do that, and it takes even more courage to battle a disease like cancer with such grace and determination, and I know her family is here and they're working and fighting with her every inch of the way," he said. "Laura's story is incredibly moving. But sadly, it's not unique. Every day in this country, more and more Americans are forced to worry about not just getting well, but whether they can afford to get well."

Obama returned to the White House later that day to hear a bad political prognosis. Axelrod walked into the Oval Office with a new batch of polling data that pointed to a gloomy conclusion. "This thing is going to be costly, at least in the short term politically," said the perennially downbeat adviser. "You need to know that."

"I'm sure you're right," Obama said, after listening closely. "But I just got back from Green Bay, where I met a woman. She's thirty-five years old, has two children, and she's got breast cancer. They're going broke because the insurance won't cover most of her treatment. She's terrified that she's going to die and leave her family bankrupt.

"So you know," he said as he ushered Axelrod out of the door, "this fight is worth it. We have to keep going."

It was supposed to be a quick hit, not unlike Bush's invasion of Iraq: a lightning strike with few casualties, with a self-financing future. Health care could be finished in a matter of months, thanks to a popular president, consensus on the need for change, and ample work already completed in Congress. "There was a strong feeling that we could get it done quickly, and the act of getting it done would be a liberating and empowering thing for Congress," said one senior Obama staffer. "Then we could move on to everything else. But it turned into 1918 on the Somme rather than a blitzkrieg. Everyone dug into their trenches for a war of attrition."

The pace of the battle was not their only surprise. It turned out they had built their Maginot Line of defense in the wrong place. In the early summer, the White House agreed to what looked like a smart deal with the drug companies: the industry would cut the cost of drugs by $80 billion over ten years, and spend $150 million on TV ads to support health care reform. The idea was to blunt the opposition that helped kill the Clinton health care effort: to divide and conquer the health care industry. "The lesson from '93 was: pick one or two of the largest industries, cut a deal, and they'll spend their money on your TV ads," said the senior staffer. "But the reality of '09 is that TV advertising—as much as was spent by both sides—was irrelevant compared with the press, and the Internet, and cable TV driving the narratives." The deal with the drug companies only seemed to confirm a trend of cozy backroom fixes costing billions and often involving big business. There was the Recovery Act, the continued bank bailout, the rescue of the auto industry, and a huge spending bill. "The context of starting health care then was it came right out of the box after four huge spending items that were very unpopular," said the senior staffer. "Part of the problem was that the president ended up looking somewhat tone-deaf to a large group of people."

Obama wasn't just cutting deals with big business. The rap was that his White House was too hands-off, too detached to push reform through a timid Congress. But that criticism overlooked the constant deal making in Congress. At both ends of Pennsylvania Avenue, there were serious, engaged attempts to push along health care reform. Out of public sight, DeParle and other senior Obama officials met with committee chairs and their aides in the House and Senate each week. She talked about new health insurance exchanges and sub-sidies. She even initiated something unheard-of on Capitol Hill: joint meetings between House and Senate Democrats, which both sides were initially reluctant to start. "Meet with the Senate Democrats?" one House staffer told DeParle. "Don't they talk to Republicans? I don't know if that would be useful now. We usually see them in con-ference." DeParle said the meetings would at least save the adminis-tration time, so they began in April 2009. They grew into twice-weekly sessions and then, in the summer and fall, a 9:00 p.m. phone call between the White House and twenty Democratic staffers from the House and Senate. They shared strategy, numbers, policy details, and political analysis. "I don't think anyone can fairly characterize our position as being passive," said DeParle, who also met individually with more than 170 lawmakers.

Yet there was a point when DeParle and the White House simply had to stand back and watch. The president's team could not secure the votes, especially Republican ones, on the all-powerful Senate Fi-nance Committee. It was the single place where spending promises needed to be measured in real budget dollars, and it was also where the Clinton health care plan died, at the hands of its then-chairman Daniel Patrick Moynihan. Now the committee was led by

Max Baucus, the prickly Democratic senator from red state Montana, who was determined to move ahead with some Republican support. Baucus was very close to a key West Wing aide: Jim Messina, the deputy chief of staff, who had served as the senator's chief of staff and likened him to his own father. Baucus had already flexed his political muscles in several cases of Obama's nominees with tax irregularities, and played a key role in rescuing the job of Secretary of the Treasury Tim Geithner. Now he wanted to play the central role in health care reform. In readiness for Obama's likely health care effort, he staged hearings and a bipartisan one-day health care summit in the summer of 2008. Baucus believed there was common ground with the Republicans who showed up, including the senior GOP senator, Iowa's Chuck Grassley. In particular, they all agreed to expand coverage, as long as they stayed within the private insurance system. A week after Obama's election, Baucus released a white paper that served as a template for new comprehensive legislation to reform health care. "This is probably going to be close to the bible that everyone is going to look at in trying to figure out what our health care reform changes should be," Baucus said.

Baucus was no Ted Kennedy, yet he was thrust into Kennedy's role. He would traditionally take second place to the Democratic lion on Kennedy's signature issue of health care. But Kennedy was ailing from his brain tumor and was already a rare presence on Capitol Hill. Baucus had the power and the presence, but he had neither Kennedy's charisma nor his political sensibilities. Both men liked to build bipartisan groupings, albeit in different styles: where Kennedy backslapped his way to a deal, Baucus preferred painstaking negotiations. That caution was partly the result of personality and partly the product of Montana politics. Republicans outnumbered Democrats among registered voters by a large margin in his home state, and Baucus would never forget how he had almost lost his seat after voting for Clinton's 1993 crime bill, which included a ban on assault weapons. Baucus would tell White House officials that health care was the toughest issue for him since taking on the National Rifle Association in his gun-loving state, a comparison that left them stunned. How could he compare health care and guns? Still, he wanted to forge ahead with the biggest legislation of his career. "Health care reform is the holy grail of domestic policy, and he's in the driver's seat," said one senior Democratic staffer. "He didn't want to fuck this up."

Baucus started his long journey toward health care reform at a major disadvantage: there was little trust on either side. Within a month of entering office, the new White House team pushed ahead with a long-desired expansion of the State Children's Health Insurance Program (SCHIP), the survivor of what remained of the Clintons' health care efforts. Along the way, Democrats delivered on a promise to Latino groups to end a five-year waiting period for legal immigrants to qualify, attracting Republican accusations that the bill would help illegal immigrants. The bill passed, but so did the moment for agreement. "It made them less trustful of how this new Senate majority would work," said one senior Democratic official. "It made them a little gun-shy."

Baucus negotiated with three Republicans—Grassley of Iowa, Mike Enzi of Wyoming, and Olympia Snowe of Maine—and seemed to be making real but achingly slow progress by the summer. He began snack-filled and pizza-fueled talks in his red and beige conference room, a shrine to Mike Mansfield, Montana's legendary senator, the former majority leader who introduced the Civil Rights Act and the Great Society legislation of the 1960s. But Obama had set a deadline of August for reform, and the talks were moving far slower than the White House political calculation of what was optimal. The longer the debate dragged on, the greater the chance for Republicans and industry opponents to scare voters and lower the odds of passing a bill.

The snail-paced talks were at least moving in the right direction. Before leaving for his traditional Iowa tour in August, Grassley seemed optimistic a deal was in the works. "We have made great progress. Every day we make some progress," he told National Public Radio in late July. "We're on the edge and almost there." To those in his party advocating an end to the talks and delivery of a decisive defeat to the president, Grassley was dismissive: "I think that anything that's politically motivated when you're dealing with the life-or-death situation of every American—and that's what health care is all about—and you're restructuring one sixth of the economy, you ought to be thinking about what you're doing right for the country, and not just what's right for your political party."

In private, Grassley was feeling his party's pressure, even though he had a record of bucking its leadership. The GOP Senate leader, Mitch McConnell, had a disciplined strategy to hold his caucus together and deny Obama any claim of bipartisanship. "It was absolutely critical that everybody be together because if the proponents of the bill were able to say it was bipartisan, it tended to convey to the public that this is okay, they must have it figured out," McConnell explained. The GOP leader also wielded the considerable power to rotate committee chairs every six years, and Grassley treasured his senior position. If Grassley broke with his fellow senators, he could face a bruising primary challenge from the right as he ran for reelection in 2010. Even if he emerged triumphant, he could lose any chance of chairing another committee. He needed political cover, and that meant more than just a single moderate Republican like Olympia Snowe. Just before he returned to Iowa, he met with DeParle for another strategy session.

"If we do everything and resolve all the policy issues the way you want, with no public plan, do you think you'll be able to support the bill?"

Grassley looked away. "I don't know."

Grassley went to the Oval Office for a similar conversation with the president and his fellow Republican and Democratic negotiators. He asked Obama to say publicly that he would sign a bill without a public option of a government-run plan. Grassley believed this would be a reasonable, minimal demonstration of Obama's desire for a bipartisan deal. But the president declined to confront his own party base so explicitly. Obama asked Grassley the same question DeParle had posed: With every concession he wanted, could he support the bill?

"Probably not."

"Why not?" asked an exasperated Obama.

"Because I'd have to have a number of Republicans," said Grassley. "I'm not going to be the third of three Republicans. I've defined a bipartisan bill as broad-based support."

For all of Obama's stated desire to reach across the aisle, bipartisanship was even more elusive than the details of expanded health coverage.

Soon after, Emanuel met with Baucus on the West Wing patio of the chief of staff's spacious corner office, to push him to send his bill to the Senate floor.

"Max, this is going to be endless. You have run the course here. Why don't you just go?" Emanuel asked Baucus. "Just mark up a bill in your committee and *go*?"

"Why would we do that? Why wouldn't we want to make sure that we have a good product that we know we can sell? And that we've got sixty votes on the floor?"

"We'll get Snowe and Collins," Emanuel insisted. Baucus explained that Snowe took an eternity to make up her mind, and they needed to be patient. Besides, her fellow Maine senator, Susan Collins, wasn't part of the negotiating team. Emanuel wasn't fazed. Nor was he impressed with the whole team, especially Grassley.

"Grassley isn't going to be there. Fuck that. It's not going to happen."

"Rahm, let's assume what you're saying is true, that we have fifty-nine votes and we'll get one Republican. That means we have to hold every member of the caucus. Do you know what that's going to mean?"

"Yeah, we'll just make deals."

"That's going to be ugly. Everyone is going to extract their price. And on something like this, you want to avoid that," said Baucus. "It's *ugly*."

"Fine. We'll get it done. We'll worry about that later."

Baucus thought the go-to-the-floor approach was far too risky on something as big as health care, when failure could effectively end the presidency.

Obama's aides concluded that Grassley was torn between dismay with his own GOP senators and his desire to run for another Senate term the following year. Back home in Iowa, he had long ago alienated his own state party. He had even turned some evangelical conservatives into enemies, after launching congressional investigations into several large national ministries for lavish spending on their own preachers. But after an August touring Iowa and staging raucous town hall meetings, Grassley seemed to have made up his mind. Town hall screaming matches were taking place across the country, often with the help of conservative groups, and especially for the enjoyment of cable TV cameras. But their effect on Grassley was more meaningful than most of the spectacles. He started talking about end-of-life counseling, which would supposedly ration care to the elderly or even recommend euthanasia. He even warned against the government deciding when to "pull the plug on Grandma." With that, he pulled the plug on a bipartisan deal.

Inside the West Wing, Obama's aides aimed their anger at Mitch McConnell. "That's a power that the leader of the Republican Party has," one senior staffer said. "I respect his leverage and his power to command loyalty." David Axelrod was rather less respectful. "I think he did a great job for his interests and a bad job for this country. That's exactly what people think about Congress and exactly what they think about Washington. So he's made himself the poster boy for self-interested, partisan, phony-baloney politics," he said. "Congratulations, Mitch McConnell."

Obama's aides tried to regain control of the debate in September with their trump card: a big speech. But their preparations were only marginally less chaotic than the town halls. To reassert Obama's leadership over health care, they planned for a speech to a joint session of Congress, just like the State of the Union. However, they gave themselves no time for planning: the decision to go ahead with the speech came only a week before the address itself. Moreover, the intervening weekend included the wedding day of Ben Rhodes, one of Obama's senior foreign policy aides and speechwriters. The president's entire speechwriting team and half the press office were in Los Angeles celebrating; chief writer Jon Favreau reworked his draft through the wedding day itself. On Monday morning, as he prepared to head back, Favreau took a call from Reggie Love, the president's personal aide. "The president wants to meet with you and Axe about the speech in an hour," Love said. When he heard that Favreau would not return to D.C. until that night, Love indulged in some understatement: "That's a real problem." Several hours later, and without his security pass, Favreau ran off the plane and rushed over to the White House. He told the guards at the gate that he had a meeting inside. When the Secret Service officers asked who he was meeting with, all Favreau could say was "the president."

When Favreau, in his jeans and sandals, finally scampered into the Oval Office, he found Obama with a yellow legal pad scribbled through with notes. The president had reordered the speech and expanded his response to each criticism, from death panels to the public option. He also reworked the ending, with the help of something that had arrived just before Favreau left for L.A.: a letter from the late Ted Kennedy. Kennedy's widow, Vicki, told them about the letter only the week before and wanted to hand-deliver it to Obama.

"As we moved forward in these months, I learned that you will not yield to calls to retreat—that you will stay with the cause until it is won," Kennedy wrote to Obama. "I saw your conviction that the time is now and witnessed your unwavering commitment and understanding that health care is a decisive issue for our future prosperity. But you have also reminded all of us that it concerns more than material things; that what we face is above all a moral issue; that at stake are not just the details of policy, but fundamental principles of social justice and the character of our country."

The character of both the country and the Congress was not quite as noble as Kennedy's letter. A few days later, Obama stood before the joint session at a time of economic fear and political loathing. Before he could quote from Kennedy's letter to the members seated before him, one lawmaker took offense. Joe Wilson, from South Carolina, pointed his finger at the president as Obama denied that health care would now cover illegal immigrants.

"You lie!"

Sitting in the First Lady's box, listening to the chaos, was Laura Klitzka, the Wisconsin mother of two with terminal cancer and limitless spirit.

The distrust was not confined to southern Republicans. Soon after the speech, Obama's aides lost patience with Baucus and the Senate process. They began to look at the option of using budget reconciliation rules to pass a health care bill with a simple majority of votes instead of the sixty-vote supermajority needed to break a Republican filibuster. But that maneuver would cost them six or seven Democrats, leaving another excruciatingly close vote on a more narrowly defined bill.

They were stuck with Baucus and needed to force his hand. Baucus appeared reluctant to move ahead with a bill for consideration, or markup, in his Finance Committee. "There was pressure to move with all deliberate speed and pressure to move in a bipartisan way," said a senior Senate Democratic staffer. The White House decided to demand speed. Obama's aides privately drafted their own bill, and in September they threatened to post it on the White House website and move toward a vote. It was precisely the kind of Clinton-era tactic Obama had eschewed: to write and publish their own detailed legislation. Yet the threat seemed to work. Baucus decided it was now time to move ahead with his own bill. "It was tense between the White House and Chairman Baucus," said DeParle. "But not ugly. No one doubted that he more than anyone had staked himself on this and wanted to get it done."

In October, Baucus emerged from his committee with a successful vote on health care. After more than a year of his own talks, memos, studies, and hearings—and eight months of Obama's supervision—he won just one Republican vote: Olympia Snowe of Maine. His strategy cost the White House at least three months of delays and a summer of pain. "In retrospect, many staffers think we could have gotten the same result in the Finance Committee on July 15 that we got in October," says DeParle.

Even the effort to win the deliberative Snowe fell apart, as Baucus gave way to a broader effort in the Senate, led by the more brusque Democratic leader, Harry Reid. "People don't know how much time the president, our team at the White House, and frankly Senator Baucus spent in continuing to work with Senator Snowe," said DeParle. But now there was no one to hold her hand and coax her vote. Reid focused on getting up to the magic sixty-vote tally, while the White House worked on winning over the wavering, more conservative Democrats—Nebraska's Ben Nelson and Virginia's Jim Webb—as well as Connecticut's Joe Lieberman, now an independent, and the two Maine Republicans, Snowe and Susan Collins. But Snowe did not like Reid's take-it-or-leave-it approach and wanted to be treated as a serious negotiating partner, even though her ideas endured. "I could give you a list that would run to two pages of all the things of hers that were in the bill that passed the Senate and remain in the bill," said DeParle. "The president kept them in there, mostly because they were policies he agreed with. She's a moderate and so is he. And he wanted this to be a bill that moderates could support."

The president himself was impressed with the tenacity of the Republican opposition. "You have to give the Republicans credit, just from a pure political perspective, that they used every instrument available to them in the Senate to prolong the process in such a way that helped drive down support nationally, that gave everybody a sense that somehow Washington was broken," he told me. "At a time when everybody was worrying about jobs, for us to have to spend six to nine months on this piece of legislation obviously was not helpful."

The House voted for health care reform in early November by a margin of 5 votes out of 435. Just one Republican voted with the Democrats.

After several weeks of sweetheart state-centric deals with individual Democratic senators—especially for Louisiana and Nebraska—the Senate was now ready to move. Early Christmas Eve morning, senators voted for health care reform by a margin of 60 to 40, with no Republican support. The lawmakers promptly disappeared for their vacation, along with President Obama, who had delayed his family trip to Hawaii for the vote. "In hindsight we probably screwed up as Democrats," said one senior Democratic staffer. "All of us were just dying. Some of us wanted to come back December 26, conference this thing, and pass it January 5: 'Just finish this fucking bill right now.' But the White House wanted to cool off and take some time off: 'Our people are exhausted and can't think straight.'" At the White House, the early plans for a return the day after Christmas were shelved. "There was a feeling the Senate was leaving and there was no way of getting them back here," said one senior West Wing staffer.

Nobody noticed that Martha Coakley had effectively ceased campaigning in public.

Obama and his aides returned to the White House for surgery on the health care bill just six days before Coakley's candidacy died. Instead of stepping back, Obama was now shuttling between rooms inside the West Wing, trying to broker deals with Democrats and their supporters. On the first day, he spent six hours in talks with House and Senate Democrats, focusing especially on one emotional and contentious dispute: the terms of a new tax on so-called Cadillac, high-cost health care plans. Backed by the labor unions, the House preferred a general tax on the wealthy, especially millionaire couples, to pay for part of the health care reforms.

For House Democrats, the debate was typical of the impractical state of mind inside the West Wing. "The Cadillac tax goes after the health care benefits for working people, and it's a much harder sell," said one senior House Democratic staffer. "The bulk of the House Democrats are more progressive. The White House thinks there's a strong argument for the Cadillac tax because it reduces consumption and raises revenue. That is good in the abstract. But the House is a different animal. We stay pretty close to the ground and get elected every two years. We look at things differently."

They did indeed look at taxes differently. Obama, like the Senate Democrats, was taken with the notion that the tax on Cadillac plans could change behavior among patients and doctors. He wanted to do much more than cover the uninsured or those with preexisting conditions. Obama wanted to shift the culture of health care. "I don't just want to put everybody in the same creaky old system," he would tell his senior aides throughout the health care debate. "I want to make sure that we really are doing things that help to bring costs down." That meant siding with the economists, not his political advisers, when it came to the Cadillac tax.

Such arguments meant little to the labor unions and their advocates in the House. Inside the expansive Roosevelt Room, Obama sat through a long discussion of how the Cadillac tax would hurt working families. Anna Burger of the Service Employees International Union (SEIU) argued that the tax would hit one of her members who worked in a New Hampshire community college and made $30,000 a year, but had a health care plan that cost $32,000 a year.

"Well, she has to work in a government job, then, because no going concern can afford that," Obama replied. "That's part of what I'm trying to do with these health benefits that are that expensive. It's not in anyone's interests. It's not in your interests in labor to have those kinds of health benefits. You want people to be taking home a living wage, not spending it on health care."

Still, Obama pulled Nancy-Ann DeParle aside after the meeting to make some concessions. "I want to be sure that this doesn't affect someone like that right away," he said. "Is there some way to phase it in?"

Two days later, he faced the same arguments from a more determined opponent: House Speaker Nancy Pelosi. A prodigious fund-raiser and disciplined vote-getter, Pelosi was relentless in negotiations. When it came to the Cadillac tax, she repeated insistently how it would snag working families, not simply the wealthy. Soon Obama wearied of the harangues. "I'm not a stupid man," he told her, trying to cut her short. Pelosi seemed unfazed by the slap.

It made little difference, and he took little offense. "I don't think Nancy is difficult to negotiate with at all," he told me. "I think that Nancy is very mindful that she is the leader of her caucus. And I think Nancy is somebody who understood the sensitivities in the House, the political difficulties that her members were going to be facing in reelection, and I think in all our negotiations [she] wanted to exhaust every possibility of relieving some of the political pain on her members while still getting the job done. And I never faulted her for that. I actually had fun negotiating with Nancy."

The result was not as dramatic as Pelosi hoped: Obama agreed to minor changes, delaying the tax until 2018, well after the broader reforms would begin. But they were enough to win over the unions and the House Democrats. "It feels like a boil got lanced," said one of Obama's health care aides. "The unions are very enthusiastic about the deal."

Winning support—or neutralizing opposition—was only one of Obama's goals. In his view, all the technical details of health care, and all the feverish rhetoric, led people to forget what they were trying to do in the first place. Obama ducked out of his West Wing meetings to talk to the House Democrats at one of their brainstorming retreats in the new Capitol Hill Visitor Center. His pep talk on health care was intended not just for the broader group of Democrats but for the leaders onstage beside him. It was time, he argued, to think of the greater good—not just the personal tally of wins and losses. "Now, I know that some of the fights we've been going through have been tough," he said. "I know that some of you have gotten beaten up at home. Some of the fights that we're going to go through this year are going to be tough as well. But just remember why each of us got into public service in the first place. We found something that was worth fighting for."

Obama's high-minded oratory had little immediate impact. He returned to the White House to continue the talks that would either make or break a deal between his own Democrats in the House and Senate. Never mind the fiery attacks of Republicans and their determined opposition to health care reform. The distrust and rivalry between Democrats on both sides of Capitol Hill was just as fiery and determined. To the House, the Senate was too ready to tilt to the right and relinquish core principles that would help working folks. To the Senate, the House was hopelessly unrealistic and preferred all-out political warfare to reasonable compromise. Besides technical differences over taxes, there was one big challenge: the House bill cost some $200 billion more than the Senate version, and topped the politically perilous figure of $1 trillion over ten years. "Their negotiating style is 'No. Our way.' They don't give ground," said one senior Senate Democratic staffer. "They are not deal makers. They're not trained as deal makers over there. It's my way or the highway. It was brutal." To White House aides, Nancy Pelosi was just a determined advocate for her side. "She's a very tough negotiator," said one West Wing staffer. "She's going to stay at that table until she comes out with what she wants."

It was Obama who had to leave the table first. After a day of haggling, he needed to travel to his daughters' school, Sidwell Friends, for a flute recital at 8:00 p.m. "We have a $75 billion gap," he told the congressional leaders. "Everybody go home and figure out how to make a proposal." Both sides retreated to their conference rooms on Capitol Hill, while the Obamas attended to their parental duties. When they all returned to the Cabinet Room, the Senate Democrats offered to halve the difference.

"Here's our proposal," said Pelosi. "We don't have one. Our proposal is our position."

The meeting fell apart on the spot. The senators walked across the hall to the Roosevelt Room, shaking their heads in disbelief. Before long, Rahm Emanuel walked in. "Look," he said, "the House guys would kill me if they knew I was back here right now. This is how we tie a bow around this thing. It's what we said when we closed out deals in banking." The senators chuckled at Emanuel's obvious shtick: his hammed-up sense of secrecy and the claims of big-bucks deal making. But it was late, around 10:00 p.m., and they were ready to make one final deal to halve the difference again. "If you offer this, then we'll do this," Emanuel assured them. "I'll go home and pop champagne."

The senators returned to the Cabinet Room to make their offer of a $15 billion cut. "Here's our offer," said Pelosi. "Nothing."

This time it was the turn of the House Democrats to move to the Roosevelt Room. When they returned, Obama was ready for his final pitch. "It's a $15 billion difference and it's eleven p.m. Here's how I propose dealing with it," he said, before outlining a package of tweaks to spending and taxes. The senators agreed. Henry Waxman, one of the powerful House committee chairmen, raised his hand. "Mr. President, I think you have put together a very promising set of numbers," he said. "I can tell you I think it's a very good faith offer. I don't speak for the House, but I think we can work with this." Pelosi, sitting next to the president, was muttering under her breath, visibly annoyed. "Henry," she said, "I agree with you on two things. One, the president put forward some numbers. Two, Henry, you don't speak for the House."

Obama appeared pissed. He clenched his jaw and raised his voice in righteous indignation—an extraordinary sight for members of Congress. "Dammit, folks, this is history," he sputtered. "We're *this* close to history. We're $15 billion away. This is outrageous. I'm leaving this to Rahm. I'm going to bed. Good night. I'm out of here. You guys can figure it out." He promptly marched out of the room.

"Rahm," he said on his way out, "clean it up."

For the next two hours Emanuel tied a bow around a deal. They broke at 1:30 on Friday morning, leaving their staff to draw up the detailed proposals over the weekend.

The presidential walkout was an act, a stage show designed to shock the congressional leaders into action. And it worked. "I wasn't really that frustrated," Obama told me later, in the Oval Office. "The truth was we were very pleased that it was going as well as it was. There are certain points during negotiations where the big issues have really been settled. Everybody knows where the agreement is going to be, and people are then dickering over stuff that is not worth another hour or two of lost sleep. And we were at that stage. So I made a gesture just to remind people that we shouldn't be nickel-and-diming each other when we're talking about big historic legislation like that."

The tactic worked only up to a point. The nickel-and-diming had wasted precious time and goodwill. If the negotiations had gone smoother, and ended earlier, the House and Senate could have voted on a final bill on the day of the Massachusetts election itself. "It would have been tough. We needed drafting and scoring," said a senior Democratic staffer. "But we could have wrapped it up on election day." Inside the West Wing, the president's aides looked at that option but rejected it for the sake of political appearances. It was already clear that the country had turned against the backroom deals and the forced politics. "It would have been possible, and I believe that was considered," said one aide. "But the president didn't want to do it that way because he thought it would look like the thing we were accused of (which is not what we did): ramming it through. He didn't want to do that."

To Obama, the great irony of Scott Brown's victory was how close he felt to his own triumph on health care. "The truth of the matter is, it went surprisingly well. That was part of what was frustrating about the Massachusetts vote, was that the negotiations had gone so well during the course of the week, much better than we had expected," he told me. "There was some late-night jockeying between House and Senate members, but the fact is that we had 98, 99 percent of it settled, and had it not been for the Massachusetts vote, we would have had it settled probably that same day or the next day."

What *did* Obama want to do? Once his party lost the Massachusetts seat, how would he revive health care and his presidency? The answers were either hard to explain or not forthcoming.

When Obama met with his senior aides, he would turn his hands around each other in opposite directions. "It's like a Rubik's Cube," he told his senior advisers. "We've just got to figure out the right way to make the pieces fit together."

"A Rubik's Cube," thought Nancy-Ann DeParle. "That's not a good metaphor for me. It's a metaphor of frustration."

For Obama, health care was an even more intricate puzzle to be solved. How could he make it work? And how could he explain it to voters? It was just like one of his lowest points in the fall of 2007, as he struggled to connect with voters in Iowa. He was trailing in third place in the polls, and his donors were frustrated and angry at his flailing campaign. "I have to figure out how to connect with them," he had told his senior aides. "I'm not connecting with them. It's a safe, and I've almost got the combination of how to get it open."

His chief of staff, Rahm Emanuel, preferred a smash-and-grab raid to some elegant safecracking. He was pushing hard for a smaller, cheaper package of insurance industry reforms that both parties could readily accept. But Senate Democrats believed that approach was delusional. "It was a death spiral," said one senior staffer. "The reforms wouldn't work unless there were more people in the pool." Still, Emanuel continued to push for a scaled-down bill, even though his ally Nancy Pelosi derided that notion. Emanuel even drafted his brother Zeke, a health care expert inside the White House budget office, to write up a bill along those lines.

Inside the West Wing, the team was falling apart. Staffers blamed their political office and their communications team. They questioned the tireless and low-key congressional liaison Phil Schiliro, a former senior House staffer. Everyone blamed the Coakley campaign, the national party, and congressional Democrats in general. "It was as close to finger-pointing as I have ever seen in our group of people since the campaign," said one senior Obama aide. "You just don't finger-point. You're supposed to get over the rivalries. But there was a period when some people were starting to blame Phil Schiliro for having been too obsequious to the Hill, of having given up too much on the timetable, and keeping things behind closed doors."

As Democrats and pundits lined up to declare health care dead, the president sat down for an interview with ABC's George Stephanopoulos in the Roosevelt Room. It was the day after the Massachusetts defeat, and Obama's comments seemed to lean toward Emanuel's strategy. "I would advise that we try to move quickly to coalesce around those elements of the package that people agree on," he explained. That sound bite was replayed on cable TV shows and the evening news. They suggested Obama was ready to scale back his health care package.

But they told only half the story. A few minutes later, Obama told Stephanopoulos why a comprehensive approach was the only one that made sense.

"I don't know how we avoid taking on these big problems," he continued. "Let me just give you a very simple example, just so you get a sense of why these things are so important. If you ask the American people about health care, one of the things that drives them crazy is insurance companies denying people coverage because of preexisting conditions. Well, it turns out that if you don't make sure that everybody has health insurance, then you can't eliminate insurance companies—you can't stop insurance companies from discriminating against people because of preexisting conditions. Well, if you're going to give everybody health insurance, you've got to make sure it's affordable. So it turns out that a lot of these things are interconnected. Now, I could have said, 'Well, we'll just do what's safe. We'll just take on those things that are completely noncontroversial.' The problem is the things that are noncontroversial end up being the things that don't solve the problem. And this is true on every issue."

Even White House staffers were confused, never mind regular voters. Obama's aides were unclear whether their boss was going to bury his own plan or try to revive it. Two days later, without warning, he gave them their answer in an unscripted response to an unprompted question at his first public event after the Massachusetts defeat. At the very end of a town hall meeting in Elyria, Ohio, Obama took a question from a businessman wanting to borrow money to open a factory. Held in a darkened gym inside a community college, the whole event was designed to address concerns about the economy, to demonstrate that the president was focused on the top priority for voters.

But Obama could not resist one final discussion about health care at the end of a week when most political experts—and many in his own party—had already pronounced his effort dead. "Now, I'm out of time, but I want to say one last thing," he said, raising his hand above his head as if to halt the debate. Speaking in front of his traditional presidential podium and a low bulletproof barrier, he explained why insurance reforms could only take place if there were more people compelled to buy insurance in the first place. "A lot of these insurance reforms are connected to some other things we have to do to make sure that everybody has some access to coverage. All right?" he began, pacing up and down the small stage. "None of the big issues that we face in this country are simple. Everybody wants to act like they're simple. Everybody wants to say that they can be done easily. But they're complicated. They're tough. The health care system is a big, complicated system, and doing it right is hard . . . We can't shy away from it, though. We can't sort of start suddenly saying to ourselves, America or Congress can't do big things; that we should only do the things that are noncontroversial; we should only do the stuff that's safe. Because if that's what happens, then we're not going to meet the challenges of the twenty-first century. And that's not who we are. That's not how we used to operate, and that's not how I intend us to operate going forward."

Back at the White House, Obama's health care staffers were transfixed by the TV screen. They had no idea what he wanted to do with their work of the last twelve months. "That wasn't in the talking points," Nancy-Ann DeParle said to one of her team. "He still wants to do this."

On Capitol Hill, they were paying no attention to the president. Instead the Democrats were indulging in a mixture of mass hysteria and civil war. "The House is acting as if nothing has changed," complained one senior Democratic staffer in the Senate. "They think we're fucking idiots. They win their special elections." Inside Capitol Hill and the West Wing, the more experienced principals and staffers knew there was only one realistic course of action: for the House to pass the Senate bill, and then for both sides to pass a package of fixes under budget rules of reconciliation that only required a simple majority. "Coakley may be a blessing in disguise," said one senior Obama aide. "If progressives realize that we don't have sixty votes, it takes that monkey off our back. As long as the House acts like grown-ups and takes the Senate bill, then deals with other stuff through reconciliation. But Schiliro, who used to work on the House side, says you can't count on anyone being adult."

Leading the House Democrats, Speaker Pelosi was so volcanic that much of the White House strategy was shaped in terms of how to deal with her. "There was the school that wanted a smaller plan, and there was the school that wanted to get Nancy Pelosi to come over," said one senior West Wing staffer. "She was enraged. She blamed us and thought we blew Massachusetts. She thought it would have huge consequences for everyone."

At her first West Wing meeting with the president and Harry Reid, two weeks after Coakley's defeat, Pelosi emerged into the hallway next to the Oval Office looking beet red. When Emanuel suggested a smaller-scale approach, focusing on just the popular insurance reforms, Pelosi snorted. All along, she felt that Emanuel, Axelrod, and Vice President Biden wanted to go small. There was no way she would sign up to "kiddie care," as she told Obama.

"Why don't you pass the Senate bill?" asked Reid.

"I can't do it because I don't have the votes," she shot back. "And don't you ever say the House has to pass the Senate bill," she warned Reid and Obama, raising her voice. "I need time. I have to bring people along. People have to get over the shock. They have to see what the consequences are if we fail. If you people tell everyone to pass the Senate bill, I won't have any room to maneuver."

The price of Pelosi's room to maneuver was no room for Obama. If he couldn't talk about a game plan, then he looked weak and indecisive. "For two weeks he got the shit kicked out of him in the press for not being a leader," said one senior staffer. "Everyone on cable TV got their pound of flesh."

Obama's aides knew that their work with Congress had now taken on a new dimension: they had to overcome not only the Republican opposition but also the distance between House and Senate Democrats. "One of our objectives here is the House has got to stop distrusting the Senate and start distrusting the Republicans," said one senior Obama official. "If you need—and I'm not saying this neg-atively or cynically—if you need an opponent for motivation, it's not the Senate Democrats, it's the House Republicans that should be your motivation. And getting them to focus on that is important."

The result of the infighting was that Obama could barely men-tion health care in his own State of the Union speech delivered little more than a week after the defeat in Massachusetts. In the absence of any public strategy, his aides were at a loss to figure out how to talk about their domestic priority. In their planning sessions for the big-gest presidential speech of the year, they needed some kind of guid-ance from their boss. "We came to the topic of health care and it was an open question," said Dan Pfeiffer. "We just lost Massachusetts. No one knows where it's going to go. People are going to read a lot into whatever it is the president says about health care. But we still don't know. There was all this frustration of people who wanted to move forward, and people who wanted to do other things. We just needed an answer. It was *killing* our planning not knowing what was going to happen. So it came up, what are we going to say?"

Obama appeared somewhat less stressed. "Well, here's what I want to say," he told his aides. "I'm still committed to a big health care bill. But I think we should take a step back after Massachusetts, pass a jobs bill, see where we are, and then come back to health care." His aides sighed with relief; they had the bare bones of a plan.

To those who wanted him to punch back against Congress, Obama had a simpler message. "Relax," he said. "They will come to understand that they can't walk away."

His mood seemed frustratingly familiar to those who had worked with him through the long presidential campaign. When Valerie Jarrett asked him how to respond to the public attacks, he smiled calmly before saying, "Valerie, this is just the first quarter." In his own mind, he was the basketball star who would raise his game just when everyone else was flagging. He had done it in the primaries, and again in the general election. At each stage, when his supporters began to doubt his determination, his stamina, or his abilities, he believed he would be the clutch player. "Oh no," thought Jarrett. "Don't do this to us again. Don't wait till the fourth quarter!"

THREE

REDEMPTION

The snow started to fall the following week, muffling the White House and the Capitol under heavy layers that froze and buried the landscape. Week after week, the snow deepened and hardened in storms that subsumed even the Chicago crowd. In their first winter in Washington, Obama and his friends found it all too easy to mock the nation's capital for its readiness to capitulate to a dusting of flakes. In their second winter, all they could do was join the rest of the city to pick up their shovels, trudge through the slush, and hunker down. Four snowstorms in three weeks snapped all records since 1899, when William McKinley lived in the Executive Mansion, not long after the

United States annexed Hawaii and the Supreme Court found that segregation was legal. For all that had changed since then, such heavy snow could still close down most of the federal government, leaving few people at work beyond the White House.

Outside the Oval Office, the Rose Garden was thick with snow that clumped in the joints of tree branches. The steps down to the lawn were cleared, but they led nowhere. A branch broken by the weight of flakes hung limply in front of the tall windows of the outer Oval, where Obama's personal aides managed his time and space. The only disturbances were the paw prints left by the frolicking first dog, Bo.

Obama's comments on health care in his State of the Union made little impression and even less news. As the House and Senate Democrats struggled to clear their own path to a health care bill, he could only stand back and watch. He asked for bipartisan ideas; he half blamed himself for failing to sell his own plan; he pleaded for patience and perseverance. "As temperatures cool," he said weakly, "I want everyone to take another look at the plan we've proposed."

Now that the temperatures were sufficiently chilled, he was starting to reheat the politics. Inside the Oval Office, gathered behind the *Resolute* desk and in front of his family photos, were a clutch of cabinet secretaries. His wife, Michelle, stood with her hand on his red leather chair as he talked about the virtues of her new plan to reduce obesity among children. His head scanned from left to right as he spoke to an imaginary audience on either side of his desk. In fact, there were photographers crouched in front of him, TV cameras opposite him, and staffers pressed behind the sofa against the back wall. The desk was polished and empty, save for two sheets of paper in a black folder, his gray presidential phone, and a single pen in an oversized wooden holder crafted from the timbers of a British antislavery ship. The papers were an executive order giving his administration ninety days to write a plan of action to turn his wife's health care ideas into reality. He scribbled his name on the second sheet and turned to look up at his wife. "It's done, honey," he said, sounding like he had just finished another family chore.

"Now we work," she replied as her own staff applauded.

This was the easy end of health care: a feel-good campaign with an unimpeachable message of healthy food, regular exercise, children's fitness, and the support of the private sector. It was pulled together by a coalition of officials led by the Obamas' smart young personal chef, Sam Kass, and the president's domestic policy chief, Melody Barnes. But its rollout lacked energy and inspiration. Three hours later, at a formal event in an overheated State Dining Room, the D.C. schoolchildren sitting onstage beside Mrs. Obama were struggling to control their yawning mouths and drooping eyes as the grown-ups droned on about their calorie intake. An issue that united red and blue America, black and white, urban and rural, young and old—the very promise of Obama's breakthrough speech at the 2004 Boston convention—was simultaneously desirable, doable, and earnestly dull.

As the First Lady prepared to move ahead with her version of health care, her husband was sitting in the long Cabinet Room overlooking the snow-covered Rose Garden. He sat opposite a portrait of Teddy Roosevelt that possessed more vitality than the congressional leaders around his own cabinet table. Less than eighteen months earlier, he had sat at the same table, with the same leaders, as the financial sector was melting down and Congress seemed incapable of responding. At the time, the antagonism and distrust between him and the GOP leaders were already in place. The passage of time had not warmed the room. Now John Boehner, leading the GOP in the House, sat with a thinly veiled disdain for Obama's rhetoric. "I think it's fair to say that the American people are frustrated with the lack of progress on some key issues," Obama began with just a hint of understatement. Boehner sighed out loud and stared at the president, as if to underscore his own frustration with the man he blamed for the lack of progress. The architect of the frustrating stalemate was his counterpart in the Senate, Mitch McConnell—a man whose mission was to block bipartisanship. His waxen face was emotionless and unflinching, unlike that of his Democratic opponent, Harry Reid, whose eyes scanned across the wall of TV and still cameras in front of him. As Obama outlined his hopes for agreement on a jobs package and deficit reduction, just one leader seemed to relish the moment. Nancy Pelosi sat still and licked her lips continuously, as if the White House was readying a large steak for lunch.

After the cameras moved out, the leaders set aside their table manners. Both parties liked to talk about the deficit, and senators from both sides had proposed the idea of a fiscal commission that would make binding recommendations to cut the government's debts. But now the Republicans were blocking the commission, fearing they would be forced to agree to higher taxes in the process. "Math is not partisan," Obama told them, as he asked the GOP leaders to stop the grandstanding and join the process.

"If you're serious about cutting spending," Boehner replied, "why don't we do it now?" He didn't need to wait for a commission, Boehner argued. He already had the authority to send Congress specific cuts to spending bills, which the same Congress had just approved. "Let members vote up or down on wasteful Washington spending!" Boehner said later.

There were few bigger grandstands than health care, although both sides only spoke briefly about the president's biggest domestic priority. Obama wanted to hear the other party's ideas as long as they were serious about lowering costs, reining in insurance abuses, and making health care more affordable. Boehner and McConnell agreed that the status quo was unacceptable, but they wanted him to start again from scratch.

Never mind the subject—they could barely agree on a definition, or a purpose, of bipartisanship. McConnell said he supported Obama on nuclear energy and offshore drilling for oil. But that was only half the deal—the Republican half. In exchange, Obama wanted their support for ways to limit carbon emissions and climate change. "Bipartisanship can't be that I agree to all the things that they believe in or want, and they agree to none of the things I believe in and want, and that's the price of bipartisanship, right?" Obama told reporters a few hours later. "I'm willing to move off some of the preferences of my party in order to meet them halfway. But there's got to be some give on their side as well. That's true on health care. That's true on energy. That's true on financial reform."

All he could do was crack a joke about how little common ground there was between his party and his critics. It was five years since he talked of the shared values of red and blue America. It was two years since he turned his convention oratory into reality in the snowfields of Iowa, attracting independents and even some Republicans to his campaign. Now, at a surprise appearance in the narrow press briefing room just a few paces from the Oval Office, he was left with not much more than a punch line.

"A little while ago I had a meeting with the Democratic and Republican congressional leaders, and it went very well. In fact, I understand that McConnell and Reid are out doing snow angels on the South Lawn together," he began, as the reporters laughed, among them Chuck Todd of NBC. "Can you picture that, Chuck? Not really?"

In fact, McConnell and Boehner went outside to the White House driveway to shiver in the snow with the press. In front of them, a construction team was sawing its way through the frozen earth to dig up two trees on the North Lawn. Watching the GOP leaders from the warmth of the press office, Obama's aides were experiencing a rare feeling: happiness at the political and physical discomfort of their opponents. "It sure feels different from a normal day," said one of them. "It's hard to stay on offense the whole time when you're running government. You could do it every day in the campaign, because it's easier to find those opportunities. But it's hard to do that in government. Are our poll numbers higher at the end of the day? I have no idea. But it just *feels* better."

Was the promise of the 2008 campaign just a joke, a ruse about some new kind of politics? In the winter of early 2010, the very notion seemed in deep freeze. The White House blamed determined Republican opposition; the GOP blamed the Democrats for jamming their agenda through. There were few who would venture between the two. The real answer lay less with the partisans and more with the character of the man who had promised to unite his own country.

What kind of politician was he, and what did he represent? Was he a reasoned and reasonable negotiator or a driven and competitive alpha male? Was he trying to change Washington's ways or master them for himself? These questions were not intellectual exercises, and they were not easy to answer. They represented the central axis of disagreement inside the Obama White House, the dividing line that separated two powerful and self-righteous camps: the Revivalists and the Survivalists.

The Revivalists were campaign loyalists who believed in the transformational spirit of Change. They nurtured a sense of mission and a sincere belief in the unique talents of their leader to bend the arc of history and reform the culture of politics. Above all, they believed the White House had erred by drifting away from its campaign identity.

The Survivalists were political insiders who measured Change in the smaller increments of the here and now. They saw themselves as scrappy realists who used any means necessary to advance their leader's agenda. They believed the campaign was a useful but childish thing unable to survive in the harsh world of Washington's hyperpartisan politics.

One group saw itself as the keepers of the flame of the Obama campaign; the other saw itself as the pragmatic experts who pulled the levers of government.

Obama himself straddled both groups, leaving the questions about his character and purpose unresolved. He was an unconventional outsider who could break the established rules of politics to dramatic effect; yet he was also a conventional insider with an innate aversion to risk and a commitment to compromise. His mistake, if not his hubris, was to assume that others would either share his powers of reason or understand the sincerity of his motives.

These were questions that remained unanswered even after extensive debate, both internally and externally, through twenty-one months of a presidential campaign. John Edwards argued in Iowa that Obama did not have the stomach to change the system and challenge its vested interests. Hillary Clinton argued that he did not have the experience to manage the system and its vested interests. His own staffers sometimes found it hard to reconcile the new, mostly positive politics Obama wanted with his determination to win. For his part, Obama argued that Clinton embodied the same old failed system, and that only a new force could reform it and win. That was his message in the final days of the Iowa caucus campaign, when he spelled out the choice in the basement of a Masonic temple in downtown Des Moines. "The real gamble in this election is playing the same Washington game with the same Washington players and expecting a different result," Obama said. "This has been our message since the beginning of this campaign. It was our message when we were down, and our message when we were up. And it must be catching on, because in these last few weeks, everyone is talking about change. But you can't at once argue that you're the master of a broken system in Washington and offer yourself as the person to change it."

Two years later, in Washington, the choice was not so stark between mastering the system and changing it. The petty pace of day-to-day government, of negotiating with members of Congress and battling with the media, had altered the forces of Change. "The president said during the campaign, 'I don't want to be the master of the system. I want to change it.' But we have to do both," said David Axelrod, speaking on the eve of the anniversary of Obama's inauguration. "In order to get things done, you have to work with the Congress and you have to work with the system, which runs contradictory to the notion that you are going to change it. So there's this tension between getting things done and taking a strong stand on reform. How deeply should the president be involved with the legislative process? He has been deeply involved and we should probably be less so. He can't be a prime minister."

Health care reform was not just the biggest domestic legislation in a generation but the biggest test of Obama's style of governing and of his political identity. The struggle to define his character and politics was hard fought inside an inner circle that melded political and communications aides. For this was a battle of style as much as of substance. Of the president's five closest aides, no fewer than three saw themselves at the intersection of politics and messaging: chief of staff Rahm Emanuel, senior adviser David Axelrod, and press secretary Robert Gibbs. The other two embodied the insider and outsider of Obama's character: Pete Rouse, his former Senate chief of staff, and Valerie Jarrett, his family friend and a former Chicago city official. The balance was almost as exquisite as it was in flux.

First among these equals was Rahm Emanuel, the Survivalist leader and the loudest advocate of a Clinton-style mastery of the system. He served as pseudo–prime minister, über–press secretary, and strategist in chief. Where normal staffers struggled to cope with one job, Emanuel's capacity for three was merely a fraction of what he thought his brain could handle. Often his motormouth could barely keep pace with his machine-gun mind. Phrases popped out of his lips like lead slugs. If he was feeling generous, he might try to cushion the impact with a sentence; if not, he would take another shot. The performance almost lived up to the legend of the profane, hyperpartisan, hyperactive political hack. Like some Brazilian soccer star, the chief of staff went by one name in staff conversations across the administration: Rahm.

But for all his macho bravado, the tufts of graying hair and the deep, dark rings around his eyes pointed to an inner insecurity. Emanuel was a worrier—a teeth-clenching, dissatisfied ball of incessant nervous energy. The contrast with his boss was as striking as it was unnerving. Obama was preternaturally calm, content with his own company, and inclined toward complete sentences. Emanuel was unnaturally neurotic, in need of others to affirm his self-worth, and spoke in a shorthand of half-formed shapes.

His burden and his drive came from a sense of destiny, duty, and impossibly great expectations. Both his parents were political activists: his Israeli-born father was part of the militant Irgun group; his American mother embraced the nonviolence of the civil rights movement. They marched with Martin Luther King in Chicago, and raised their three sons to strive, to succeed, and to have some sense of public service.

Rahm, the middle son, learned his purpose on Earth at an early age. "Look, I share this story because it's telling," he explained to me.

"In our family room in our house are *all* the pictures—downstairs in the basement—of *all* the relatives on my mother's and father's side who never made it to the country. Pogrom. Holocaust. War of Independence. In the middle are the passports and the purse of my grandmother—paternal grandmother—and my two great-aunts, who came to America. It was very simple. And there was nothing subtle about it, as you can imagine. *You are lucky sons of bitches and you better not waste your time.* So I loved politics. I got in to politics to *help.* I consider it community service, in the sense of what you're doing . . . representing constituents, putting policies in place that you care about. However you want to divide it, slice and dice that thing, you can."

Young Rahm was especially close to his mother's father, whose life story merged personal courage with family support, ethnic persecution, and immigrant dreams. His grandfather had arrived in America as a teenage illegal immigrant, with no resources, no papers, and few friends. Emanuel could still get emotional talking about his grandfather, a union organizer and sometime boxer, years later, inside the White House. His survival story led directly, and indirectly, to Emanuel's own public service in Congress:

"My grandfather on my mother's side is a classic story. Moldavia, Russia-Romania border. Thirteen years old. Right at the height of the pogroms, 1917 revolution. And his relatives, or his parents, put him on a boat with a note to a third cousin from a different part of Moldavia, who he had never met when he was in Moldavia, with a note to ask him to help him. Lands in New York, as a thirteen-year-old on a boat, and makes his way to Chicago to meet his cousin, who he's never met. Basically puts him up for a temporary period of time, so he can get established. The irony of the irony of the irony of the story: it's Albany Park he settles in, which is the area I represented in Congress. Which is also the area where my dad first moved to from Israel to the United States, and opened up his private practice, set up a practice in . . . Albany Park."

Serving in Congress, Emanuel believed he was a lucky son of a bitch. A former Clinton White House staffer, he had successfully managed the 2006 Democratic takeover of the House. Before the call came from Obama's team two years later, toward the end of the general election, he had good reason to think he could one day become the first Jewish Speaker of the House. Besides, he and his wife, Amy, liked their life in Chicago. So when the job offer landed, he made it clear to friends—including those in the press—that he was ambivalent.

"It's simple and complicated," he told me. "If all you were about was your career—which I know people think I am?—you'd have stayed where I was, in the House. If in fact you got into public service because you wanted to do things with it, not to accumulate power for the sake of power but to do something with it, this was a unique president at a unique time in history, where you can make an impact. If I was doing it just for my personal life—and I mean personal life for my kids' health, the health of my family life in its totality—you wouldn't do this. Truth is, Amy and I had a pretty good gig going on. Gone three to four days a week. Kids were in a great school. Had a summer home I haven't now been to in sixteen months that I'm paying for. We had a great life. On the other hand, this is a once-in-a-lifetime and a *unique* moment in time, and, you know, it's like this is the obligation you have and the responsibility you have."

Emanuel was the master of the system, not the man to change it. As a product of the Clinton era, he represented much of what the Obama campaign fought against in the extended primary season. Emanuel was the most visible source of the tension between governing and campaigning—someone who was ready to compromise and cut deals rather than stick to the spirit of Change. However, that was precisely the reason why Obama chose him for his own chief of staff. It greatly perplexed some of Obama's most faithful aides and distressed many of his supporters. Yet Obama appreciated in Emanuel all that he lacked on his own. "Obama didn't choose Rahm because he was so much like him. He chose him because he complemented him," said Axelrod. "He brought a set of skills and experiences that Obama didn't have and an orientation that was necessary. So they're not alike. But as should be the case, the president sets the direction and Rahm has faithfully executed that job. And that's what a chief of staff is supposed to be."

Emanuel's leading presence in the transition, alongside other Clinton veterans, dismayed many of Obama's most loyal aides. To those who endured the wrath of the Clinton machine for daring to work for the upstart senator's campaign, it seemed like betrayal to watch a transition run by Emanuel and John Podesta, who had been chief of staff in the Clinton White House. "When I walked into the transition offices, there was Rahm and Podesta and Hillary," said one senior White House official and Obama loyalist. "I was astonished." Those loyalists blamed the Clinton officials for something that never happened inside the campaign: the regular leaking of news, especially appointments. "It was so unlike the campaign and it was just wrong," said one longtime Obama adviser. "Before someone got announced, their name was leaked so everybody could shoot at that person. It was to see if there was any dirt on someone, rather than doing your own vetting, and that's the way the transition was handled. It wasn't done by someone who was involved in the campaign."

To those involved in the campaign, the Clinton clique wasn't the only shocking part of the transition. Even before the election, in early October, the transition team wanted to move away from the campaign's core commitments to keep lobbyists out of the transition and the new administration. After two weeks of back-and-forth, the two sides clashed on a conference call with Podesta. "The assumption from the transition team was that we were looking for cover, a way to shed that particular pledge," said one longtime Obama aide.

"We felt very strongly that Obama didn't just make that up out of nothing." Podesta said there were talented people, whom they all knew personally, who would not be able to join the administration. He began to name names, but the campaign team was unimpressed. "Okay," they said. "Tough."

The Revivalist who ran the Obama campaign was not part of the transition or the White House. David Plouffe was burned out after the general election; in fact, he felt that way as early as the end of the extended primary season. He chose to step aside, write a book, make money giving speeches, and save himself for some unspecified role in Obama's reelection. In fact, he worked hard to make sure that Emanuel took the job of chief of staff. Plouffe believed Emanuel was a warrior with the political brain and congressional experience that made him uniquely qualified for the job. That confidence paid off, but it opened the door to huge differences in style and discipline. "Rahm is in a class all by himself," said one Obama aide who worked closely with both Plouffe and Emanuel. "But who he is and what the campaign was are two separate things. There have been identity issues. People had to unlearn the way they were conditioned to think about politics, which is that you don't need to win every little battle or news cycle. Decisions are made now, and the group that doesn't win tries to canvass support to undo the decision. We didn't have a lot of that in the campaign."

West Wing staffers saw Emanuel as the second most powerful figure in the White House—far more influential than Vice President Joe Biden—and Emanuel enjoyed that power and status. Yet he remained unsure of his own relationship to Obama and suffered a deep fear of failure. He would approach those with longer ties to the president with a nagging question. "You know him better than I do," Emanuel would say. "What do you think he thinks of how I'm doing?" "He is deeply insecure," said a senior Obama aide. "He cares about every detail and keeps himself up worrying about everything. It's not about his agenda, which may make things harder, because he used to be a principal." That worry took a visible toll on the man who liked to look and sound like a dynamo. "Don't be fooled by Rahm," said another trusted Obama aide. "He may look like he's got a lot of energy. But he's burned out like the rest of us."

The Emanuel mythology ran deep inside the West Wing: the chief of staff was exceptional. His old Chicago friend David Axelrod liked to retell the story of how Emanuel asked his advice on whether he should run for Congress for the first time, in 2001. "Do you think I can win?" Emanuel asked Axelrod, who was the best-established Democratic political consultant in Chicago.

"I *know* you're going to win," said Axelrod, even though Emanuel was no shoo-in.

"How do you know I'm going to win?"

"Because you're not allowed to lose," replied Axelrod. "You're like a heat-seeking missile."

The contrast with Obama—who rarely appeared flummoxed by his own failures—was unsettling to Emanuel. Obama behaved as if on the edge of victory; Emanuel lived on the edge of defeat. To those who knew him best, Emanuel's insecurity intensified around the seemingly secure Obama. "Rahm is a guy whose insides are constantly churning. That's his nature," said Axelrod. "And so this kind of cool, centered quality of the president, his sort of tranquillity, is sometimes hard for Rahm to understand when he's dealing with the pressures of the job in his own way."

Unlike his boss, Emanuel wasn't interested in looking reasonable with Republicans; he wanted to look victorious. He didn't care much for uniting red and blue America; he wanted blue America to beat its red rival. He didn't really agree with some of the core values of the Obama campaign—especially the notion that the new politics could be cleaner than the old. And he wasn't much convinced by Obama's reasoning on health care: that this was a once-in-a-generation chance to pass comprehensive reform. He saluted and followed orders. He fretted about turning the orders into action. But if the orders needed modification on the long road to victory, then he was ready to use the older politics, or be less comprehensive. The logic of deal making was not the logic of Change.

Obama was prepared to sacrifice time and political capital to make his policy bipartisan and more ambitious; Emanuel believed Obama did not have that luxury. "Time is your commodity. That answers everything," Emanuel said. "But a lot of us thought we didn't have the amount of time that was being dedicated. If you abandon the bipartisan talks you get blamed. He still wanted to try to achieve it that way. But that's one of a series of things you can look back on and be a genius about.

"My job as chief of staff is to give him 180-degree advice. He hired me, as he asked, to learn from the past, or to use my knowledge from my time in Congress and in the Clinton administration. Watching '94, watching '97 when we did kids' health care, and then studying Medicare, what were the lessons? The lesson about time as a commodity is not mine, it's Lyndon Johnson's. You got X amount of time; you gotta use it. And my view is, given where we are in politics and given where everything is, understand the trade-offs here. If you stay big, given where the clock is, what are the trade-offs and the equities you have to weigh?"

He plainly didn't agree with Obama's trade-offs. "Rahm is 100 percent loyal to this president, but he thinks half his decisions are insane," said one senior West Wing staffer. "And he viewed health care in that context."

Still, Emanuel did have a degree of sympathy for the daunting nature of his boss's job. After all, the voters had chosen to trust Obama's judgment, even if it differed from his own. "Look," he said, turning around in his chair to point at the Oval Office behind him, "you know what ends up down in that office? Bad and worse. Those are your choices. And the time frame they're on is immediate and crisis. That's the axis. Up here in the right-hand and the left-hand top corners are bad and worse choice; immediate and crisis are at the bottom. And that's it!" Emanuel clapped impatiently. "And then you gotta now choose! I gave him advice, but it's like everything. What are the equities you're weighing against each other, and where do you make those choices? And so, part of electing a president—and people know this instinctively—is where are they on policy and where are they on judgment? And he made a judgment based on, 'This is a once-in-a-lifetime to get this done.' I'm not sure, to tell you the truth, that I made that same judgment; that there's not another chance, and therefore this is the opportunity. I can see, and I understand exactly, this is the moment in time to make this political capital expenditure. That's what he did. And that's what a president is supposed to do. And that's his strength."

Emanuel wanted to shift from defense to offense as soon as possible. He saw two moments of opportunity. The first was the Republican House retreat in Baltimore, just ten days after the disaster in Massachusetts. The other was to create something similar to Bill Clinton's work session on welfare reform in 1995, staged at Blair House, across Pennsylvania Avenue from the White House. Emanuel didn't care for working with the Republicans. He wanted to force them to choose sides, and to turn the cameras on how they justified those choices. Either they wanted to oppose the president at all costs, or they wanted to help govern the country. Emanuel felt they could not have it both ways.

Obama wanted to engage with Republicans for entirely different reasons. He had long toyed with the idea of his own version of the British prime minister's question time: a televised exchange of questions and answers with the opposition party. He thought the regular debate would be very useful for the White House, Congress, and voters. He had wanted to go to the Republican House retreat in early 2009, at the start of his presidency, but his senior staff shot down the idea. He liked the idea of testing himself and his ideas in public; it might even allow him to find common ground with the more reasonable Republicans. It would certainly signal a change in the politics of Washington.

It was unusual, but not unprecedented, for presidents to visit the other party's retreat; Bush had done the same with the Democrats in 2007. Three days before the House GOP retreat, Dan Pfeiffer briefed Obama's senior staff about the event at their daily 7:30 a.m. meeting in Emanuel's office. Someone suggested opening up the whole event to the TV cameras, inviting them to stick around for the questions and answers after the president's set-piece remarks. It was an unconventional idea, and they loved it. But when Phil Schiliro, Obama's congressional liaison, called the Republican leadership to discuss the idea, the response was hesitant. The morning of the retreat, the White House leaked to reporters that the GOP was refusing to open up the session. The private response from Republicans was furious, but they caved. Emanuel liked to take credit for opening the session to the cameras, arguing that it was just the kind of transparent exchange the Republicans wanted the president to stage throughout the health care debate.

Whoever was responsible, and whatever the reasoning, the back-and-forth was unlike any other scene in the health care debate. Obama spoke from a presidential podium inside the newly remodeled Renaissance hotel in Baltimore's redeveloped Inner Harbor. His Republican opponents were dimly lit, or stood in darkness, with few microphones able to pick up their faint voices. The staging and sound were tilted in his favor. So were the debate skills. During the long presidential campaign, Obama had seized on moments when his opponents played political games. He loved to call out the gimmicks of his rivals, such as aggressive personal attacks or policies designed to grab the headlines. Those moments allowed him to look like a political outsider, a more authentic and honest voice than the tired and discredited politics of his Washington opponents, whether they were Democrats or Republicans. Now he could do the same, while also taking credit for exposing himself to unscripted and televised questions from his harshest critics.

The only irony was that he was using an Emanuel tactic—confronting the GOP—to profess his commitment to reach across the aisle.

Little more than halfway through, he took a question from Marsha Blackburn of Tennessee, who was concerned that her party's ideas for health care were not reaching him. When would he sit down and work with Republicans on health care? Obama assured her that he had seen their ideas and embraced some of them. His plan now looked a lot like the one proposed by a group of former Senate leaders at the Bipartisan Policy Center: Republicans Bob Dole and Howard Baker, and Democrat Tom Daschle, who was originally supposed to be leading the health care reform drive for Obama.

"Now, you may not agree with Bob Dole and Howard Baker, and, certainly, you don't agree with Tom Daschle on much, but that's not a radical bunch. But if you were to listen to the debate and, frankly, how some of you went after this bill, you'd think that this thing was some Bolshevik plot," he said with a hint of surprise, as his audience laughed a little nervously. "No, I mean, that's how you guys presented it. And so I'm thinking to myself, 'Well, how is it that a plan that is pretty centrist . . .'" This time, his audience grumbled out loud at the idea. "I'm just saying, I know you guys disagree, but if you look at the facts of this bill, most independent observers would say this is actually what many Republicans—is similar to what many Republicans proposed to Bill Clinton when he was doing his debate on health care. So all I'm saying is, we've got to close the gap a little bit between the rhetoric and the reality.

"You've given yourselves very little room to work in a bipartisan fashion because what you've been telling your constituents is, 'This guy is doing all kinds of crazy stuff that's going to destroy America.' And I would just say that we have to think about tone. It's not just on your side, by the way. It's on our side, as well."

When asked if he could stick around for a few more questions, Obama seemed happier than he had been at any time in the health care debate for weeks, if not months. "You know," he said, "I'm having fun."

"Okay," said Mike Pence, the Indiana congressman who chaired the meeting, trying to jump in on the president's fun, "so are we."

"This is great," Obama deadpanned, as the Republicans laughed and applauded.

Obama and his senior aides found the session more than just a source of fun. It revived their spirits after Massachusetts and the bleak anniversary of the inauguration. And it reminded them of the original playbook they had used to such dramatic effect through the presidential campaign. Perhaps the fourth quarter was about to begin.

The next day, Obama drove with a group of his closest aides to the Verizon Center in downtown Washington to watch the college basketball game between Georgetown and Duke, Reggie Love's alma mater. In the second half, Obama joined the CBS announcers Verne Lundquist and Clark Kellogg. "After retirement, I'm coming after your job, Clark," Obama said with his trademark grin. "I'm just letting you know. So you either have three more years or seven. You need to plan accordingly." Striking back, the CBS team aired some tape of Obama's breathless scrimmage with the University of North Carolina team in the 2008 campaign.

"You're obviously a left-hander," said Lundquist after watching tape of Obama missing an easy layup with his stronger left hand. "Do you have any problems at all going to your right?"

"You know, I went to the Republican House caucus just yesterday to prove that I could go to my right once in a while. But there's no doubt that I've got a stronger left hand." His coannouncers shook their heads and smiled at the layup of a one-liner.

That night he called his own time-out inside the Roosevelt Room with his most trusted aides. For some time Obama had been asking for strategy meetings on domestic and foreign policy, as well as communications, for the coming year. The message planning normally came last, once the policy outlines were clear. But now, at the point of his political collapse, the president did not want to wait. The politics and communications efforts were paramount to him. What was his message, and was his team as tight as they could be in their operations? For more than two hours, he grilled his senior advisers, along with his former campaign manager, David Plouffe, and his former communications director, Anita Dunn. The meeting took a familiar tone and shape for those who sat through the postmortem discussions after their primary losses in states like Ohio and Texas. Obama went around the table asking each of them for their thoughts. How had they all performed last year? What could they do differently?

The team's conclusion was gloomy. They had chosen to defer their course corrections time and again through the fall. Everything needed to wait until health care, but the wait had been almost fatal. They had lost one of the defining qualities of their campaign days: focus. "We weren't as disciplined as we used to be," said one participant. Instead of following their own priorities, they were following those of Congress. That might have made sense in politics, but it made no sense for their own message. They couldn't push back on members of Congress for fear of alienating them, even when the town hall meetings were spewing out rumors and lies. With no idea of the scope of any congressional deal, the White House could not easily sell health care reform in media interviews. "When Harry Reid and Nancy Pelosi's decision making drives your strategy, it's just hard," said another aide. Everyone knew the communications effort was struggling, including Dunn and her successor, Dan Pfeiffer, who had spent several weeks reviewing their operations. He wrote his critique in a seven-page memo and delivered a forty-five-minute version of his conclusions to the team in the Roosevelt Room. Pfeiffer believed the cabinet was underused in 2009. They had failed to coordinate their message with Democrats in Congress and Democratic pundits on cable and in print. Rapid response and planning were both in trouble. Above all, they needed to be more strategic in using the president's time. They relied too much on him to deliver the message.

Obama agreed. He was out there all by himself. There were a few cabinet officials out there, but most were hardly seen or heard. The other side was running a campaign against them, but they weren't running a campaign back. It was all defense and no offense. And they needed to accomplish what he had always set out to do as a community organizer, as a writer, and as a presidential candidate: to tell a story. "We did a lot of good things last year, but we could be a lot tighter in how we operate," said Obama.

To the campaign veterans, the flashbacks to Ohio and Texas were vivid: they were repeating many of the same mistakes they had made as they tried to close out the primaries early in March 2008. They had grown conventional in their politics and message, forgetting their identity as outsiders in their desperation to win. Back then, they played old-style pro-union politics, railing against the North American Free Trade Agreement (NAFTA). It was the kind of game Obama could never win against Clinton. Now, in the dying days of the health care debate, they were playing conventional politics again. There were special deals for Nebraska senator Ben Nelson, who won extra federal funds for the expansion of Medicaid.

Louisiana senator Mary Landrieu secured extra Medicaid funds to fix budget distortions that lingered after Hurricane Katrina. The unions extracted their own deals on high-cost, Cadillac health insurance. "We could *taste* victory in Ohio and we made decisions and compromised some things in order to try to just throw the knockout punch," said one longtime aide. "We thought it's okay to be a little cheap on NAFTA to help us win Ohio and then it's done. We've won. We've done this amazing thing. We can have a week off. We're exhausted. And that's how we were on health care. It's so close. This is our one chance to do this historic thing. We can do some things we're maybe not comfortable with. Not bad things, but outside of our general lane, to get things done."

Health care fatigue was much like primary fatigue, only it lasted longer, the stakes were higher, and the voters were a tiny group of anxiety-filled elected officials. The first one hundred days had been relatively simple: the administration would bring Change to Washington, rescue the economy, and clean up the Bush mess at Guantánamo and beyond. Health care was the president's big priority, and it was supposed to be completed by the summer. As that dragged on and on, Obama's team drifted into a tactical, day-by-day disarray. "I think we got sucked into trying to win news cycles and part of it is when you are in a campaign, you're just telling a story to voters," said a senior Obama staffer. "In health care we had all of our chips in the middle of the table and felt we couldn't afford to lose and every day we were forced to do certain things. You just don't want to make a decision with your life savings in the middle of the table when you're holding two sevens. We knew during health care that we were being too tactical and didn't know how to get out of it. We thought, 'Once we finish health care we can solve all our problems.' I've come to the view that maybe some tactical strategic decisions might have added three to six points to approval ratings." Three to six points might sound small, but on the scale of Washington nerves, it was the difference between sub–50 percent weakness and plus–50 percent strength.

Plouffe's presence in the Roosevelt Room was a clear sign of the kind of revival Obama was looking for. The president had just asked Plouffe to become more involved in helping merge the political and communications efforts inside the White House. Obama's goal was to bring more strategic discipline to his entire presidency in the election year of 2010, and there was no one better at the job than Plouffe.

Plouffe was just as driven and competitive as anyone around the table, including Rahm Emanuel. But his mind was far more focused than Emanuel's scattershot brain, and he reveled during the long campaign in saying no to what he considered distractions. No to state or congressional officials who wanted a candidate visit. No to staffers who wanted to waste money. No to lobbyists getting favors inside the campaign. No to the national media and national advertising when they needed to win a handful of states. In many ways Plouffe was a reflection of Obama. He was skinny in physique and intense in character, with a love of grassroots politics and a disdain for official Washington. Plouffe said Obama picked him as his manager because of his "judgment, temperament, organization, and strategic sense." He wanted a campaign with a small circle of decision makers and zero tolerance of leaks. That was what Plouffe pursued with a single-minded purpose, to the point where he would strain his best friendship of the campaign, with his business partner David Axelrod. When Axelrod wanted Obama to meet with an editorial board in the closing weeks of the campaign, Plouffe said no, insisting on discipline.

Plouffe had declined to join the administration, but he never really left the Obama orbit, and he continued to offer strategic advice. What he couldn't do was give them discipline. Inside the campaign, Plouffe had kept the core team on a single strategic track and tied together their political and communications efforts. Where Axelrod took the stratospheric view of themes and narratives, Plouffe kept an eye on the ground truth. Where Robert Gibbs wanted to get down in the weeds to win, Plouffe elevated the discussion. Now he could only offer occasional advice, at least until he returned full-time for the president's reelection.

Did they lack strategic focus compared to the election of 2008? At times, Plouffe thought yes. But he also thought the errors were understandable. "It's easier to be strategic and laser-focused on a presidential campaign, as complicated and hard as it is, compared to government," he said. "I do think there's a special burden given the range of things that intrude on your best-laid plans, particularly in our cultural and media environment. There has to be a thread that ties together everything that you're doing, and it was easier sitting in Chicago, not judging your day based on what the pundit class was saying. It's harder now because you have to deal with Congress. Many in Congress consider MSNBC and Fox and Politico to be reality, even though the rest of the country doesn't."

Plouffe's bigger problem was how Congress—and especially its love of backroom deals—had undermined Obama's identity. He thought Obama would succeed in Washington because "he is a chess player in a town full of checkers players." Yet sometimes the checkers players seemed to run the show. "I think they've done a terrific job on lobbyists and transparency," Plouffe admitted. "But to get things done, there's a tension there. Sometimes that's because others want to play by the Hill's set of rules. My sense is that we'll be strongest if we are clear about our identity and are ruthless in our pursuit of trying to improve the country, but doing it within certain boundaries. We promised to drain the swamp, but the swamp is still there."

Other Obama aides saw the problems extending far beyond Congress, to a Washington mind-set embodied by the Survivalists and adopted by the president at times. "The president was so annoyed at himself for having gone so far afield from where he had meant to go," said one senior aide. "He's the non-Washington guy. He's the change-the-system guy. The transparent guy. The get-rid-of-business-as-usual guy. And everything about this process at the end was exactly what he said he wouldn't do."

Emanuel himself had little problem with business as usual, nor did many of those Obama aides who also wanted victory as badly as he did. It was only in hindsight that they realized how far they had strayed. "During the campaign we had a unified view of taking the long term over the short term, being strategic over tactical, and being willing to lose news cycles to tell a larger story. That isn't a strategy embraced by anyone who came up in the Clinton culture—in the campaign and the Clinton White House," said one Obama loyalist and West Wing staffer. "Rahm wants to win every battle, and we couldn't have achieved most of what we accomplished without Rahm. I'm not sure in this environment anyone absent Rahm's hard-charging personality could have gotten us to the point of getting things done. He's basically had to run the Congress and run the White House and push all of it by sheer force of will. The problem is less the addition of Rahm than the absence of Plouffe." Other Obama aides were less forgiving. "We thought Rahm would learn the ways of the campaign," said one senior adviser. "We had no idea how he would work to undermine them."

It fell to Axelrod to try to rein in his old friend Emanuel. Axelrod was hardly the most disciplined man in the West Wing. He could rarely keep track of his own BlackBerry, never mind his own schedule. He could be as indecisive and messy as the daily splash of food on his shirt and tie. Yet he had an acute sense of the changing mood of voters and the grand themes of the Obama narrative.

Nobody knew the president's political persona better than Axelrod, but he often seemed ill equipped to translate the big picture into the real world. His distant thoughts became something of a running joke inside the West Wing. At one Oval Office meeting, he walked the senior team through the latest polling and focus group data on health care.

"You know," he said, "it turns out that the hard stuff is really hard."

"That's what we get for all this polling we're paying for?" asked Obama.

Axelrod continued to fumble through the kind of health care message that might resonate with the American people, but the president was none the wiser.

"David, you're supposed to be my message guy, but I can't comprehend a word you just said."

West Wing aides described how Axelrod would often argue with Emanuel that his latest idea, policy initiative, or media message would not work or was not in keeping with the spirit of the Obama campaign. "That has been the nature of our relationship for twenty years," Axelrod said. "Rahm is an absolutely brilliant guy and a force of nature. There's no doubt that Rahm wants to win every single day, and that's a strength of his. But sometimes you've got to take the long view. That's sort of our *gestalt,* the Obama thing."

Their gestalt was not quite as organized as appearances suggested. It was more a combination of long bouts of indecision, moments of sharp insight, and a dogged sense of discipline. Take the defining line of the Obama campaign: Change We Can Believe In. The same slogan appeared on the same plastic banner at almost every campaign event of the extended primary contest. But it didn't emerge until the late summer of 2007, some six months after Obama announced his candidacy, after months of hand-wringing by Axelrod and his team. "It's my least favorite thing," said Axelrod. "We all struggled with it." The idea first came from Jason Ralston, a member of the media team handling the campaign's ads under the superconsultant Jim Margolis. But the candidate didn't much like it because it conveyed nothing about his position on what he called "the issues." To Axelrod and Plouffe, it was imperfect but it spoke to their rationale for believing in Obama and signing up to one more exhausting election. "It was good because it went to a lot of the character questions," said Axelrod. "We were running against the inauthenticity of Washington. We were appealing to everyone's sense that we needed real change, not phony change. But it took several months before we finally persuaded ourselves that we had to have it."

Once they were persuaded, it was far too much trouble to dream up—and agree on—a new slogan. So the candidate, and the campaign, stuck at the same message week after week, month after month. It was a repetition that Obama hated, even when the lines were his own. Early in the campaign, Margolis and pollster Joel Benenson urged Obama to repeat the lines from his breakthrough convention speech in 2004, about uniting red and blue America. "He didn't want to do it," said Benenson. "He thought everybody had heard it. But we tested it in polls and ads and people were crazy for it. They said, 'I've been waiting for somebody to say this.'"

Now, inside the White House, some of his closest staffers thought he needed to return to the days when he repeated himself. "We have not done a good job of saying what our message is, a simple message of what we stand for or what we're trying to do, especially on health care," said one senior Obama aide soon after the Massachusetts defeat. "In the campaign it was Change We Could Believe In, and it was simple. It was always there. We don't have the same message from one week to the next. I told the president, 'In the campaign you were sick and tired of giving the same stump speech over and over. But it worked. Now you don't say the same thing from day to day.'"

The Bush White House was sharply divided along ideological lines between moderates and conservatives, doves and hawks, realists and neocons, deficit haters and tax cutters. Obama's White House divided less on policy than on personal lines and political style. The Survivalists were represented by Emanuel, senior adviser Pete Rouse, deputy chief of staff Jim Messina, and congressional liaison Phil Schiliro. And the Revivalists were represented by Axelrod, senior adviser Valerie Jarrett, press secretary Robert Gibbs, former campaign manager David Plouffe, and two communications directors, Anita Dunn and Dan Pfeiffer.

Personal friendships and rivalries cut across both groups. Axelrod and Emanuel were close friends, and Obama had initially been worried that their friendship might come to dominate the West Wing. For much of the first year, Axelrod seemed to side with Emanuel in turning his back on the campaign days and concentrating on politics inside the Beltway. Some of his political consultant friends urged him to reconsider at the regular midweek strategy sessions he held in his apartment. "This is a campaign," one told Axelrod, as Republicans rejected Obama's outreach through 2009. When Axelrod insisted that they needed to focus on governing rather than campaigning, his team of consultants sharply disagreed. "Tell that to the other side," said one. "They're running a campaign." By the time of the Massachusetts defeat, Axelrod had shifted to telling everyone they were now in a campaign.

Among the Revivalists, Axelrod and Gibbs were once distant and even rivals. Gibbs was wary of Axelrod's presence on his own turf of communications and messaging before they started traveling around Iowa together with Obama. Having been pushed out of his last presidential campaign with John Kerry, Gibbs seemed determined not to lose another boss. "I think Robert had gotten burned before in some of his relationships," said Axelrod. But the experience of fighting through the primaries together had brought them closer. "I love Gibbs and wouldn't want to do this without him," Axelrod affirmed. "I was standing with him on the platform in Denver when the president gave his acceptance speech and I saw the tears streaming down his cheeks. People don't realize what it means to have been a part of this. Robert is a genuine progressive and a total soul mate when it comes to the reform agenda."

To the press, the division was about Chicago versus Washington, placing Emanuel at the center of a hometown cabal that was imperiling the presidency. That story line proved as popular as it was simplistic. It evoked the old critique of Bill Clinton's initial White House team: that he promoted too many inexperienced or unqualified Arkansas friends. But Chicago was a place, not a state of mind. The Chicago figures—with the exception of Valerie Jarrett—did not lack experience in national politics. Emanuel was no rube, and he was not particularly close to Obama, either. The conceit began with a *Financial Times* analysis of Obama's woes, depicting a closed inner circle of Chicago and campaign acolytes. It continued online with the think-tank blogger Steve Clemons and the Daily Beast columnist Les Gelb, who both narrowed their fire on Emanuel. When the *Washington Post*'s Dana Milbank crafted a defense of Emanuel, the capital parlor game of "who's up and who's down" was playing itself out in public. The attention troubled Emanuel even as he claimed to ignore it. For someone who carefully nurtured his pet reporters and continually dabbled in communications, the coverage was too hard to ignore.

To the Survivalists, the division was not about reform versus resistance, but idealism versus realism. And the dividing line ran not just through the West Wing but through the personality of the president himself. "The fault line is how to reconcile the two different themes of Change and getting stuff done," said one Survivalist.

"You can't get stuff done without some of these special deals to get bills passed. It's the fault line of naïveté. These naive people choose an idealized image of Obama versus the reality. It's about how you keep Obama true to himself and advance his agenda. The fact is that Obama is much more pragmatic. Is it better to have no deals and no health care reform, or minimal deals and pass health care reform?"

The Revivalists saw that thinking as little more than capitulation. The first year was not about idealistic campaigning versus realistic governing. It was about fighting for what you believe in. "Governing is campaigning for your agenda," said another trusted aide. "As opposed to this idea that you're 'governing' and that many of the policies in the campaign not only could be changed but had to be adapted to 'governing' or else we risked having the agenda go down. It was like appeasement by the Neville Chamberlain wing rather than 'We came here for a reason.'"

In the middle of the dispute, Barack Obama acknowledged that his first-year strategy was misguided. They had played too much of an inside game. He preferred to portray the mistakes as matters of communication. But inside his own team, and perhaps inside his own head, politics and message were deeply intertwined. "Thinking more about communications during that first year probably would have been important," he told me in the Oval Office in the early spring. "There's probably even a certain pride that we took in ignoring the polls because we felt like that wasn't the right thing to do for the country. And I think the Massachusetts race was a good reminder that if you aren't thinking about public opinion, there's a lot of good policy that is going to be left on the shelf because you're only going to be able to go so far."

★ ★ ★

On the day of the health care summit on February 25, the forecast snow and hurricane-strength winds did not whip through the streets of Washington. Instead, on the morning that Obama would finally deliver on a campaign pledge, there was a bright blue sky streaked with light white clouds above the White House. He was at last going to allow the TV cameras of C-SPAN to broadcast at least part of his health care negotiations. The summit was a mix of Rahm-like realism with campaign-style idealism: Obama was both confronting his opponents and broadcasting his openness. He was also taking a Renegade-style risk that he might stumble through several hours of live television, or that his own Democrats might publicly bicker among themselves as they had for several months in private. They needed self-discipline inside the room, and they needed to connect with the increasingly skeptical voters watching at home. White House aides scurried across Pennsylvania Avenue to Blair House, the guesthouse normally used by visiting world leaders. The sidewalks were lined with snowbanks and black metal barriers; three white patrol cars were parked in the middle of the unnaturally empty street. Secret Service agents checked off names outside the building like flustered party organizers outside an L.A. nightclub. Across Lafayette Square, hanging along the facade of the Chamber of Commerce building, was a giant banner urging America's capitalists to "Dream Big." Obama's former campaign aides, now serving in the White House, were dreaming on another scale. "You're going to enjoy today," said one. "It's time to kick ass."

Obama had long ago promised to open up his health care negotiations to C-SPAN, and his failure to do so was an embarrassment. The C-SPAN promise was one of those campaign markers that never survived the demands of government—until the Massachusetts defeat, when Obama needed to revive the campaign spirit for himself, his supporters, and his party in Congress. "None of us could believe how much traction the Republicans got from us having given up our pledge to do it on C-SPAN," said one senior aide. This C-SPAN session would not be with the drug industry and insurers, and there would be no working doctors, nurses, or experts present, as promised. During the twenty-one-month presidential campaign, Obama had thought the toughest opposition would come from the health care sector. Instead, his die-hard opponents worked at the other end of Pennsylvania Avenue, and it was members of Congress who would appear before the C-SPAN cameras.

As a candidate, Obama told voters that he would not allow business to buy every chair, because he would be in charge. Besides, he said to chuckles of laughter at rallies across the country, "I'll have the biggest chair because I'm president." But businesses did not need to buy every chair when they had already won over a significant chunk of Congress. And Obama didn't need the biggest chair, because he controlled the microphones and the clock—in this case, an antique-style pocket watch encased in a glass paperweight that sat on the table in front of him. It was solid and heavy enough to hurl at an unruly lawmaker, but also thick enough to make it hard to read. Instead of a bigger chair, he had a bigger sense of self-belief than anyone in the room. "He has a supreme amount of self-confidence in his ability to deal with this kind of thing," said one senior aide.

That confidence included little preparation about what kind of message he would deliver in front of the cameras. He sat through a few half-hour meetings about possible scenarios in the summit, where his communications team highlighted three points: that health care was a big problem; that his own plan was not radical, as the GOP myths suggested; and that there were broad areas of agreement.

Beyond those outlines, Obama crammed on his own for the highly public event, drawing on a vast memo prepared by Nancy-Ann DeParle. In the days after the House Republican retreat in Baltimore, DeParle had examined the GOP's health care proposals and found them limited to just three pages. So she and her team studied every recent Republican health care bill and wrote a thirty-page memo with many more pages of appendix documents.

"I've gone through it all, and you're going to see exactly what you've been saying, which is that there are so many of their ideas in our bill," she told Obama.

"Well, I want to see that," he said.

"We're not supposed to send you memos that are this long, Mr. President. It's eighty pages."

"I think I can handle it."

Obama read the whole memo, making notes throughout, and called back DeParle to discuss the real differences between the two parties. The night before the summit, he sat with DeParle and Phil Schiliro going through technical questions about health care. "He and I are both lawyers, and I had the sense it was like preparing for a trial," said DeParle. "What are my arguments? What are our weaknesses? Are there places where I can give in to them? He was trying to make sure the policy made sense." That left little room for his political and communications aides. "I think he felt comfortable with the message," said Axelrod. "He wanted to be sure he was right on the facts."

Obama walked into Blair House with a head full of facts. It was still frigid outside, but the room was overheating as it filled with the members of Congress who controlled the health of millions of Americans. White House aides were worried that the air-conditioning could not cope with the cramped confines of politicians and press. The electrical circuits had already blown that morning as the TV lights and cameras, as well as dozens of laptops, sucked too much power from the overloaded circuits.

The summit was staged in the so-called Garden Room, an overwrought 1980s confection of summer images that bore little relation to the bare trees in the brick and concrete courtyards outside. Little was real in a room filled with fakery. Behind Obama's seat was a curved wall depicting a stone balustrade and a rose garden. Opposite was another mural of a balustrade with flowers in full bloom, a lazy lake, and an idyllic bridge. There were plantation shutters on the windows, peacock designs on the seats, and a chandelier with fake candles overhead. The scene looked like a weekend retreat in the country, not a made-for-TV game of political poker.

As they entered, the members of Congress mugged for the cameras. They slapped backs and feigned surprise with their hellos. The tables were laid out in a giant square, with blue place cards set before each seat, alongside a Blair House notepad declaring they were staying at The President's Guest House. In fact, the guests had set their own conditions for their stay. Phil Schiliro spent hours negotiating the shape of the table and the number of Republican guests. He ultimately yielded to their wishes for more members, even though it made for poor TV angles and an excessive demand on time as everyone wanted to hold forth.

The senators were seated along one side of the square table, with Obama's election rival John McCain seven places away from him. Members of the House were seated along the right side of the square. Opposite was a mixture of House and Senate types. In case they got confused, Obama and Biden both had the benefit of a seating chart in front of them. To Obama's left sat his congressional foes: John Boehner and Mitch McConnell. To his right sat his feuding congressional friends: Nancy Pelosi and Harry Reid.

Some chose to study ostentatiously for the day's summit. Representative Joe Barton of Texas, seated close to the reporters and photographers squeezed into the Garden Room, took out a yellow highlighter to work his way through the legislation. His tie was a gaudy homage to the Tabasco sauce bottle, and despite his studious reading, he stopped to take a photo of the scene with his BlackBerry. Senate leader Harry Reid and House leader Steny Hoyer stood at the fireplace to chat. Hoyer hitched up his pants and buttoned his jacket, and Reid followed suit. Then Hoyer saw two prime targets on the other side of the room and the aisle: John McCain and Chuck Grassley. He slapped both senators heartily on the back. Grassley, for so long the object of Obama's attention on health care, had been looking at the bill he just pulled out of a small, green canvas tote bag. McCain preferred to confer with his leaders, especially McConnell. John Boehner walked in later with a subtle prop: a huge pile of legislation that he dumped on his desk. He stared blankly at the room full of lawmakers and media, and wiped his lips like a parched man bellying up to the bar at the end of a long, hot day.

Obama and Biden walked in and worked their way around the room. The president greeted everyone and moved on quickly; his vice president stopped to talk to most of his former colleagues. "Come on, Biden," Obama said after urging everyone to have a seat.

This was Obama's preferred setting and style: a professorial seminar where he could synthesize differing views and attempt to arrive at some consensus. And it was, by now, his specialized subject. He spoke without teleprompter and without notes, opening the first few minutes with several stories. He drew on the letters he received from regular Americans struggling with health care, then turned to his own experiences with his family. He recounted how he rushed his daughter Malia to the ER for her asthma because she could not breathe. He told how his younger daughter, Sasha, suffered meningitis as a baby, and how he sat in the ER, not knowing if she would make it, but thankful for his reliable health care. Finally he recalled his mother's suffering:

"My mother, who was self-employed, didn't have reliable health care, and she died of ovarian cancer. And there's probably nothing that modern medicine could have done about that. It was caught late, and that's a hard cancer to diagnose. But I do remember the last six months of her life—insurance companies threatening that they would not reimburse her for her costs, and her having to be on the phone in the hospital room arguing with insurance companies when what she should have been doing is spending time with her family. I do remember that."

His most personal stories had no apparent impact on the room. He tried an old strategy from his community organizing days: weaving together everyone's stories, and everyone's positions, to build a bigger narrative. "Now, everybody here has those same stories somewhere in their lives," he said, trying to find common ground. "Everybody here understands the desperation that people feel when they're sick. And I think everybody here is profoundly sympathetic and wants to make sure that we have a system that works for all Americans."

It was only five years earlier that Obama had endured hours of listening to his fellow senators drone on, as he tried to establish himself as a respectful junior senator, despite an outsize national following. He cursed his staff, and the boredom was almost insufferable. But now it was his place to inflict such suffering on others, including his former committee chairman, who used to treat him with little respect in the Senate: Joe Biden.

Obama dug into his research memo for material to tweak the conscience of the Republicans seated near him. He cited McCain's comments about the devastating impact of rising health care costs on middle-class families. But his old rival could only raise his eyes and smile wryly. Mike Enzi, the Wyoming senator, had worked with Ted Kennedy and spoken of the health care burden on small businesses. But Enzi only nodded gently. Obama turned to Mitch McConnell, who was seated closer to him on the same side of the square. "And, Mitch, you've said that the need for reform is not in question," he ventured. McConnell blinked rapidly and kept his eyes fixed on the cameras. His face did not flinch.

Obama appealed to them to move beyond politics to what he called common sense. But the other side had already figured out that playbook. McConnell and Boehner gave up their chance to respond and handed the responsibility to someone who sounded much less partisan and much more like common sense: Senator Lamar Alexander, the former Tennessee governor, who came armed with his own anecdotes.

"Your stories are a lot like the stories I hear. When I went home for Christmas, after we had that twenty-five days of consecutive debate and voted on Christmas Eve on health care, a friend of mine from Tullahoma, Tennessee, said, 'I hope you'll kill that health care bill.' And then before the words were out of his mouth, he said, 'But we've got to do something about health care costs. My wife has breast cancer; she got it eleven years ago. Our insurance is $2,000 a month. We couldn't afford it if our employer weren't helping us do that. So we've got to do something.'"

That something was to start all over again. Obama scribbled down notes as he spoke, but it was deadlocked from the beginning: he was using the same arguments and tactics to come to the opposite conclusion. Alexander ended with an appeal to bipartisanship, alongside references to Alexis de Tocqueville on democracy and Lyndon Johnson on civil rights.

Obama rested his hand on his chin and smiled. On the facts and the stats, he could outpace Alexander, and he did so. He cited Congressional Budget Office figures to show that his bill would reduce premiums. Alexander looked flustered and suddenly sounded far less fluent. "Rather than argue with you in public about it, I'd like to put my facts down, give them to you," he explained. He later asked an aide to write a letter to make his case to Obama, which the aide delivered to a White House staffer that afternoon.

Not to be outdone with all the storytelling, others also tried to strike a folksy note. Nancy Pelosi told her own health care stories of traveling the country, where she'd "seen grown men cry." Harry Reid, locked in a difficult reelection fight in Nevada, trumped her with a story about a Latino voter called Jesus, whose newborn baby had a cleft palate. Reid told how Jesus's insurance refused to pay $90,000 in hospital bills for surgery, before switching to a subject that he felt more pressingly: a defense of a partisan vote using budget reconciliation rules. "Health reform shouldn't be about political parties fighting each other," Reid concluded. "It should be about people fighting for their lives and fighting for a better quality of life, people like Jesus and that little girl."

How true, and how unrealistic. At this point, health care was all about parties fighting each other. Just before lunch, Obama tried to focus the discussion on insurance reform and invited McCain to speak. McCain had little interest in insurance and much more enthusiasm for turning the clock back to 2008. His arguments were not unlike the ones raging between the Revivalists and the Survivalists inside the West Wing.

"Both of us during the campaign promised change in Washington. In fact, eight times you said that negotiations on health care reform would be conducted with the C-SPAN cameras. I'm glad more than a year later that they are here. Unfortunately, this product was not produced in that fashion. It was produced behind closed doors. It was produced with unsavory—I say that with respect—deal making," he began, before detailing some of the backroom deals with individual senators and industry groups. "And at the town hall meetings that I conduct all over my state, people are angry. We promised them change in Washington and what we got was a process that you and I both said we would change in Washington."

Obama tried to interrupt, but McCain was in no mood to give way.

"Let me just make this point, John, because we're not campaigning anymore," Obama said when McCain finished. "The election is over."

"I'm reminded of that every day."

"Yes. So we can spend the remainder of the time with our respective talking points going back and forth. We were supposed to be talking about insurance," Obama said testily. "Obviously I'm sure that Harry Reid and Chris Dodd and others who went through an exhaustive process through both the House and the Senate, with the most hearings, the most debates on the floor, the longest markup in twenty-two years on each and every one of these bills, would have a response for you. My concern is, is that if we do that, then we're essentially back on Fox News or MSNBC on the split screen just arguing back and forth. So my hope would be that we can just focus on the issues of how we actually get a bill done."

"Could I just say, Mr. President, the American people care about what we did and how we did it. And I think it's a subject that we should discuss. And I thank you."

"They absolutely do care about it, John."

Obama had no interest in rehashing the arguments about the deal making. He had come to hate it, too. He wanted a clean break from last year, and a clear decision on how to move forward. Soon after, Obama broke the session for lunch and walked back to the West Wing. "I don't know if it's interesting watching it on TV, but it's interesting being part of it," he told reporters as he crossed Pennsylvania Avenue. "I think we're establishing that there are actually some areas of real agreement and we're starting to focus on what the real disagreements are." He returned to the Oval Office to review the summit with his senior staff. "It's actually going pretty well," they told him. "The one thing that is important is to show openness to specific Republican ideas. You're coming in open and nobody believed us."

The idea was not really to win over Republicans at this stage;

they wanted to give centrist Democrats the space to move forward. Obama closed the summit having gained little ground with Republicans, but embracing the idea of a continuous campaign. "The question that I'm going to ask myself and I ask of all of you is, is there enough serious effort that in a month's time or a few weeks' time or six weeks' time, we could actually resolve something," he said. "And if we can't, then I think we've got to go ahead and make some decisions and then that's what elections are for. We have honest disagreements about the vision for the country and we'll go ahead and test those out over the next several months till November."

Instead of uniting red and blue America, Obama had brought together two groups who were just as distrustful as Republicans and Democrats: the members of his own party in the House and those in the Senate. Nancy Pelosi emerged from the summit sounding victorious. She had beaten down the Emanuel option of trimming the bill down to size. "Start over, eentsy weentsy spider, little teeny tiny," she told reporters the day after the summit, "you can't do it." And she had won Obama's support to amend the Senate version to address her own members' worries. "I believe that we have good prospects for passing legislation, in light of the recognition the President gave to the concerns of the House Members," she explained.

Her comments were the turning point that Obama's aides were searching for. "What happened in that room wasn't just Barack Obama talking to the American people about health care," said DeParle. "It was also the Democratic House and Senate becoming a team, as opposed to the House versus the Senate, which is basically what it had been for the last year. If you watched Pelosi and Reid, just look at the body language. Watch them chatting. I think that was a big part of her developing the confidence that she could go back to the House with the Senate bill."

* * *

The revival began partly in an ugly concrete block a few minutes' walk away from Blair House and the West Wing. There, one of the most overlooked operations of the White House deals with the one part of Washington everyone professes to care about: real people. The White House Office of Presidential Correspondence relies on fifty employees and twice that number of volunteers to answer thousands of calls on the president's comments line. The office sends out some 100,000 greeting cards a year for birthdays, wedding anniversaries, Girl Scout and Boy Scout awards. They respond to seniors and veterans needing assistance with federal agencies. They dispatch help to those writing suicidal thoughts, and they send condolence messages to the bereaved. Within forty-eight hours, the office responds to some 20,000 e-mails—a fraction of its total in-box of around 400,000 a day. It is also the first White House operation to reply in kind, via e-mail, rather than on paper. It has to process and report as many as 40,000 gifts each year, coming from foreign leaders and working Americans. The gifts are an eclectic collection. When the Obamas were picking out a dog, the office was swamped with dog toys, dog beds, and dog books. When the First Lady exercised with a hula hoop, they received hundreds of plastic hoops. One man sent a book he borrowed from his public library; another sent five hundred personalized coat hangers from Britain.

Despite the overwhelming volume, the office wielded real influence. With a selection of ten letters each day, including a handful of e-mails, they could reach the leader of the free world and shift his thinking, insult his ego, or offer a political opening. Each night, a purple folder with the letters traveled to the White House residence with the presidential briefing book for the next day's work. The letters' outsize influence lay in the hands of a quiet, unassuming former Peace Corps volunteer from Illinois. Mike Kelleher had ambitions to enter Congress in 2000, at the same time as Barack Obama. Kelleher was running in downstate Illinois, while Obama was running in Chicago. They met at a Chicago hotel, at a cattle call of candidates searching for the support of some liberal interest group. They both lost. Kelleher lost again when he ran for lieutenant governor in 2002; he supported Obama in his next race, for the U.S. Senate, two years later. Kelleher went on to find a job working in then-senator Obama's office in Chicago and Washington. Obama went on to run for president.

Now Kelleher was working on letters, facing an unprecedented volume of correspondence. For much of Obama's first year as president, health care represented about half of the calls, e-mails, and letters arriving at the White House. Most told personal stories of health care problems; some were about children or parents struggling with the same issues; others combined economic woes, such as a lost job, with the loss of insurance. And then there were what Kelleher called the big three: job loss, sickness, and facing imminent foreclosure. In making a final selection, Kelleher looked for something compelling, including letters that were highly critical of everything Obama was trying to achieve.

After a few months of seeing the letters, Obama called him into the Oval Office to sit down and explain his work.

"He said he didn't want to change the process," Kelleher recalled, but Obama wanted to know about his decision making. Kelleher explained how he tried to make a selection that was in proportion to the overall mailbag, in both subject and tone. "That was good enough," Kelleher said. "I try to be fair. I try to be as objective as I can."

"What are some things that surprise you about this mail?" Obama asked.

"A lot of folks that write will not necessarily ask for help for themselves," Kelleher said. "They say, 'I want you to think about people like me.' Or they say, 'I know you may not be able to help me in my particular case, but please think about my family when you are making these decisions.'"

Obama said the letters had an impact, and he explained that he would show the letters to others. Some would get personal, hand-written responses; others would prompt him to ask questions of Treasury or the Pentagon.

One letter surfaced at the top of the pile early in 2010. It was from a fifty-year-old Ohio woman, Natoma Canfield, who was a cancer survivor struggling to pay for her own health insurance. In 2009, her premiums increased by more than 25 percent, but her insurer paid out less than $1,000 after collecting more than $6,000 from her. This year, her insurance was going up again, this time by 40 percent. "I need your Health reform bill to help me!!! I simply can no longer afford to pay for my health care costs!! Thanks to this incredible premium increase demanded by my insurance com-pany, January will be my last month of insurance," she wrote. "I live in the house my mother & father built in 1958 and I am so afraid of the possibility I might lose this family heirloom as a result of my being forced to drop my health care insurance. The health insurance industry technically has not denied me insurance di-rectly, but indirectly they have by increasing my costs. They per-ceive me as becoming a higher risk factor to them despite being a loyal customer. I will never be able to obtain new health insurance due to the lack of real competition."

One of Kelleher's letter readers picked it out, marked it with a code saying "sample/health care," and put it in a pile in his office. Kelleher selected it for its impact and relevance, and placed it in a folder to head to the president's staff secretary. Canfield earned a rare, handwritten response from the president. "Natoma, thanks for your letter," he wrote. "It's because of folks like you that we are still fighting to get health care done!"

It was a touching exchange, but it turned into something more. For a White House trying to resurrect its campaign spirit, the letter—and the issue it highlighted—represented a priceless opportunity. Hikes in insurance premiums first appeared on the White House radar a little more than two weeks after the Massachusetts defeat. Anthem Blue Cross in California was sending letters to customers about raising their premiums by 40 percent. Nancy-Ann DeParle got an instant e-mail from an ally on Capitol Hill and couldn't believe it was true; she thought it must be some kind of early April Fools' joke. At the same time, David Axelrod was e-mailed the story by a friend outside the White House. Dan Pfeiffer noticed the item in the daily White House stack of news. They all came to the same instant conclusion. "Our big challenge this whole time is that health care is a competition between fear of the known and fear of the unknown," said Pfeiffer. "And fear of the unknown was trumping fear of the known. Our challenge was to show people who had health insurance why reform would make their life better. People needed to understand a fear of the status quo." Obama's senior aides talked generally about the issue at their early-morning meeting in Emanuel's office. But they did not jump on the story for several days, until the president sat down for an interview with Katie Couric of CBS News, just before the Super Bowl game.

From there, the White House stepped up the pressure. The next day health secretary Kathleen Sebelius wrote to the insurers demanding an explanation, and the story went viral. Having walked away from reform in the fall, the insurers were far more attractive opponents than the Republicans. "We needed the struggle against the insurance industry," said one senior aide. "We couldn't get it done without them." Now the insurers were penalizing their own customers. Pfeiffer's mother, who lived in Delaware, mentioned it after seeing a news crawl on CNN, confirming to him that the issue was breaking through the noise of the twenty-four-hour news flow.

"It was the first piece of momentum we had in the health care debate that wasn't tied to a specific legislative action like the Finance Committee markup," said Pfeiffer. "This was the first time we felt like we were winning the message war."

Momentum was what they had tried to achieve in the 2008 campaign: a sense of gathering force through the early primaries, and then the later stages of winning superdelegates. Now they had to conjure up some pace with no pressing deadlines or voting days, other than ones of their own making. On the Sunday after the health care summit, Obama gathered his senior aides, along with David Plouffe and Anita Dunn, inside the Roosevelt Room for another weekend communications meeting. There they reached back to the campaign for redemption as they tried to close out health care reform. One of Plouffe's favorite ads was a late September spot in the general election, defending Obama's plan as a centrist position between two extremes.

The image was simple: a double arrow pointing to either side of the debate. "On health care reform," the voice-over said, "two extremes. On one end, government-run health care, higher taxes. On the other, insurance companies without rules denying coverage. Barack Obama says both extremes are wrong." The images switched to photos of Obama talking to voters. "His plan: Keep your employer-paid coverage. Keep your own doctor. Take on insurance companies to bring down costs. Cover preexisting conditions, and preventive care. Common sense for the change we need."

Plouffe and Axelrod wanted to try to recapture that kind of message now. Three days later, on March 3, Obama stood in the East Room alongside a handful of doctors and nurses to deliver his closing arguments on health care:

> On one end of the spectrum, there are some who've suggested scrapping our system of private insurance and replacing it with

a government-run health care system. And though many other countries have such a system, in America it would be neither practical nor realistic. On the other end of the spectrum, there are those, and this includes most Republicans in Congress, who believe the answer is to loosen regulations on the insurance industry—whether it's state consumer protections or minimum standards for the kind of insurance they can sell. . . . Now, the proposal I put forward gives Americans more control over their health insurance and their health care by holding insurance companies more accountable. It builds on the current system where most Americans get their health insurance from their employer. If you like your plan, you can keep your plan. If you like your doctor, you can keep your doctor.

He ended with a late addition, on the morning of the speech, which reminded many of his staffers of the old candidate days when he was campaigning against Washington. "At stake right now is not just our ability to solve this problem, but our ability to solve any problem. . . . I do not know how this plays politically, but I know it's right."

The sun shone brightly through a blue sky the next morning, melting the icy remains of the giant snow piles outside the White House. On the North Lawn, the buds on the magnolia trees were light green and growing rapidly. Inside the West Wing, Obama was prepping for a presidential drop-by at a meeting of insurance executives with Secretary Sebelius and a group of state insurance commissioners. Pfeiffer and the health care team thought it would be useful to brief him ahead of the meeting with a health care letter, so they called over to Kelleher. Two letters came back, with Obama's reply attached; one was Natoma Canfield's. Obama's aides thought the letter would fire up the boss ahead of the confrontation.

Holding the letter, Nancy-Ann DeParle walked into the Oval

Office. "Mr. President," she said, handing it to Obama, "we wanted you to see this just to remind you why we're doing this and what you're talking to the insurers about."

Obama sat down, read the letter, and grew visibly emotional. "This is exactly what we've got to stop," he said. "This is the kind of thing that just makes me sick."

He walked into the Roosevelt Room across the hallway and read the executives the same letter. "Mr. President," said one of the insurers, "when our customers suffer, we suffer." Obama's aides wanted to laugh, but the president pressed on, asking why the rate increases were so much higher than the rising cost of medical care.

"Here's what I don't get," he said. "The medical trend is high single digits, say 8 or 9 percent. How do you get from that to 40 percent?"

Obama left without an answer that made sense to him or his aides. He left Sebelius to browbeat the executives, most of whom sat opposite her across a large table under a portrait of FDR. "The meeting was really prompted in part by the rate increases which have been announced all over the country and the input I have had from people across America who are frightened that they are being priced out of the market," she said. "They want some information about how this is happening and what strategies we have for looking at costs in the future."

That Sunday was warm, sunny, and springlike, and Obama played basketball at Fort McNair, close to where the Potomac meets the Anacostia River. It was an increasingly rare pleasure for Obama, and it evoked the time when he played as a token of good luck on primary days.

The next day, March 8, he staged the closest thing to one of his old campaign rallies in a university gym in the Philadelphia suburbs. Three giant Stars and Stripes stretched down at the back of the stage at Arcadia University in Glenside. The basketball hoops were raised to the ceiling and a brown tarp covered the floor. All that was missing was the blue banner promising Change We Can Believe In. The invocation included prayers for a resolution to the health care debate, and the bleachers started chanting: "What do we want? Health care! When do we want it? Now!" His introducer was another woman who wrote to the White House with her story of woe: Leslie Banks of Philadelphia, a self-employed single mother with diabetes, whose premiums were set to rise by more than 100 percent.

Obama bounced onstage to screams and cheers, and waved at the bleachers. "I'm kind of fired up!" he said, kind of resurrecting his campaign chant.

"We love you!" shouted one of the students. "Love you back," he said, sounding less and less like a president, before rattling off an official thank-you to elected officials in an unofficial style. "One of the finest governors in the country, Ed Rendell is in the house," he said of the man who helped kill his primary effort in Pennsylvania. "Everybody notice how good Ed is looking, by the way? He's been on that training program, eating egg whites and keeping his cholesterol down. Your senior senator who has just been doing outstanding work in the Senate, Arlen Specter is in the house." Specter looked confused, perhaps still struggling with his recent conversion from Republican to Democrat. "One of my great friends, somebody who supported me when nobody could pronounce my name, Bob Casey is in the house," Obama continued, praising the senator who was his traveling buddy and biggest endorsement in the state two years earlier. "Your congressman, the person who gave me confidence that I could win even though nobody could pronounce my name: Chaka Fattah is in the house," he continued to applause and laughter. "I figured if they could elect a Chaka then they could elect a Barack."

There were four members of the House in attendance, and they were his real target, not the people in the gym or at home. He needed their votes—each and every one—to pass the Senate bill, and many of his words were directed literally and metaphorically at them. He took off his dark jacket, rolled up his sleeves, and got to work taking apart the mind-set of many members of Congress:

"It is great to be back here in the Keystone State," he said, forgetting what he used to call the death march through the Pennsylvania primary in 2008. "It's even better to be out of Washington, D.C. First of all, the people of D.C. are wonderful. They're nice people, they're good people; love the city, the monuments, everything. But when you're in Washington, folks respond to every issue, every decision, every debate, no matter how important it is, with the same question: What does this mean for the next election? What does it mean for your poll numbers? Is this good for the Democrats or good for the Republicans? Who won the news cycle? That's just how Washington is. They can't help it. They're obsessed with the sport of politics. . . . You want people in Washington to spend a little less time worrying about our jobs, a little more time worrying about your jobs."

Obama was campaigning against more than just the Republicans when it came to health care. He was campaigning against a whole political and media culture: the same old Washington game that he had decried through most of his presidential campaign. Never mind that he was now at the heart of that game, or that his inner circle obsessed about the very people they disdained. This was candidate Obama, not President Obama. "Now, since we took this issue on a year ago, there have been plenty of folks in Washington who've said that the politics is just too hard. They've warned us we may not win. They've argued now is not the time for reform. It's going to hurt your poll numbers. How is it going to affect Democrats in November? Don't do it now. My question to them is: When is the right time? If not now, when? If not us, who?"

It was an old line attributed to Bobby Kennedy. But he could just as well have evoked King and called for the fierce urgency of now, as he did so many times in the primaries. He talked about his introducer, Leslie, as a single mom, "just like my mom was a single mom." He talked about Natoma Canfield from Ohio and Laura Klitzka from Wisconsin. "I just talked to Laura this past weekend, and let me tell you, she knows that the time for reform is right now," he said. "So what should I tell these Americans? That Washington is not sure how it will play in November? That we should walk away from this fight, or do something like some on the other side of the aisle have suggested, well, we'll do it incrementally, we'll take baby steps. So they want me to pretend to do something that doesn't really help these folks."

"No!" shouted his supporters, as Obama stared directly at the group of lawmakers sitting down to his right. Backed by a cheering crowd, he was daring his own party, his own members of Congress, to gamble their careers. "So let me remind everybody: Those of us in public office were not sent to Washington to do what's easy. . . . We were sent there to do what was hard." At the barnstorming end of his speech, he slung his jacket over his shoulder and walked straight down into the cluster of members of Congress.

Laura Klitzka's name became a talisman as Obama struggled to reach his destination with health care reform. He invoked her as he stood alongside several doctors in the East Room. And he rallied his supporters with her story in the final days. As the legislation was tweaked and rewritten in the last days and weeks, Obama would often ask Nancy-Ann DeParle a simple question: "How will this help Laura?"

For the next two weeks he needed a combination of Revivalists and Survivalists. He played the outside game with a series of old-style rallies that returned to his campaign themes. And he played the inside game with the single-minded pursuit of individual House votes. The hunt was not unlike his charm offensive for the party's superdelegates to secure his nomination as a presidential candidate less than two years earlier.

He was risking his presidency like a renegade. But he was working the phones and pressing the flesh like a machine politician. Two days after Arcadia University, he flew to St. Louis, Missouri, for a fund-raiser for Senator Claire McCaskill, one of his earliest and feistiest supporters in his own election. At a raucous reception in the Renaissance Grand Hotel, he said he was tired of talking about health care; it was time to get it done soon. His supporters started chanting the rallying cry from his defeat in the New Hampshire primary: "Yes We Can."

"See, I want every member of Congress to hear this chant," he said. "You know, we were meeting with some supporters back here, and a couple of them said the same thing. They said, 'Don't let them wear you down.' And I tried to explain I don't get worn down; I wear *them* down."

Obama and his aides knew they needed to apply as much emotional pressure as political arm-twisting. Above all, they needed to look like they were gathering pace and supporters as they neared the finish line. In public, Obama challenged Congress with the big rallies that Hillary Clinton had come to hate watching during the primaries. In private, he and his aides—especially Emanuel and Schiliro—leaned hard on the wavering House members. "As long as it looked like it was more and more likely to pass every day, that would encourage more people to do it," said one senior Obama aide. "In the superdelegate world, new superdelegates were good to get out there every day, but superdelegate switchers were always huge. It counted as two, and it was seen as a gain of momentum and a blow to the other side. We relished those and saved them for big days.

Here, our focus was on pushing and pushing and pushing to get people who voted no before to come out and say yes. And Rahm and Phil worked with that group to get them out. We tried to sequence them so we had something every day."

The week after St. Louis, on March 15, Obama traveled close to Natoma Canfield's hometown, where her story had only worsened. She had given up her insurance in January after the hikes in her premium. Then two months later, she collapsed while working on a farm nearby. She was rushed to the hospital and diagnosed with leukemia, just a week before Obama arrived in the nearby town of Strongsville, Ohio.

"So you want to know why I'm here, Ohio?" he asked. "I'm here because of Natoma."

In truth, he was also there because he could target two congressmen who had voted against health care reform in 2009. One was John Boccieri, a young and vulnerable first-term congressman representing a conservative district, where Canfield lived. The politics were so tough for Boccieri that a plane flew over his district with a banner urging him to vote no "for abortion funding." He was in Ohio on the day of Obama's speech, but declined both an invitation to the rally and a ride on Air Force One back to Washington, choosing instead to travel six hours by car, while reading the health care bill.

Obama's event was held in the neighboring district, represented by the unpredictable, attention-seeking Dennis Kucinich. The two former presidential rivals traveled together on Air Force One, and Obama gave him the hard sell on health care reform. Obama recalled how Kucinich had helped on the eve of the Iowa caucuses by freeing his voters to side with Obama in case of his own poor showing. At the start of the rally, as he was thanking all the elected officials for being there, Obama mentioned Kucinich, and a supporter piped up: "Vote yes!"

"Did you hear that, Dennis?" Obama said, looking over. "Go ahead, say that again."

"Vote yes!" It was quite possibly the only time Obama had asked a heckler to repeat an interruption.

Two days later, on March 17, Kucinich became the first House Democrat to switch his vote from no to yes, saying he wanted to be "very careful that the potential of President Obama's presidency not be destroyed by this debate." White House staffers who thought of Kucinich as an unlikely savior were nevertheless impressed. "Kucinich is a man who knows his moment, and he milks it for all it's worth," said one senior Obama aide. "And it led the news. It was seen as a huge deal."

By the end of the week, the last remaining bloc of Democrats to oppose the bill were switching sides. A pro-life group led by Bart Stupak of Michigan was crumbling. Dale Kildee, an eighty-year-old congressman also from Michigan, switched sides, saying there would be no federal funding of abortion. Sister Carol Keehan of the Catholic Health Association spoke out in support of the health care bill, as did the leaders of religious orders representing fifty-nine thousand nuns. When Stupak met with White House officials in the Cannon House Office Building on the Friday before the final vote, he was sold on a solution: the president would sign an executive order restating the ban on federal funding for abortion. "That's when I knew we had the votes," said DeParle.

John Boccieri, half Kildee's age, stood outside the East Front of the Capitol in the bright spring sunshine to announce his decision to reporters. Standing beside several constituents, he said that he would switch to yes, even though that meant he could lose his job. One of the reasons he gave for taking the gamble was a leukemia patient, hospitalized but with no insurance, living in his district. Her name: Natoma Canfield.

"Her story took me back to a place that I haven't been in a long time. I remember standing at the foot of my mother's bed as she told me that she had breast cancer. As a young boy I didn't know what that meant. Thank God she had health care insurance," he began. "Mom survived breast cancer. But I remember her always saying to me, 'Don't tell me what you believe in. Show me what you've done and I'll tell you what you believe in . . .' There's this one person today I want to make proud. I want my mom to know I'm standing up today and doing what I believe in. Natoma, I wish you could be with me here today."

Watching the rapid flow of votes from the Oval Office, Obama started to believe he was on the verge of historic change. "I think in the last week you had a lot of folks who stood up in a pretty courageous way—John Boccieri of Ohio, Betsy Markey of Colorado, Tom Perriello in Virginia—folks from very tough districts," he told me. "And them saying to me, 'You know what, I think this is the right thing to do, even though I don't know how it's going to play politically,' gave me some confidence that maybe we could pull this off."

With the arrival of spring, Obama's mood improved. He took time out of lobbying for health care votes to make his selections for the NCAA basketball championship for the ESPN cameras, adding a whole new meaning to March Madness. "This is the most important work I've done today," he quipped to ESPN's Andy Katz as he walked into the Map Room inside the Executive Mansion. He picked Duke for the final four, in honor of Reggie Love. But he chose Kansas to win outright, saying he wanted to please his health secretary, Kathleen Sebelius, formerly governor of Kansas.

With the cameras off, Obama had a few special requests. "Last year I beat Reggie but Axelrod won the whole thing. It was *shocking*. The first round killed me. So I'm counting on a little bit of improvement this year," he began, with a distinct sense of injury. "Can I only just say one thing? I noticed last year after I got hammered on the first round, you guys kept running the loop on *SportsCenter* about how bad I had done during the first round. Come on, man. Help me out. You know that's my job, by the way, when I'm ex-president. *SportsCenter*. I want to pick the top ten. Who has *that* job?"

By the end of the week, as the House votes started to trickle in, Obama's aides were watching the basketball games in their West Wing offices, and the president's schedule began to shift suspiciously in line with the start and end of big games. The fourth-quarter player was enjoying his own comeback.

Obama made one last effort to revive his own party in the House. On a hot, sunny Saturday afternoon, with the White House magnolias in full bloom, Obama's aides gathered outside the Oval Office. Once the closely fought Villanova versus St. Mary's game ended, the president walked out of the West Wing with Phil Schiliro to the waiting motorcade. On the streets outside, there were hundreds of antiwar protesters demanding that Obama's predecessor be indicted. But along Pennsylvania Avenue, toward Capitol Hill, the signs turned more personal and more concerned with health care. "Socialists 'You Lie'" read one. Another called Obama a tyrant. His armored limo pulled into the Capitol and the president walked into the underground auditorium in the new visitors' center. He waved at the House Democrats seated inside and took a seat onstage along with the House leaders, Nancy Pelosi and Steny Hoyer, and their favorite object of suspicion, Senate leader Harry Reid. As Pelosi promised to make history by giving 32 million people health care insurance, Obama stroked his lips and seemed lost in the remarks he was about to deliver. Reid promised to make his "good bill even better," and the entire House caucus—including those who would vote against the bill—stood to applaud and cheer. "Mr. President, I know you know basketball," Reid ventured, as Obama smirked. "You're a big fan. I know many are fixated on the national college basketball tournament going on now. So Mr. President, we're in the last minute of play. The shot clock is turned off. Everyone knows what the outcome will be. So they are trying to foul us and foul us and foul us and foul us again, just to keep the clock from reaching zero . . . Every time they foul, we'll keep hitting our shots."

Obama reached for inspiration not from a ball game but from one of his personal role models, the man he called, at the start of his presidential journey in early 2007, "a tall, gangly, self-made Springfield lawyer." Lincoln spoke to Obama—himself a tall, gangly, self-made former Springfield senator—in a way that continued to lift his spirits. Early in his presidency, it was clear how important the sixteenth president's example was to him. "I do still use Lincoln's writings as a touchstone," he told me one day in the Oval Office.

Depending on his mood and his needs, he reached for different Lincoln texts for guidance. Three years ago, Lincoln's lesson was that "there is power in words . . . there is power in conviction . . . there is power in hope." Now, Lincoln's message was that success was not as important as principle. "I have the great pleasure of having a really nice library at the White House," he explained. "And I was tooling through some of the writings of some previous presidents and I came upon this quote by Abraham Lincoln: 'I am not bound to win, but I'm bound to be true. I'm not bound to succeed, but I'm bound to live up to what light I have.'" The people who passed Social Security and civil rights felt the same way as Lincoln, he argued. The current Congress was no different now. He told how he started out as a community organizer who was "skeptical about politics and politicians" but decided to get into politics to change the system. All of the House Democrats had felt the same way early in their careers. Then they made compromises and family sacrifices. And they wondered why they got involved in the first place.

> But you know what? Every once in a while, every once in a while a moment comes where you have a chance to vindicate all those best hopes that you had about yourself, about this country, where you have a chance to make good on those promises that you made in all those town meetings and all those constituency breakfasts and all that traveling through the district, all those people who you looked in the eye and you said, "You know what? You're right. The system is not working for you and I'm going to make it a little bit better." And this is one of those moments. This is one of those times. We are not bound to win, but we are bound to be true. We are not bound to succeed, but we are bound to let whatever light we have shine.

Obama was playing one of his favorite roles: the narrator of the great American story, merging together his own narrative with his audience's, and tying both to a historical tale. The only problem was that the quote was not from Lincoln. It was from Ronald Reagan, who misattributed the lines to Lincoln as he laid a wreath at the Lincoln Memorial. Obama admired Reagan's ability to redefine the political landscape for a generation. But the fortieth president was an improbable person to spur Democrats to push ahead with health care reform.

The error was innocent, but the story was embellished in a telling way. Obama's source was not some tome in the White House library but his own diary. There was often speculation that a writer like Obama would keep extensive journals of his own unlikely journey from the Illinois state senate to the presidency. He had kept journals as a young community organizer, and he told me early in his presidency that he still relied on the words of Ralph Waldo Emerson, the great journal writer and advocate of self-reliance. But the speculation was never confirmed, and Obama's aides appeared to know little about what their boss was writing, if anything. The Lincoln quote was part of an extensive collection of Obama's writings, including inspirational thoughts and words from people he admired. "It turns out that it wasn't from a book of Lincoln quotes," he admitted to me in the Oval Office. "It was actually something that I had written. Sometimes I keep notes, I keep a diary, and I was looking over some old volumes that I had written. And that quote was there that I had gotten from somewhere else." He had copied the quote some time ago, he explained. "I always liked the quote, and it spoke to what I thought was the spirit that members of the House and Senate needed to go into this final stage with: a sense that we're here for a reason. We're not here just to manage our poll numbers. We may not win, but we can be proud if we feel like we're doing the right thing."

No doubt such diary entries would form the basis of a future autobiography, just as his Chicago journals were the foundation for his memoir, *Dreams from My Father*. But they also suggested something about Obama's self-reflective moments. They were the result of a methodical harvesting of other people's ideas and words: a conscious effort to weave his own thoughts and experiences into some kind of literary compendium. They also served to reinforce his self-image, as a self-disciplined, strategic mind that could find solutions to emotional challenges. As the Reaganesque version of Lincoln revealed, this was not a scholarly attempt at research; the writings served the twin purposes of private self-improvement and public inspiration. They were a record of how far he had traveled and a road map to how he might reach his destination.

As Obama left the auditorium, the House Democrats started up an old chant: "Fired Up! Ready to Go!" They were still chanting as Obama walked to his presidential limo and traveled back down Pennsylvania Avenue. Past the protesters shouting, "Kill the Bill!" Past one tourist wearing a Palin 2012 T-shirt, and another tourist giving the thumbs-up. Past the cherry blossoms outside the White House. Back in the Oval Office, you could still hear the peace activists angrily shouting, "No More War!"

The next day his staff showed up to work early for a Sunday. The House planned to vote late in the day, and the legal team was finishing the wording of the final deal: the executive order reaffirming no federal funding of abortion. Obama's senior aides met in Emanuel's office at 9:30 only to find an unusual addition: the president himself. He was rattling around the West Wing looking for something to do. There were no calls to make and no members to meet. He sat down and said simply, "Today's a big deal. If we get it passed."

"Well, it's a big deal if we fail, too," quipped one aide.

They laughed grimly and talked about what he should do in the event of a late-night vote.

"This could go until nine or ten at night," said Dan Pfeiffer. "Even though you're going to miss the news, we think you should go out no matter what."

"Absolutely, we'll do it," said Obama. "I think this is important."

With the meeting over, time passed slowly and anxiously, as it had on election day sixteen months earlier. Nancy-Ann DeParle went home for a run. Pfeiffer joined his regular basketball team for a league game. Many spent the afternoon watching NCAA tournament games.

They gathered in the Roosevelt Room to watch the voting begin even later than they anticipated. They were assured the votes were there, but after Massachusetts—after all the false starts and misplaced hopes over the last year—they were still holding their breath as the numbers on the screen edged upward to 219, three more than they needed. There were no Republican votes and 34 Democratic defections. Inside the House chamber, the Democrats started chanting "Yes We Can!" Inside the West Wing, Obama's staff cheered and applauded as the president walked in and high-fived Emanuel.

Obama placed a call to his toughest political partner: Nancy Pelosi. Just two months earlier she had erupted in anger in the same room as they negotiated how to save health care. Now she had just made history. "I'm happier passing health care than I was after the election," he gushed.

"Well I'm *not* happier than after the election," she said matter-of-factly. "Because without the election, we would have none of this."

It was shortly before midnight when Obama walked over to the East Room to talk to the news media. "This isn't radical reform," he explained. "But it is major reform. This legislation will not fix everything that ails our health care system. But it moves us decisively in the right direction. This is what change looks like."

For a man who often seemed to prefer his own company, Obama now wanted to share the moment of change with the people who made it happen. He first asked his staff to find DeParle, the health care aide he leaned on most heavily, who was watching the votes in person in the House of Representatives. She rushed to the White House and was pulled aside by Reggie Love. She found the president next door to the East Room, having just finished his remarks to the cameras. There, he put his hands on her shoulders and they hugged. "Can you believe it?" he said. After all the months of technical talks, after all the wonkish details and congressional maneuvers, DeParle felt overwhelmed with emotion.

Even more rare than the open emotion was the president's idea for a staff party on the Truman Balcony of the residence. He wanted to share his thanks with every staffer—senior and junior—who worked on health care. "I don't want to ruin a good party with a long speech," Obama told his team. "We've had tough times, but we've done something big. We just accomplished what we all came here to do." He thanked his key aides, including DeParle, and set about talking to each one in person.

It was, like election night in Chicago, unseasonably warm as they drank beer and champagne overlooking the South Lawn, the Washington Monument, and the Eisenhower Executive Office Building, where many of them toiled in obscurity. Ann Widger was a junior staffer who talked daily with Natoma Canfield and her family, but she had never met Obama until now.

"I really feel like I should thank you not just on behalf of someone on your staff but on behalf of Natoma, because I am now so invested in her life," she said, as he put his hands on her shoulders.

"Go back and tell Natoma that you talked to me and I said to tell her that she's the reason I fought so hard."

To those who knew him best, Obama seemed unusually, exceptionally at ease. He took his tie off and was laughing and smiling. He could pause and savor the time in a way that was impossible on the night of his own inauguration.

"How does it feel?" asked Valerie Jarrett.

"I am *so* happy," he said. "It feels far better than election night."

"Why?"

"Because election night was just a means to get to this night.

That was not nearly the cause to celebrate as actually accomplishing something."

Jarrett thought he was happier than any other night since his wedding day. In fact, he was celebrating this historic moment without his wife and children. Michelle Obama and their daughters were spending the weekend in New York to make up for a long-promised White House trip to Indonesia and Australia, which was canceled for the health care vote.

Three of Obama's longest-serving staffers sat together sharing war stories. Robert Gibbs, Jon Favreau, and Dan Pfeiffer recalled their first foray into health care. It was early in the presidential election, when they were still working in Washington rather than Chicago, under the auspices of an exploratory committee, not the formal campaign. Obama had committed to talking to a conference staged by the Families USA activist group. They had no health care policy and no idea what shape their plan would take. Their rival John Edwards was already promising a big focus on health care, and Hillary Clinton would likely do the same. But they had no policy and no news. "Just on a whim, Gibbs has the idea of putting in the speech that we would pass universal health care by the end of our first term," recalled Pfeiffer. "But we never did a conference call on it. We didn't poll it. We just threw it in there. And it was like a bomb set off when he said it. Because everyone who knew anything about Washington thought we were crazy. And it became a part of his stump." Soon after, Clinton was asked if she would commit to the same timetable, but she declined. Health care might take *two* terms, she warned.

Three years later, they were sitting on the Truman Balcony, close to President Obama, having beaten their first-term goal by a wide margin. This revival was the result of a renegade mix of hubris and stubbornness. "Every once in a while there's a moment when you realize how far you've come," said Pfeiffer.

Soon after one in the morning, Katie Johnson, Obama's personal secretary, walked over to her boss, who was talking with DeParle, and asked if he wanted to wrap up the party.

"No," Obama said. "I'm having a great time."

"I think, sir," DeParle ventured, "people probably won't want to leave until you do."

FOUR

RECOVERY

Joe Biden and Barack Obama walked onstage in the makeshift auditorium with two supporting actors: one ran a solar energy company in Boulder, Colorado; the other, a construction company in Imperial, Pennsylvania. They were mute endorsements of the biggest economic gamble of the new presidency. Now a year old, the $814 billion American Recovery and Reinvestment Act represented more money than President Bush had spent in more than seven years of waging the war on terror in Iraq and Afghanistan. Obama had handed over to Biden the task of spending the colossal amount of cash on the homeland in just two years. To mark the anniversary of their effort to rescue the economy from collapse—and their administration from the early disaster of a prolonged recession—they staged an uninspired event in the easiest location. The real auditorium inside the White House office building was undergoing extensive remodeling; this replica was even closer to the Oval Office than the original. The result: four men in suits speaking to a room full of staffers and supporters inside a temporary metal box, on what used to be a courtyard next door to the West Wing.

Biden spoke first, his forehead still smudged with the Catholic mark of Ash Wednesday, the start of the Lent season that leads to the Easter resurrection. It was Biden's job to supervise the sprawling billions, to minimize waste and embarrassment, and to sell the policy to voters still struggling with job losses. He told how he had traveled to sixty cities to talk about the Recovery Act, and the stories of recession and recovery seemed to blur into one rambling journey through his thoughts. He had just been to Saginaw, Michigan, where he met someone whose name he half remembered—"his name is Gonzalez, Mr. Gonzalez"—who had a B.A., a wife, and two kids. Gonzalez got laid off from a car company, took a job-training slot at a community college (funded by the Recovery Act), and now had a job at Dow Corning, working with chemicals used in solar panels.

"They added a thousand people over the last year because of some help they got as well, and in their great reach, he's now working. He's working at a decent salary. And that community college is going to train this year—another hundred people are going to go right from that training program directly to a job. The other thing I've noticed is—and I notice particularly from you all, and I use 'you' in an editorial sense—is this emphatic, unrelenting belief that there is no reason why America has to be number two. None whatsoever. I find even that laid-off worker refuses to believe America is going to be number two in the world—whether it's in ultimately the construction of wind turbines, or whether it's in any other renewable energy form, or new automobiles and battery technology. I mean, there is this sense, there is this sense among Americans, even in these tough times, there's no reason we're not going to come out of this stronger than when we went into it."

Somehow he lurched from Saginaw to a sound bite from his boss's most recent State of the Union. "I do not accept second place for the United States of America," Obama had said about global economic competition, including clean energy investments. The only problem was that White House research suggested the phrase didn't resonate with the right voters. "It doesn't poll well," said one senior Obama aide. "Women don't like it in the focus groups because they don't like the competition. They tend not to like the Darwinism."

Obama himself had no problem with competition. Reading from two teleprompters, he was both more focused and more nuanced. He poked fun at Republicans who opposed the controversial Recovery Act but showed up at ribbon-cutting ceremonies when the money was spent. Yet he also admitted that the enormous sums of money had fallen short. "If we're honest, part of the controversy also is, is that despite the extraordinary work that has been done through the Recovery Act, millions of Americans are still without jobs. Millions more are struggling to make ends meet. So it doesn't yet feel like much of a recovery. And I understand that. It's why we're going to continue to do everything in our power to turn this economy around."

Obama also wanted to turn around the story about the stimulus package. First he wanted to correct the idea that billions were wasted. "Joe and I were just talking in the back—when this thing passed we said, '$787 billion; somewhere there's going to be some story of some money that ended up being misspent,'" he explained. "$787 billion spent out over 18 months, that's a lot—that's a lot of money. And it is a testimony to Vice President Biden and his team that, as Joe puts it, the dog, so far at least, hasn't barked."

He also wanted to do a better sales job on some of the key industry investments of the Recovery Act. For months Obama had felt frustrated that voters had no idea that his administration had helped fill a critical hole in the clean energy economy, which would hopefully add to the auto industry's prospects for survival. It fell to the president, in a contrived and unimaginative press event, to make the case:

> Because of the Recovery Act, we have finally jump-started the clean energy industry in America, and made possible 200,000 jobs in the clean energy and construction sectors. Just take one example: Consider the investment that we've made in the kind of batteries used in hybrid and electric cars. You've heard about these, right? Before the Recovery Act was signed, 98 percent of the world's advanced battery production was done in Asian countries. The United States did less than two percent of this advanced battery manufacturing that's going to be the key to these high-mileage, low-emission cars. Then we invested in new research and battery technologies, and supported the construction of twenty battery factories that will employ tens of thousands of Americans—factories that can make enough batteries each year to power half a million plug-in hybrid vehicles. So as a result, next year—next year, two years after the Recovery Act—the United States will have the capacity to produce nearly 20 percent of the world's advanced batteries. From less than two percent to 20 percent. And we'll be able to make 40 percent of these advanced batteries by 2015. An entire new industry because of the Recovery Act.

The meandering event encapsulated much of what was wrong and right with the recovery and the Recovery Act. For all the money spent on preserving existing jobs and investing in new ones, unemployment remained stubbornly high. Obama's economic team had forecast that the stimulus would keep unemployment below 8 percent, but it rapidly rose to near 10 percent by the fall of 2009 and stayed around that level for several months. Voters might find it hard to assess the relative merits of rival economic policies, but they could easily assess a failed forecast and a miserable job market. To make matters worse, the White House had never explained the gargantuan stimulus effectively from the outset, while its Republican opponents were disciplined in caricaturing its efforts. The White House was hampered by the chaos of the transition, the internal strife of a fractious economic team, and the pace and scale of the economic collapse. But it was also deluded, at the time, by its own high poll numbers and the imperative of governing in the midst of a crisis. A year later, Obama and Biden were passionate believers in the positive effects of the Recovery Act, and they traveled the country to demonstrate them. But too often their efforts seemed too little, too late: a slapdash speech in a makeshift theater before their own fans.

The problems began before they arrived in Washington. Bad news beats out good news at any time, and the disastrous developments in the economy overwhelmed any impact of the Recovery Act. But there was something more than just a tidal wave of job losses during the transition. Burned by their support for Bush's efforts to bail out the banks, Republicans were in no mood to bail out a new Democratic president. There was a political determination on the other side to deny Obama even minimal help at a time of crisis.

Obama's aides were shocked at the united Republican front against them. "What was surprising was the degree to which we got no help from the Republicans. In the entire U.S. Congress, three Republicans stepped forward to support the Recovery Act, and one of them isn't a Republican anymore," said Axelrod. "At every juncture of our history when we were facing a national catastrophe, there were those in the other party who were willing to stand up and risk themselves politically. We didn't see that." There were still some principled Republicans, in the view of Obama's inner circle. But the combined pressure of an ideological leadership and grassroots anger left those Republicans in an intolerable situation. "I think there are good people on the Republican side. I genuinely do," said Axelrod. "I think there are people who want to be helpful, who want to do the right thing. I think they're terribly frightened right now. They're frightened by their own leadership, and they're frightened by the sort of rage within their own party. So the reasonable people are running for the hills."

Obama's team was looking at the mirror image of how they had built support around his opposition to the war in Iraq. No matter what the national security interests, Democrats were burned by their compromised positions on the invasion, and were late to recognize when a new military strategy turned successful through the election year. At a time of public anger, the politics could lag behind the news just like unemployment could lag behind the recovery. For many Democrats and independents, it was hard to believe there was any good news coming out of Iraq for a long time. For many Republicans and independents, it was now hard to believe there was any good news coming out of the economy or Obama's economic policy. "First of all, people didn't believe that we put money in their pockets," said Axelrod. "People don't think we've created a couple of million jobs when we've lost more than eight million in the last two years. People don't see the evidence of progress, and it lends credence to the Republican argument that we somehow wasted $700 billion, even though $250 billion went to tax cuts for the middle class. The hardest argument to make in politics is that things could have been worse, when they are not good. I think they had an easier message. It's easier when things are bad. They say we spent all this money and it didn't work, even though every economist will tell you that the Recovery Act made a substantial difference."

However, the slow recovery in jobs was only part of the political context. Obama's aides were blindsided by the sustained anger at something begun before they entered office: the Troubled Asset Relief Program, or TARP, which helped to halt a collapse in confidence in the financial sector. "In most people's minds, there's a great deal of confusion," conceded Axelrod. "They think the Recovery Act was made for the banks."

Rather than focus on the politics of the stimulus—or communicate the policy better—Obama's team pushed hard and fast, believing they needed to act urgently as an economic imperative. They felt they could not slice up the components of the stimulus package into chunks that were easier to digest, or engage in traditional gimmicks. "If you had the luxury of doing the Recovery Act the way you'd like to, you'd have done it in phases," said Axelrod. "You'd have done tax cuts in one bill. You'd have done unemployment insurance and so forth in another. And you'd have done infrastructure in another. We didn't have that luxury. We had to move all at once. George Bush sent checks out to people so they knew they had gotten a tax cut. Our people said, 'It won't get into the bloodstream fast enough if you do it that way.' So we governed. And we did what governing required. But we did it at some cost to politics and our message."

The Bush White House believed that its numbers were tied to rising gas prices: as prices rose, Bush's numbers declined. Now the Obama team believed their numbers—and the fate of Democrats in the midterms—were tied to employment numbers. "It's very hard to govern at a time of high unemployment," said Axelrod. "If employment is going up in the six months before the next election, we're going to have a better outcome. We're at the mercy of the economic numbers to some degree."

That kind of passivity—along with the declining polls and a sluggish recovery—led to widespread second-guessing inside the West Wing. Obama was unhappy with having no clear story to tell about the economy, and he was not alone. He insisted that the economy was a disaster when he entered office and was now better than before. But he rarely told how his policies had made the economy better or how he would improve the economic outlook. "I strongly believe one of our biggest deficiencies right now is that we have no overarching message framework on paper," said one senior Obama aide. "The fact is that we don't have an economic message to deal with this problem. It needs to be addressed."

The vice president agreed. Biden believed from the outset that it was a bad idea to talk about job creation. The focus was employment, for sure. But the immediate priority was to help people in desperate need. "I was of the view that you shouldn't talk about the employment piece of the act in the front end because it was bigger than that, although that's the central underlying rationale—to get us out of the ditch," Biden told me. "The way I would explain it the first six months, when no one else wanted to talk about it, was that this was about saving a hell of a lot of people from falling into the black abyss, with everything from unemployment insurance at the front end, straight through to COBRA." The Recovery Act spent billions on keeping Medicaid alive at the state level, but nobody knew about it. One-third of the money was spent on tax cuts, but again, nobody knew about it. Very few people knew how the money was spent, allowing Republicans to complain about trivialities such as the expense of road signs proclaiming projects funded by the act. As Biden traveled the country to highlight the spending, he would ask congressmen if anyone realized where the tax cuts were coming from. "I'd say to the congressmen, 'Has anyone come up and thanked you for the $250 lump sum payment the seniors got?' No. 'Has anyone said anything to you about the $250 payment to veterans?'" At one event in New York, he heard about a nanny who believed the tax cut was a pay raise from her employer. "Nobody associated that with the act," Biden said with exasperation. "Talk about signage. That's where we should have put signage, to let people know it's a part of it."

For the communications and messaging aides, there was an air of resignation about the economy. There was little they could say to make it better. Indeed, they believed that even an attempt to highlight positive news might backfire. "I think the economy isn't something you can spin your way out of," said Dan Pfeiffer. "The fact is, people are hurting. And there's a real danger of sounding out of touch with the reality that people have on a day-to-day basis. The economy was on the cusp of depression. We're still feeling the hole left by the financial crisis and the recession. But there are a lot of good signs and evidence of a stronger economy. You have to find this balance between sounding optimistic and hopeful, and staying in touch with how people really feel. That's a challenge."

For Pfeiffer, the frustrations were only heightened by all the external advice from wealthier supporters living in parts of the country that were already enjoying the recovery. "*Everyone* has an idea of what we should do and shouldn't do," he said. "One of the facts is that many people in Washington, New York, Boston, L.A., and Chicago—and other places like that—are having a very different economic experience than people in the Rust Belt, the Deep South, and the Midwest. They think things are going great because their 401(k)s have bounced back and the sales have probably come back in the company they own, and they want us to start talking up the economy. You just have to try to keep one foot tethered to reality."

Obama's team found their consolation in the experiences of one of their favorite predecessors: Ronald Reagan. Not because they admired his policies; they opposed them viscerally. But because he was a role model in terms of political style and communications, of reaching beyond his base and changing the course of history. Senior Obama aides liked to brandish charts showing the decline of jobs under Reagan, Bush, and Clinton, overlaid with the loss of jobs under their boss. Obama's decline was more sharp and rapid than any of his predecessors, but it also started earlier than theirs. They liked to point out that the number of jobs lost in the most recent recession was greater than the combined number of jobs lost in the previous three recessions. The only president with a similarly steep drop was Reagan, whose political fortunes in his first year were dreadful. "Reagan's numbers were worse and the recession wasn't as deep," said Axelrod. "There were a whole bunch of things that I told Obama before we took office. I told him that he was going to have middling poll numbers a year later because we all had heard the economic forecasts by our economic advisers. And you can't have sharply rising unemployment and not have an impact on your standing politically. The other was that we were going to lose a whole lot of seats because we just had two extraordinary elections."

Reagan provided no model for what came after the knife-edge votes on the Recovery Act. Instead they looked at one of the signature laws of the man who campaigned against them in the primaries: Bill Clinton. Joe Biden and his chief of staff, Ron Klain, wrote a memo to Obama drawing on their experience of the 1994 crime bill, at a time when the Clintons' health care efforts were finally pronounced dead. As tough as it was to find Republican support, the most perilous part came after it was signed into law. The crime bill was almost as controversial as health care, adding 100,000 new police officers but also banning assault weapons. Biden wrote the bill and believed it carried important lessons for Obama: especially the need to continue to sell the bill long after it passed through Congress. He thought that perceptions of the crime bill turned around because every time a new police officer earned his or her badge, the administration trumpeted the crime bill. The same was true of the

Recovery Act. People wanted to see results, and Biden believed they needed to demonstrate them.

Obama agreed and handed the first new job of the Recovery Act to his vice president. It quickly grew into both the biggest demand on Biden's schedule, and the biggest success of his time in office.

During the election, Biden had been frozen out of Obama's inner circle and felt isolated from key decisions and information. He was working with a staff picked by Obama's aides rather than his regular group of current and former Senate staffers. The results were not pretty. Instead of seeking his contribution, Obama's team was troubled by his gaffes and indiscipline. Biden's move into the White House represented a fresh start, with a staff that he was comfortable with. He insisted on having a place at the table for himself and his aides during key decisions and debates inside the West Wing. He was there at Obama's daily intelligence and economic briefings, and he was present at sessions with cabinet secretaries.

His performance, while not perfect, was vastly improved from his campaign days. He learned that he could no longer think out loud and tried to choose his words more carefully. His staff decided to stop apologizing for his gaffes and started characterizing them as plainspoken moments. There were still highly public stumbles: he told NBC's *Today* show that he didn't want his family traveling on trains and subways because of the H1N1 "swine flu" virus. Even his long-time aides acknowledged that Biden was finding the transition difficult at times. "He can't ever say now, 'This is my view, but it's only my view.' If the vice president says something, it's imputed to the administration," said Ron Klain. "He has to make sure that his views have gone through a process and reflect the collective views of the team here. That has been a change. The flip side is that he appreciates as vice president that he has the ability to impact the words and policies coming from the president."

He certainly had the ability to impact the perception of the president's economic plan. As he set about managing the Recovery Act, Biden focused on two areas as the administration tried to spend the money quickly: fraud and stupidity. His first act was to choose a fraud-fighter: Earl Devaney, who previously headed the Secret Service's fraud division. A former police officer, Devaney was inspector general at the Department of the Interior, where he had uncovered the influence-peddling of lobbyist Jack Abramoff and a culture of corruption among regulators of the oil and gas industry. Devaney was supposed to be a tough deterrent against fraud. "We figured if we had a high-profile and highly empowered cop, if you will, that would deter crime," said Klain. "Our view was, we're building this superhighway and we're going to put a highly visible policeman in the middle of the street in a well-marked car and that would discourage speeding." Instead of pretending there would be no fraud, Biden wanted to be public and high-profile about cases of fraud. He met early and often with Devaney and told cabinet secretaries their priority was to act as watchdogs. Biden's reward: a presidential moniker. "To you, he's Mr. Vice President," Obama said as he committed $28 billion to transportation projects and unveiled the Recovery Act's logo and website. "But around the White House, we call him the Sheriff. Because if you're misusing taxpayer money, you'll have to answer to him."

Sheriff Joe busied himself with the kind of bureaucracy that would frustrate real law enforcement. The Recovery Act required people who received funds to file a report, but it failed to say what should happen to those who were delinquent with their paperwork. Biden's team chose to make its first example out of a child-hunger group called Share Our Strength, which failed to file reports. "A perfectly nice organization," said Klain. "These weren't mobbed-up contractors. But we cut them off and said, 'We know you're good people, but if you don't file your reports, we're not going to send you money.'" The group admitted its mistake and expressed its regret.

When he wasn't busting hunger groups, the sheriff was sniffing out stupidity. Even on projects worth less than $1 million, he and his team took an unusual—and often idiosyncratic—interest. Working under Ed DeSeve, a former deputy director of the Clinton White House budget office, Biden's team searched for the projects that might embarrass them, even if those projects rated highly by other measures and enjoyed political support from powerful members of Congress. They supported rejection of a $12 million bike path in Missoula, Montana, because of the state's harsh winters. "It was an *excellent* bike path," said Klain. "But the team's view was that a $12 million bike path in a part of the country where for several months of the year it's too cold for people to ride bikes, it just seems like it's not going to restore public confidence." They drew the line at dog parks and skateboard parks, even though the projects would employ people in construction. Senator Barbara Boxer fought hard for a $650,000 skateboard park in Santa Barbara, California. But her friend Biden insisted on rejecting the proposal. "We came to the conclusion early on that if people thought that is what their tax dollars were being spent on, at a time of great recession and great unemployment, people would think that's just *stupid*," said Klain. "Our argument was 'No. There's some things that are good to do but not good enough to justify use of the Recovery Act funds.'"

Biden's team knew that public confidence in the Recovery Act was shaky, in spite of its work. But they believed that confidence would be even shakier if there had been more stories of frivolous spending. In any case, such stories circulated, whether or not they were factual or involved Recovery Act funding. Senator Tom Coburn of Oklahoma, a conservative Republican and sometime friend of Obama's, detailed one hundred projects he found questionable.

Some were so questionable that Biden's team agreed to review them; others were either inaccurate or misleading. Many more were only questionable because Coburn disagreed with environmental programs like weatherizing old buildings for energy efficiency. Biden's aides believed their work would ultimately pay off—but only once the job market turned around. "We put ourselves in the place where, when the economic news gets better, we've got a story to tell that people will accept," said Klain, "that we were responsible stewards of this money, tried to spend it the right way, and tried to avoid bad things from happening."

Could they have won more public support by spending the money on a few big items instead of many small ones? Some critics on the left believed the Recovery Act would have been more popular if the administration had spent the cash on big infrastructure projects, like a contemporary version of the interstate highway system or the Hoover Dam. That critique annoyed Biden intensely. "The Hoover Dam took six *years,* man," he told me. "This bullshit about a Hoover Dam. It's like *the Hoover Dam.* Okay, in six years I can build a Hoover Dam. We can say look at what we did." Biden recalled that he and Obama both proposed building a new high-tech electricity grid across the nation during the transition in Chicago. "We had this great idea because we both talked about it separately in our competing campaigns—to the extent that I competed in Iowa—which was look, how about if we dedicate $100 billion to building a new grid, a twenty-first-century highway for energy? We kept going to our people and they came back and said maybe we can do seventy. It got down to three. And the reason it got down to three is because you can't build it!" The federal government could not order states and local governments to site the lines of a new grid. Even Biden and Obama's pet project of high-speed rail—which received an $8 billion down payment from the act—would take a long time to come to fruition. "By the time the act is over, they're going to see the beginning," said Biden. "It just takes that long."

It did not take a long time to realize that Obama's economic team was the most dysfunctional group of the president's advisers. And at the heart of the dysfunction was the person tasked with bringing the team together: Larry Summers. Summers was a brilliant academic economist who had served as Treasury secretary at the end of the Clinton administration. But he was socially charmless, professionally competitive, and politically clumsy. Fueled by an endless supply of Diet Coke, he appeared to suffer from his own medical condition of restless head syndrome. At times, the jitters transferred to his leg, but more often they emerged from his mouth, as his thoughts sputtered toward the end of a sentence. During the Bush years, he had led Harvard University as its president, but he stepped down after a faculty vote of no confidence as he was variously accused of both sexism and racism. He liked to think of himself as having strong political abilities, but his record at Harvard and inside the White House suggested otherwise. "Larry is a complicated character," said one senior Obama aide. "He never should have taken this job in the first place. He was trying to rehabilitate himself after Harvard."

Many of the economic team's problems began with Summers moving into his West Wing office. He wanted his old job back at Treasury, but his main rival for the position was Tim Geithner, his former protégé. Geithner lacked Summers's academic credentials but had risen fast within government as a specialist in international economics. As president of the New York Federal Reserve, he made it clear he felt no need to rehab his career, even as Wall Street was collapsing in the fall of 2008. As Obama's team urgently sought to name the new economic team after the election, the debate went back and forth between Summers and Geithner for Treasury secretary. The president-elect saw benefits to both and could not make a clear decision. So he struck on the idea of offering one of them the position of his chief economic adviser, as director of the White House National Economic Council (NEC). "It was a great way to have both, rather than one or the other," said Rahm Emanuel. "It was my view, given that you were in the heart of the crisis, that Larry should be at Treasury because he had been there. But both were going to be reassuring, and they were, and still are."

But the political context, as well as personal political talents, moved against Summers. Obama's aides began to feel constrained by the choice of Hillary Clinton as secretary of state. Could they also afford to have a former Clinton cabinet official serving alongside her in Obama's cabinet? They felt the markets leaned toward Geithner, who was himself playing the transition with remarkable skill. Geithner set down a simple condition: if he wasn't offered the Treasury job, he would stay at the New York Fed. Obama's aides had no idea whether this was a negotiating tactic or not, and they did not want to find out. For his part, Summers believed the White House job was critical at a time of economic crisis, and he could not refuse the president's offer. But he told Obama that management was not his strength. "I talked to the president about it to make sure he understood I was going to be a person who had strong views," he told me. "And if what he wanted was the most harmonious management of the paper flow, that I wasn't probably the right person. But if he wanted all positions represented with open debate, I felt I could make sure I would be able to help him in that regard."

Open debate was one way to put it. Summers clashed with almost every other member of the economic team, and his love of contrarian argument seemed to aggravate technical policy differences. If he had served simply as an economic counselor, his personal manner would have mattered little. But as director of the NEC, he was supposed to bring together the economic team. The results were the opposite. "He's the president's economic adviser. At the same time, as NEC director, he's supposed to run an honest policy process," said one senior Obama aide. "He's told me at least three times he's the only person in the executive office of the president who is running an honest policy process. But he comes in with his point of view and tries to drive it." Summers locked horns repeatedly with Peter Orszag at the budget office, and Christina Romer, who led the more technical Council of Economic Advisers. By the one-year anniversary of the president's inauguration, Obama's senior staff were hoping that Summers would leave of his own accord, perhaps to return to Harvard, rather than force a confrontation that would push him out.

For his part, Summers thought that he struck a middle tone between economics and politics. "I frankly don't feel like I'm doing my job right unless many of my academic economics friends are concerned that I'm giving excessive weight to factors outside the economic model," he told me, "and unless my political friends are frustrated that I'm being a little rigid in insisting on economic efficiency." Summers almost enjoyed frustrating others, and did little to hide it. "Larry is just a contrarian," said one colleague. "He likes to think of himself as a political operative but he isn't. It's more of an academic's contrarian point of view."

Obama himself believed that his economic team—for all their personal rivalries and tensions—had taken vital steps in the midst of the recession to help revive the economy. "The president believes that the decisions that were made last year saved the country from a much larger economic catastrophe," said David Axelrod. Obama bristled at the notion that his own team of aides was dysfunctional, even though that was the opinion of most of his own West Wing staff. Instead, he appreciated Summers for his economic expertise but did not rely on him exclusively. "He benefits from Larry's advice," said one senior

Obama aide. "But because he's smart, he doesn't just take it because Larry says it. He validates it." Others saw Summers as making far less of a contribution. "Larry is brilliant," said one of Obama's economic advisers. "But he was put in the wrong job. He belongs in a senior adviser role instead of running a process. Because he isn't a process person. He isn't an honest broker. He litigates things until he wins."

That litigation could turn into an endurance test, even on big policy initiatives favored by the president. Two days after Scott Brown's victory in Massachusetts, Obama, flanked by several economic heavyweights, delivered some brief comments to the cameras in the White House. On one side stood advisers whose experience leaned toward the financial industry: Summers was next to Chris Dodd, the Connecticut senator with close ties to the industry. Dodd himself was next to Bill Donaldson, the former CEO of the New York Stock Exchange and Bush's chairman of the Securities and Exchange Commission. On Obama's other side were those more skeptical about the industry: Massachusetts representative Barney Frank, most of Obama's Council of Economic Advisers, and a tall, bald, elderly former chairman of the Federal Reserve—Paul Volcker. Obama compressed two years of turmoil in the financial markets into a few dense sentences of outrage and explanation. The banks binged on risk in pursuit of profits and bonuses, then the American people were forced to rescue them with bailouts that were deeply offensive. Now the system needed reform, and new laws, to protect the banks' customers and taxpayers. "Never again will the American taxpayer be held hostage by a bank that is 'too big to fail,'" he promised. His solution: to stop banks from both trading for their customers and trading for themselves. "I'm proposing a simple and commonsense reform, which we're calling the 'Volcker Rule'—after this tall guy behind me. Banks will no longer be allowed to own, invest, or sponsor hedge funds, private equity funds, or proprietary trading operations for their own profit, unrelated to serving their customers."

But those simple, commonsense reforms were not so simple or sensible to Larry Summers. Summers had earned millions advising a hedge fund and giving speeches to Wall Street institutions in the year before he entered the White House. He did not always side with the industry: he could also be the advocate for the little guy, and he pushed hard for the creation of a new consumer financial protection agency. But now he leaned heavily toward Wall Street. He felt that the Volcker Rule was unrealistic and unworkable. He thought the line between trading for customers and trading for yourself was hard to define. What if you were Goldman Sachs and your customers were all the players in the foreign exchange market? Would you stop trading currencies? He feared the rule would push some banks to drop their bank status and lean more heavily on hedge fund–like trading, which would destabilize the system again. Maybe they just needed to limit the size of these institutions or require them to hold more capital.

His doubts sat there in the West Wing, blocking the Volcker Rule for months. Obama had signaled that he wanted the rule to proceed back in October. The banks were on safe ground again but could still benefit from subsidized lending by the federal government. That seemed wrong when they could use the money to trade for themselves rather than lend it to customers in the real economy. "Several of these guys, like Goldman Sachs, are engaged in massive amounts of investment for their own accounts, at the same time as getting cheap money from the government," said Austan Goolsbee, who worked closely with Volcker on the president's Economic Recovery Advisory Board. Biden was an old friend of Volcker's and started to press for the rule to take force. But as the weeks dragged on, Summers rehashed his same old questions and concerns. At one fall meeting with his economics team in the Oval Office, Obama wanted to know why nothing had moved yet. Summers dug in once again, while Geithner—whose media coverage cast him as a supposed ally of Wall Street—wanted to push ahead. Obama noted dryly, "I think I can argue everyone's position now." Volcker represented an important new voice inside a debate, and an economic team, that had grown deadlocked. "The president had to kick the economic team in the ass from time to time to get them to do things," said Axelrod, "just like he's kicked all his staff from time to time to get *us* to do things."

But the blame for the delays in reforming the banking system also lay with Obama himself. He was in no rush to change Wall Street while it looked like the industry was still fragile. And he was cautious enough about risk that he wanted to be sure his reforms were on target. In that regard, Summers's questions were giving voice to his own doubts and concerns. "I think there are very complicated issues surrounding financial regulatory reform, and my first charge to them early on was we've got to get this right," Obama told me. "Some people have wondered why we didn't do Wall Street reform first; that it would have been better politics than health care reform. Well, part of it was (a) it's highly technical and we wanted to make sure that we got it right; (b) the markets were very fragile and us trying to move forward massive legislation around banks and the financial markets at a time when they were still healing would have been policy malpractice."

When the industry bounced back, Obama already seemed to be skeptical of the advice from his economic team. He based that judgment in large part on the fierce criticism of their efforts by opponents who suggested they were too close to Wall Street. "By the time my economic team presented me with their basic framework, I think I agreed with 90 percent of it," he explained to me. "But I also felt that it was important to look at some of the critiques of our plan that were coming from other quarters and make sure that what we were doing was rigorous enough to prevent future problems. And the Volcker Rules were an example of that." Inside the West Wing,

Obama's aides found the media reporting about Volcker excessive: first Volcker was ignored, then he was dominating economic policy. The reality was that this was Obama's reawakening on the issue, and he was moving as slowly as the economic recovery.

A week after embracing the Volcker Rule, on January 29, Obama visited a factory to reassert his economic leadership and proclaim some big economic news to a skeptical public. Wearing blue safety glasses that looked like designer shades, he made a brief tour of the Chesapeake Machine Company, which manufactured special machines, including ones that produced solar panels. It was just two days after the State of the Union, and he wanted to promote one of his new policy ideas: a tax credit for small businesses to hire new workers or raise salaries. The economy was bouncing back, growing at 5 percent at the end of his first year in office, the fastest growth in six years. To help turn that growth into jobs, the tax credits would go to more than a million small businesses, including the machine company, which was ready to hire some new workers. "Now, it's true that in some instances this tax credit will go to businesses that were going to hire folks anyway," he explained. "But then, it simply becomes a tax cut for small businesses that will spur investment and expansion. And that's a good thing, too. And that's why this type of tax cut is considered by economists—who rarely agree on anything—to be one of the most cost-effective ways of accelerating job growth, especially because we will include provisions to prevent people from gaming the system."

Obama knew something about economists who rarely agreed on anything: his chief economist was deeply skeptical and critical about the small-business tax credit. Summers liked to argue that he had backed the idea of a jobs tax credit in the first year of the presidency, but it failed to win much political support. So he was reluctant to see it return the following year as a major policy, not least because his conversations with business executives suggested there were practical problems in making it work. "In general the overall determinant of how many people businesses hire is how many people they need," said Summers. "So I prefer to put emphasis on things like infrastructure that would affect the demand for products, which I thought was the particular determinant of hiring."

Summers was squabbling with Christina Romer, whose academic credentials were hardly superficial: she was an economics professor at Berkeley and a specialist in the Great Depression. Romer began to build economic models of the tax credit to boost what little academic literature existed. But Summers would often say he did not believe her arguments and models, demanding new tests and new assumptions. So Romer dutifully reworked the models and talked to outside economists who were just as skeptical as Summers. She found that many well-established economists were initially hostile but would change their minds on hearing about her studies. Even if most of the jobs would have been created anyway, Romer found the fraction generated by the tax credit was still cheaper than the Recovery Act. Much of Romer's work was designed to convince one man—Summers, not Obama—that her calculations made sense.

In fact, Summers seemed to care little about pleasing Obama. He had been a dogged opponent of another approach to helping small businesses: new lending. The idea was to divert surplus cash from the bailout of the banks to loan $30 billion to small businesses. Obama thought the amounts involved were relatively small, but Summers argued that small businesses were inherently more at risk in terms of defaulting on their loans. "It was incredibly frustrating for the president," said one senior aide. It would take almost a year for the administration to fully develop a set of programs to increase lending to small businesses.

At other times, rather than roadblock a policy, Summers tried to hijack one. Each day, at the president's daily economic briefing, Summers led a discussion about recent economic news or some broader issue of current interest. He could also move beyond organizing and facilitating the debate to skewing it in his own direction. No matter how big or small the subject, Summers fought for intellectual superiority in spirited turf wars. One concept that attracted his attention in the early spring of 2010 was the way cost-benefit analysis applied to new regulations. The analysis could effectively block or approve environmental, health, and safety rules. "Larry's basic thinking is the cost-benefit analysis ought to reflect the impact on the economy rather than just the environment or public health," said one senior Obama aide. Not surprisingly, that view alarmed the environmental regulators, especially Lisa Jackson, the administrator of the Environmental Protection Agency (EPA).

The flashpoint was an environmental disaster that occurred just before Obama entered the White House. An earth wall, built to hold back a giant pond of coal-ash sludge, collapsed west of Knoxville, Tennessee, in December 2008. The disaster filled the Emory River with coal ash, destroyed wetlands, and drove hundreds from their homes. It also renewed environmental efforts to regulate coal ash, which contains mercury and arsenic. If the EPA treated coal ash as the hazardous waste that it is, the coal industry would face new costs of $1.5 billion a year for many years to come. Summers sided with coal's political allies, especially Senator Jay Rockefeller of West Virginia: the economy and the industry could not afford the new costs. "It's complicated, because the EPA has the authority to do this, and you don't want political pressure telling them what to do," said one senior West Wing aide. "But you have eight years of pent-up frustration in the EPA and they think they have finally got a chance to repair the damage."

Rather than build support among his natural allies inside the White House, Summers attempted to control them. There was someone already tasked with the EPA cost-benefit analysis: Obama's friend Cass Sunstein, a former University of Chicago Law School professor. His office was part of the White House budget apparatus under Peter Orszag, one of Summers's rivals. Summers won Obama's approval to review the analysis, as he tried to barrel through the bureaucratic politics. But Orszag threatened to boycott the president's briefing if Summers pushed ahead with the presentation—an extraordinary expression of the personal rivalries at the heart of Obama's team, at a time when the economy was still struggling to emerge fully from recession. Summers concluded that the fault lay not with him but with the chief of staff's office. The EPA ultimately issued two alternative rules—one strong and costly, the other weak and cheaper. But inside the West Wing, the collateral damage was clear. "It was dumb, terrible procedurally, damaging internally, and damaging institutionally," said one member of the economics team. "I think there were a variety of perceived slights. Larry wanted to put a marker down and overstepped the mark."

Summers was a Survivalist, and his opposition often lay among the Revivalists at the Council of Economic Advisers: Romer, as well as Obama's campaign economist Austan Goolsbee, a young University of Chicago economics professor. Romer played no formal role in the election other than sending the occasional e-mail to Goolsbee. But she was a true believer in Obama, and had been since his breakthrough speech at the Boston convention in 2004. She admired his smart economic policy, but she *loved* his speech. "I said, 'This is the man I want to be president,'" she recalled on hearing Obama talk about uniting red and blue America. "On a grim day, my husband would see me listening to it again on YouTube." Halfway through her job interview with Obama in Chicago, the president-elect offered her the position to chair his group of economic advisers. She accepted on the spot.

"Don't you need to call someone or ask someone?" Obama wondered.

"No," she said. "I never had a candidate I felt so strongly about. You've asked me to do this. I'm not negotiating over anything. I'm in."

It was Romer's job to deliver Obama the worst economic briefing of his political career, in mid-December after his election, as he worked on his transition to the presidency in Chicago. They had just seen the extraordinary job loss numbers of November, announced a week earlier at more than half a million. At the same time, the official job loss statistics for September and October were revised upward from more than 500,000 to more than 700,000. "That's when it really hit me that this was not an ordinary recession," said Romer. In the new economic team's first meeting with Obama, Romer's job was to be blunt. "Things are grim and deteriorating fast," she told the president-elect. "This is horrible." Romer's position was that the size of stimulus they were thinking of—in the range of $400 billion to $600 billion—was nowhere near enough.

Romer had little idea what would be sufficient, and her forecasts on unemployment turned out to be too rosy. Most of her focus was on forecasting GDP, and her predictions proved largely correct. But the normal relationship between growth and jobs collapsed in the great recession of 2008, and she had no idea that unemployment would worsen in January, at almost 700,000 lost jobs. Obama's new economic team debated whether the rest of the world might survive the downturn better than the United States, but those hopes were dashed, too, in the first months of the presidency. "We knew it was horrible, even if we didn't know how horrible it would get," said Romer.

Around the same time, the incoming White House chief of staff was trying to figure out how to frame the giant stimulus that was now needed. At a Chicago party, Rahm Emanuel chatted with Jim

Crown, a director of JP Morgan Chase and the son of the billionaire investor Lester Crown. "You know, when you're management," Crown told him, "a crisis is an opportunity to do things you couldn't otherwise do." As he drove home, Emanuel had a eureka moment. "That's *it!*" he told himself. "It was an organizing theory about what we were facing," he recalled. His conclusion was that the economic meltdown was an opportunity as much as a disaster. "Never allow a good crisis to go to waste. It's an opportunity to do things you could not get done otherwise," he explained. "It's an opportunity because people will finally let go of positions *to* get something done. Which is true about the Recovery Act—which was, we have made investments you could not otherwise get."

Unfortunately, his opportunism was combined with some deeply flawed economic forecasts. The combination exposed the White House to a line of political attack for the next two years. Romer and her small team were struggling with a fast-moving crisis, which the statistics would not fully capture for several months. Yet the political demands of the time required them to put precise numbers on their vast request for taxpayer dollars. Romer felt pressured to bring her dire predictions in line with those of the more optimistic blue-chip business economists. She was rushed by the accelerated process and lacked confidence in her own numbers. "You'll have done a good job if you match the blue chip," said one Obama aide. Deep down, she thought the blue chip was wrong.

Less than two weeks before Obama's inauguration, Romer co-wrote a report that would be cited and twisted until the next election. She and Jared Bernstein, the vice president's economic adviser, predicted that unemployment would peak at 9 percent without a Recovery Act, but stay under 8 percent as long as the new administration spent billions of dollars in stimulus. They warned that there was "considerable uncertainty" in their estimates, especially around the link between economic growth and jobs. But they felt they were "relatively conservative" to assume that a 1 percent rise in GDP would lead to an additional 1 million jobs. "In truth," said one senior Obama adviser, "where we goofed was what was going to happen in the absence of that big stimulus."

That was not where the left thought they had goofed. Nobel Prize–winning economist Paul Krugman argued in the *New York Times* that they had failed to push for a larger stimulus to avert the worst. But Larry Summers believed the narrow votes in the Senate proved how they could not push for more money, even as they wanted much more. "The fact is that we pushed for a larger stimulus package than the Congress would consider passing into law," said Summers. "We fought hard for a package that was $900 billion, and that did not include an AMT [tax] fix. We pushed as hard as we could and got $787 billion, including the AMT [tax] fix, bringing the amount of stimulus down to $700 billion. And we were only able to pass it by a one-vote margin. Some people argue that we should have done $1.2 trillion. That insinuation, that we chose to have less stimulus than was achievable, is not grounded in fact."

A year later, the left and right were hurling the same arguments at the White House. With unemployment far above either the positive or the negative scenario, the debate about the value of the Recovery Act raged on. In public, the economic team appeared optimistic, even as they suffered internal divisions and external attacks. Romer was an irrepressibly upbeat presence inside the West Wing, even when delivering downbeat news. Inside the White House briefing room in mid-February, she beamed as she showed reporters a copy of her team's economic report to the president. The report suggested that unemployment would remain at high levels through the end of Obama's term, but you could hardly tell that by Romer's tone. "All right," she began jauntily. "Well, it is a pleasure to be with you all.

You have to know that for a chair of the Council of Economic Advisers, there's no bigger day than the day that her first Economic Report of the President comes out!" Behind the smiles and perky delivery, Romer saw her role as a macroeconomist whose primary focus was simple: "We need to worry about jobs." She had good reason to worry: her own economic report showed unemployment in 2012, at the time of Obama's reelection campaign, as high as 8.2 percent. If Obama won a second term, unemployment would not return to 2008 levels until his final year in office.

She wasn't the only one worrying about jobs. Republicans knew the White House was vulnerable on unemployment and spending, and they skewered Democrats on the false forecasts of the transition team. House Republican leader John Boehner wrote in a press statement that the Democrats were clueless. "Washington Democrats still don't get it," he said. "Two days after the president brushed off Republicans' concerns that Democrats' job-killing policies are causing great uncertainty for small businesses, the White House is now declaring in a new report that the trillion-dollar 'stimulus' will be one of history's 'great triumphs.' The very same report, however, notes that unemployment will average 10 percent for the rest of the year. The Obama administration promised the trillion-dollar 'stimulus' would create jobs 'immediately' and keep joblessness below 8 percent." That was true up to a point. But it also ignored the forecast that joblessness would rise to 9 percent without the stimulus—a figure that was just as wrong.

The half-truths were entirely predictable to Obama's political aides but nonetheless effective. Axelrod believed the economic team had predicted everything correctly, except for unemployment projections that were wrong as soon as they were written. In any case, the politics would have been no different had the forecasts proved accurate. "No matter what we did, things were still going to be bad,"

Axelrod said. "I think that's the calculation that Republicans made as well: 'Why should we help them, even though we created the problem? Why should we help them if we can say at the end of the year that things are still bad or worse, and he spent all this money? So it didn't work.' I think it was a very shrewd calculation. I think if you don't really care about the country, you don't put that as your primary focus. Their primary focus from the beginning has been to win an election. Our primary responsibility has been to save the country from economic catastrophe. And that put us in a very difficult position."

The GOP strategy also put Obama in the impossible position of demonstrating on a weekly, if not daily, basis that he was always focused on jobs. The vast sums of cash spent on the Recovery Act were largely forgotten in the political and media debate on the right and left. Obama needed to *show* his commitment in just the kind of dog-and-pony events he shunned during his campaign—until late in the primaries.

Two years ago, when he was struggling to close out the primary contests in Indiana, Obama feigned interest in photo ops. He greeted early-morning workers wearing hard hats at a construction site in Evansville, before moving to a nearby union hall for a so-called labor breakfast of eggs and home fries. He struggled to ingest the greasy eggs and fries just as he struggled to pretend that he needed to be there to understand their challenges.

Now, as president, he was pretending that he needed to tour factories and training centers. A few days after the book-length economic report landed, Obama rode in his motorcade through the snow-filled streets to suburban Maryland. Past the parked plows and the road repairs funded by the Recovery Act, he traveled to a union hall and training center run by the International Brotherhood of Electrical Workers that stood opposite a Maryland Lottery Claims

Center and a Realtor's office. The president toured a computer design class. ("Man, that's a lot of stuff up there. You're going to have to translate for me.") He moved on through another room full of energy-saving devices that are used inside the White House. ("Is that right?") At a wall full of fire alarms, his guide asked him to pull one of the alarm triggers. ("I need this whenever the press is around.") When he finally spoke to reporters from the podium about the future of job growth in a clean energy economy, his official remarks lasted all of ten minutes.

The political pressure to concentrate on jobs became all-consuming, and the longing for good news began to distort his economic advisers' reactions. When the huge February storms dumped record snows in the Northeast, the White House economics team answered extensive internal inquiries about the impact on jobs. The major blizzards struck in the very week the jobs survey took place. The last time anything similar happened, in 1996, the snow knocked 200,000 jobs off that month's employment figures. At the Council of Economic Advisers, Austan Goolsbee started to call any experts he could find. He asked Fed officials about the impact of snow on jobs. He tried to figure out how plowing capacity would affect different regional economies. Emanuel wanted to know how the snow would impact jobs. Axelrod wanted to know when job growth would be sustained month after month, and if that would happen in time for November's elections. Goolsbee concluded that as many as 120,000 jobs would likely be lost in February.

When the statistics finally landed, Goolsbee could barely contain his excitement: the job losses stood at only 40,000. "There's hardly ever a time when you can get me to say a minus number is a good sign," said Goolsbee. "But when I saw it was minus 40,000 and it was supposed to be minus 120,000, I was encouraged. So even though to the outside world maybe it was an almost positive, to us it was a much better than expected sign about the economy. And a sign that perhaps we were over the threshold and we're going to start seeing positive job growth, maybe on a sustained basis." From that point, Obama's economists started to see a marked shift among private sector forecasts: the economy was moving decisively away from a double-dip recession.

For most of their first year inside the White House, Obama's aides believed they were on a patriotic mission to govern the country and save the economy. If they needed to trim and hedge their promise of change, to bend to the hard realities of politics in Washington, they justified the compromise as a question of survival. After jamming through the Recovery Act, with little of the obvious pet projects that plagued traditional spending bills, Obama faced an immediate challenge. It was a giant leftover of budget legislation from Bush's last year in office, rolling nine bills into one omnibus spending package that looked like an overflowing barrel of pork. The overall cost of $410 billion included more than nine thousand pet projects, or earmarks, worth at least $5 billion. They included cash for a lobster foundation in Maine, manure research in Iowa, and a dance theater in Brooklyn. Obama tried to rationalize it in public by talking to reporters about earmark reform. "I ran for President pledging to change the way business is done in Washington and build a government that works for the people by opening it up to the people. And that means restoring responsibility and transparency and accountability to actions that the government takes," he explained. Then he admitted that his campaign spirit was taking second place to the needs of governing and the economy. "I am signing an imperfect omnibus bill because it's necessary for the ongoing functions of government, and we have a lot more work to do," he said. "We can't have Congress bogged down at this critical juncture in our economic recovery." But he promised that this was the end of such politics, as he tried to inject some last-minute hope into the story: "The future demands that we operate in a different way than we have in the past. So let there be no doubt: This piece of legislation must mark an end to the old way of doing business, and the beginning of a new era of responsibility and accountability that the American people have every right to expect and demand."

The truth was that Obama got rolled. There were powerful advocates of the old way of doing business inside his own West Wing: the Survivalists who believed they understood the ways of Washington and who appealed to his sense of pragmatic realism. Behind the scenes, Obama made clear to his senior aides that he hated the bill and wanted to veto it. "It was exactly full of the kind of crap that he felt he shouldn't be signing at this time of economic distress," said one senior West Wing official. "It was a piece of legislation laden with pork. He signed it because the congressional wing of the White House convinced him that in order to achieve health care and his other many large agenda goals, he couldn't pick a fight with the Democratic leadership on earmarks that early in his presidency. It was, 'Swallow this, and later on we'll try that line with them again.' That was a conversation that was had with some regularity over the spring and summer."

A year later, as the jobs numbers began to turn around, Obama tried to revive his campaign spirit when it came to the politics of runaway spending. That spirit was not just about high-minded transparency and accountability. It was also a political maneuver. During the campaign, he could distinguish himself from the political establishment by attacking the same old, tired politics. The strategy allowed him to side with incredulous voters who had lost faith with career politicians.

The moment for a revival came with a new effort to curb spending and cut the deficit. It was February 18, 2010, the day after the anniversary of the Recovery Act, when Obama tried to restore his reformist credentials by meeting with two old Washington hands, one Democrat and one Republican, inside the Oval Office. Erskine Bowles was a Clinton White House chief of staff, while Alan Simpson was a former Republican senator from Wyoming. Obama needed them both to lead a bipartisan commission on fiscal responsibility that would otherwise lack authority and support across the party divide. After talking for half an hour in the Oval, they walked over with Joe Biden to meet the press in the Diplomatic Reception Room, an elliptical space decorated with elaborate wallpaper showing classic American scenes, including Native Americans as they met white settlers. "What sequence are we speaking?" asked Obama outside, discovering that he was the only speaker. "All right," he told his gray-haired partners, "start walking right to the other side of the podium."

The event was choreographed for Congress as much as for the cameras. The media stood opposite a presidential podium, a small presidential signing desk, and two flat-panel screens with the president's remarks running in teleprompter fashion. The scene was either a grand exercise in presidential bluff-calling or a historic first step in the long journey to manage the deficit. The eighteen-person commission would be evenly divided between Democrats and Republicans, with two-thirds named by congressional leaders and one-third named by Obama. The panel needed a large majority— fourteen out of eighteen members—to make recommendations by their target date of the end of the year. Their goal: to bring the deficit down to 3 percent of GDP within five years (minus interest payments), and explain how to return to something like responsible spending in the nation's capital. That was no small challenge, at a time when the current deficit stood at more than 11 percent of GDP. The president praised Simpson as a fiscal hawk who previously worked to lower the deficit. "If you look in the dictionary it says 'flinty,' and then it's got Simpson's picture," Obama joked. Then he praised Bowles for his work on Clinton's balanced budget. "Although one is a strong Democrat and one is a strong Republican, these are examples of people who put country first," he gushed. "And they know how to disagree without being disagreeable, and there's a sense of civility and a sense that there are moments where you set politics aside to do what's right. That's the kind of spirit that we need."

Obama liked to believe he shared that spirit. He saw himself as being able to disagree without being disagreeable, as putting country first and setting politics aside—even as he played politics with the other side for failing to live up to that spirit. Case in point: the commission itself was the brainchild of two senators—Democrat Kent Conrad and Republican Judd Gregg—but their proposal died in Congress as soon as Republicans realized they might be accused of raising taxes. Seven GOP senators who cosponsored the idea ended up voting against a bill that would have given the panel the power to force Congress to vote on its recommendations. Another twenty-three Democrats voted against the panel, leaving both sides looking timid in the face of a crisis of their own making.

That left ample room for Obama to occupy his favorite territory: the middle ground. "I know the issue of deficits has stirred debate," he said with considerable understatement. "And there's some on the left who believe that this issue can be deferred. There are some on the right who won't enter into serious discussions about deficits without preconditions. But those who preach fiscal discipline have to be willing to take the hard steps necessary to achieve it. And those who believe government has a responsibility to meet these urgent challenges have a great stake in bringing our deficits under control— because if we don't, we won't be able to meet our most basic obligations to one another."

Without Senate support, Obama promptly sat down at the small wooden desk and signed an executive order to create the commission himself. It would not have the same power to force a vote in Congress. But it would have the power to expose those who preferred to play politics with the deficit, rather than balance the budget.

"Where's Erskine in the dictionary?" asked one reporter, as Obama walked out.

"Under 'smart,' " he quipped.

Smart was what Obama's aides thought they were in framing the fiscal commission. "It's the hypocrisy of Republicans that is breaking through," said one senior West Wing aide. "We get points on the hypocrisy on the stimulus, with them taking the checks but opposing the bill. And then the big thing that hits them is the switch on the fiscal commission and the cosponsors." The debate about the commission shifted the White House from squabbling with Democrats to an open fight with Republicans. But Obama's team ignored their own degree of hypocrisy in this maneuver. After all, it was harder to argue for bipartisanship if you seized on partisan disputes that blocked compromise.

After Scott Brown's victory, and their own near-death experience, they saw little value in purity and consistency. "Coming out of Massachusetts we developed a strategy that we were going to reach out to Republicans, and we're going to be very aggressive in our outreach, and force them to either choose to do things that are popular and good for the country, like a jobs bill and the bank tax, or have to defend their obstructionism," said Dan Pfeiffer. "They gave us a gift with the fiscal commission, where they flipped. It's a choice now. In 2009, it was a referendum on us. It was a family argument in the Democratic Party about the public option, about the size of the stimulus, about Wall Street, about earmarks. It was about what Democrats thought of each other with Republicans throwing rocks from afar. Now we're having a debate with the opposition, which is a strategically better place to be, and an easier place to plan from."

For the economic team dealing with the commission, this

strategy made their job harder, not easier. They had considered appointing a single, heroic figure to chair the panel, instead of a Democrat and a Republican. But the only heroic figure that sprang to mind—Paul Volcker—was already employed on the president's Economic Recovery Advisory Board. Obama's team felt fortunate that Simpson accepted the offer, not least because they had almost no other candidates. As congressional support started to fade, Obama's aides started to game out what steps they might need to take if the Republican leadership nominated *nobody* to be part of the panel. If that happened, they were ready to make a public appeal to any Republicans who cared about the deficit to step forward. In practice, the GOP leaders relented and named their own hawks to the commission. Still, Obama's staffers were concerned that the commission's work would falter without congressional support. They studied the last successful panel of its type, a Social Security commission chaired by Alan Greenspan three decades earlier. Their conclusion: it only succeeded because senators on both sides of the aisle pushed its recommendations into law. "We didn't know, and we still don't know, if in this political environment, this is a viable possibility," said one senior Obama aide.

The reality was that everyone from the president down liked the idea of cutting the deficit, but they *loved* the results of federal spending. The evening before he announced the chairmen of his new fiscal commission, Obama sat down at the long table inside the Roosevelt Room to hold an extraordinary videoconference call. The flat screen was hidden inside a huge antique-style cabinet that occupied most of one wall, opposite the fireplace and the classic portrait of Theodore Roosevelt on horseback as a Rough Rider. On screen was the crew of the International Space Station and the shuttle *Endeavour*, wearing red and blue shirts. Obama, sitting next to a group of schoolchildren, was as excited at the sight of the astronauts in zero gravity as were his Secret Service agents, who strained to look at the screen from their position in the doorways. The first question for the crew came from a North Carolina student who wanted to know why it was better to explore in space rather than on Earth. "You better have a good answer," warned Obama. "The NASA folks are sitting here listening."

"I can tell you your curiosity reaches far and so does ours," said one of the astronauts. "And that's sort of the human spirit, to find out what can humans really do."

One of the things humans couldn't do was to defend spending cuts and lost jobs under intense political attack. It was only two and a half weeks since news broke about one of Obama's highest-profile budget cuts: to cancel the struggling Constellation program, the successor to the space shuttle. NASA's overall budget would rise by $1 billion, with investments made in new space technologies and commercial space flight. But the notion of flying back to the moon— or even President Bush's much-mocked vision of a mission to Mars—was dead. The criticism was loud and public from NASA's supporters, including members of Congress and the *Apollo 11* commander Neil Armstrong. Less than two months later, Obama relented in part and revived the Orion space capsule in a scaled-down form as an escape vehicle from the International Space Station. With it, the White House promised to create thousands of jobs, not least in the crucial presidential election state of Florida. The move looked a lot like Obama's own escape capsule from the political pressures of spending cuts.

There was a stubborn contradiction about the politics of this harsh economy and the politics of this president. The economic pain was pulling apart the center ground between the parties and deepening the partisan divide. At the same time, voters were more disillusioned than ever with both parties and yearning for outsiders who could challenge the Washington establishment. At the heart of it all was a president who ran as a renegade against his own party's machine politicians in 2007 and 2008. Yet as president, he faced a determined and united opposition and needed his party more than ever. In short, he needed Democratic support to rise above Democratic politics. And that was a tougher sell now than it had been when he had the sole mission of beating Republicans.

He found a natural refuge with the nation's governors, including Republicans who might end up running against him in two short years. The week after the anniversary of the Recovery Act, Obama hosted the National Governors Association at a ball and a day of talks with his cabinet and White House officials. The morning after their party, the governors were served coffee in gilded china cups in the entrance hall of the Executive Mansion. Inside the State Dining Room, California's Arnold Schwarzenegger sat next to Joe Biden. South Carolina's almost-divorced Mark Sanford sat opposite the newly engaged Peter Orszag, and the new Republican star in Virginia, Bob McDonnell, sat next to the old Democratic warhorse from Pennsylvania, Ed Rendell. Larry Summers stood awkwardly in the middle of the room, seeming unsure about who, or how, he should schmooze.

With a crowd that included Republicans who decried the Recovery Act, as well as those who preferred to look more bipartisan, Obama could happily call out Republican gimmicks and embrace Republicans at the same time. "I understand that some of you still claim it's not working or wasn't worth it, but I also know that you've used it to close your budget gaps or break ground on new projects. I've seen the photos and I've read the press releases," he said as the governors chortled. "So it must be doing something right. Overall, the economy is in a better place than it was a year ago. We were contracting by 6 percent and we're now growing by 6 percent. But I know that your states are still in a very tough situation, and too many Americans still haven't felt the recovery in their own lives. So we're working to create jobs by all means necessary, be it by cutting taxes for small businesses that create them, to investing more in infrastructure and in energy efficiency, or giving you more help to close budget shortfalls." By all means necessary—whether Republican ideas on taxes or Democratic ideas on spending—Obama was trying to rise above both sides and their political games.

As a senator, Obama disliked both sides of the aisle. He was frustrated with his own party, with the Senate, and with the political ecosystem. He carried many of those frustrations with him to the White House: they were at the heart of his reforming, Revivalist spirit. At the start of his time in the Senate, Obama was tasked with leading the work on ethics reform, after the spate of scandals that would ultimately help the Democrats take over Congress in 2006. It was a disappointing experience for him. Although his own party seized on the corruption stories swirling around the lobbyist Jack Abramoff, Obama encountered sustained opposition to relatively modest reforms from his own Democrats. After one leadership meeting, he returned to his Senate office to tell his staff that his own party's leaders disliked proposed restrictions on gifts and meals from lobbyists. "I have no interest in appeasing the American people on this one," said one senior Democrat, according to Obama's staff. "I've got a lot of important work done over dinner," said another prominent liberal. Obama and his aides concluded that his own party did not grasp the mood of the country or how they, too, would be punished by voters.

That judgment did not change inside the West Wing. "Why

aren't they moving in this environment to do more on transparency and ethics reform to show that they get it, that it's not Washington as usual?" asked one frustrated senior Obama aide. "Obama isn't up until '12 and he has a lot of political skills. He'll bounce back and will be popular, if unemployment goes down to 7.5 percent. We'll probably be all right. But these guys will go down the chute and we'll be affected by it. Because we'll be blamed for it and our working majority will be gone."

The economic and political cycles were not aligned with each other—at least, not for the Democrats in Congress. The economy might well bounce back in time for Obama's reelection, but his trajectory was a familiar one for all recent presidents, with the single exception of President Bush in the year after the 9/11 attacks. Obama would lose seats, especially in a struggling economy, no matter how he performed as president. Once again, the best model for Obama's aides was a Republican president from three decades ago, who lost seats and his party's confidence before growing into a conservative icon. "If you look at where we are today versus where Bill Clinton was or Ronald Reagan was going into his first midterm and the struggles Ronald Reagan had in keeping his base together and keeping people active, I daresay we're in a great place," said one senior Obama aide. "Let's remember that after that first year, Ronald Reagan was being written off by conservatives who said that he had lost his way and ended up losing twenty-six House seats in that first term." Reagan's record was built on his landslide reelection and his communications skills. But his performance in his first midterms, and arguably in his reelection, hinged on the economy. In late 1982, his approval ratings were in the low forties while unemployment was above 10 percent and rising. In the middle of 2010, Obama's approval ratings were in the high forties and unemployment, which was already on a downward track, stood a little lower than it did twenty-eight years earlier. In any case, Reagan survived the midterms better than his party, and still managed to reform Social Security the following year.

As the economy improved, there was a tangible turnaround in the political faith of supporters, and in some of the polling numbers. Senate contests in Illinois, Colorado, and Pennsylvania that seemed out of reach began to narrow in the early summer. Even the personal response of Democrats was shifting. At the start of the year, Obama's political director, Patrick Gaspard traveled to Florida and found party activists vocal in their doubts about the direction of the White House. A follow-up trip in the spring was far more uplifting. "On the last trip it was all just hugs and people just asking what *they* could be doing," Gaspard said. "A few months ago, people were telling us what we should be doing better. And now activists are asking me, 'What can we do? Because we're ready.'"

However, the renewed enthusiasm would never match the fire on the other side. Poll after poll showed a double-digit gap between Republicans and Democrats among those professing to be very excited about voting in the midterms. Much of that excitement came from the so-called Tea Party movement, a motley crew of tax-cutters, small-government ideologues, libertarians, conspiracy theorists, and racists. They were united in their loathing of Washington and their hatred of Obama. In some states, they managed to unseat Republican members of Congress or simply the party leaders' favorite pick for a seat. Backed by hugely popular figures on Fox News and conservative talk radio, their influence was often exaggerated because it made for great cable TV images and newspaper headlines. Yet one of the biggest effects of the Tea Party phenomenon was how it normalized discussion of Obama as a "socialist." For many, the word was just a casual insult. It had no bearing on the twentieth-century ideology that demanded the public ownership of economic production, distribution, and exchange. For others, like Glenn Beck of Fox News, Obama was some kind of agent of the Soviet Union.

Beck spoke glowingly of Friedrich Hayek's *The Road to Serfdom*, suggesting that Obama's approaches to health care and the bailouts were steps on the slippery slope to Marxism. Never mind that the White House never pushed for a public option among its health care ideas, and never considered a single-payer, government-run system such as Canada's or Britain's. Never mind that the government stakes in the bailed-out banks and automakers were temporary, and allowed the businesses to survive their existential crises.

But what was Obama if not a socialist or a free-market evangelist? Was he a Clinton-style New Democrat? His economic team's experience suggested so, but the 1990s were also a period of deregulation that led directly to the bank excesses behind the financial meltdown. If Obama had a coherent economic worldview, it lay in the language and strategy of a community organizer, the street-level activism where he started his career in politics. Organizers need to share stories of motivation, to find the common ground between disparate people, in order to get them to come together to campaign for change. Obama had built an entire presidential campaign on the premise that diverse Americans could find in each other the hope, strength, and purpose to overcome their doubts and cynicism to vote for a new politician and a new political force. This was the language of the communitarian philosophy, as well as community organizing. Not communism, as his extremist opponents suggested. Not the radicalism of Saul Alinsky, the father of community organizing. Communitarian politics was a response to excessive individualism. It crossed the divide of Republicans and Democrats, with those on the right emphasizing faith-based policies and those on the left emphasizing education and the environment. That in part explained the connection between Obama and the conservative *New York Times* columnist David Brooks. One of the most influential columnists among Obama's pile of reading, Brooks declared Obama to be a communitarian on the eve of the New Hampshire primary in

2008. And he recommended a communitarian response to the public anger against big government and big business in 2010. Brooks was so important to Obama that Rahm Emanuel would call him on deadline to ask if his boss would be happy or not after reading his next column.

Obama could understand the anger. But he saw the value of both big government and big business. Tucked between his health care meetings and jobs events in late February, he gave a little-noticed speech that he toiled over to an extraordinary degree. The speech, delivered in a luxury hotel just a few blocks from the White House, tried to correct the Tea Party and Fox News caricatures of his economic policies. But it also tried to mesh the business interests of his audience with the working interests of his party. In a windowless meeting room at the St. Regis, close by the headquarters of the AFL-CIO labor federation, around one hundred chief executives from the Business Roundtable group were meeting for their quarterly session. It was a strangely low-key event. Obama walked in unannounced, and the audience almost missed his arrival. The room was long and narrow with antique pretensions: its ceiling sported chandeliers and exposed wooden beams, and the walls were plated with odd-sized mirrors. Behind the podium was a flimsy backdrop with the group's sparse red-and-white logo, and the lighting seemed barely adequate for an after-dinner speech. To add to the sense of occasion, the room also stank from what smelled like an overflowing toilet nearby.

Obama seemed to care little about the setting and far more about the substance of his speech. After a severe recession and a "lost decade" of falling wages, Americans were frustrated, he explained inside one of the city's most expensive hotels: "They're frustrated with government and they're frustrated with business. They're angry at a financial sector that took exorbitant risks by some in pursuit of short-term profits, and they're angry at a government that failed to catch the problem on time. They're angry at the price they paid to prevent a financial meltdown that they didn't cause, and they're angry that recovery in their own lives seems to be lagging the recovery of bank profitability. They're angry at the lobbyists who use their influence to put their clients' special interests ahead of the public interest."

He might not feel their pain, but he understood its causes and could analyze what it meant politically. In particular he could analyze just how twisted the political debate had become. So he set about explaining his vision of how government and business needed to work together to create growth. "Now, contrary to the claims of some of my critics and some of the editorial pages, I am an ardent believer in the free market. I believe businesses like yours are the engines of economic growth in this country," he began. But he also detailed government's role—to set the rules of the marketplace, invest in common goods like infrastructure, and provide a safety net like Social Security and unemployment insurance. "I take the time to make these points because we've arrived at a juncture in our politics where reasonable efforts to update our regulations, or make basic investments in our future, are too often greeted with cries of 'government takeover' or even 'socialism,'" he explained. "Not only does that kind of rhetoric deny our history, but it prevents us from asking hard questions about the right balance between the private and public sectors."

Neither side of the partisan divide was helping, in Obama's view: "Rather than hurling accusations about big-government liberals or mean-spirited conservatives, we're going to have to answer those tough questions. And getting that balance right has less to do with big government or small government than it has to do with smart government. It's not about being anti-business or pro-government; it's about being pro-growth and pro-jobs." He wasn't interested in long-term intervention in the auto sector; he just wanted to rescue General Motors, the financial sector, and the wider economy from collapse. He didn't even want to curb excessive salaries; he just preferred shareholders to have a say on pay. If the CEOs paid their workers well, they could count on more loyalty to the company. If financial reform took place, they could all have more confidence in the system. And if a child in the Bronx had a better education, the company that employed him would benefit, along with the rest of the country. "To put it simply," he said, "we are all in this together." That communitarian idea was so important that he said it three times, in slightly different words, in the closing minutes of his speech. He might as well have said there was no red America and no blue America, just a United States of America.

He saved his final lines for the political climate of the moment: a toxic mix that had only worsened in the last six years since he delivered his convention speech in Boston. "At a time of such economic anxiety, it's tempting, and maybe it's easier, to turn against one another and to find scapegoats to blame," he said. "So politicians can rail against Wall Street or against each other, and businesses can fault Capitol Hill, and all of it makes for easy talking points and good political theater. But it doesn't solve our problems. It doesn't move us forward. It just traps us in the same debates and divides that have held us back for a very long time and forced us to keep on punting down the road the same problems we've been facing for decades." It was a revival of his campaign promise to turn the page on the old politics. But it was somewhat diminished by his own readiness to attack Wall Street for its recklessness and self-interested lobbying, or the Republicans for their obstructionism and desire to return to laissez-faire economics.

Yet it still spoke to a central concern inside the West Wing: that the political climate had degenerated—in large part because of the news media—to the point where the country was increasingly hard to govern. Good government was now getting stymied by the political media and by politicians who measured their performance by their minutes on cable news shows. The recession, combined with the long-term business decline of traditional media, was making the culture worse. But so were the choices and behavior of elected officials, interest groups, lobbyists, and journalists, according to Obama's aides. When they complained about cable news, their critics suggested they were thin-skinned and hypocritically obsessing about something they dismissed as superficial. That was partly true. Yet their complaints were also intended to dissuade elected officials from playing to the standards of the new, sensationalist Internet and cable culture.

"I think the current state of our politics, of which the political media is a part, makes it hard to govern," said Dan Pfeiffer. "We're obviously living in a hyperpartisan world and the media is not the sole cause of it, but it contributes to it on a daily basis. The example I use all the time is the cable TV culture, which is more than just cable. It's probably most of political media these days. That culture does to politics what *SportsCenter* is accused of doing to basketball. Everyone wants to be in the top ten plays on *SportsCenter*. You only get on the top ten plays by showboating, dunks, no-look passes, at the expense of core fundamentals of sports. Politics is the same way these days. You don't get on TV for passing laws, or building coalitions, or working with the other party. You get on TV for saying the single most outrageous thing possible. Which is why Michele Bachmann and Sarah Palin are on TV all the time. And everyone wants to be like them. So in that sense, it makes it very hard to govern because the media has often come to highlight what is absolutely worst about politics."

The feeling among Obama's aides was that they were in a media transition that would fundamentally change the way future administrations dealt with the news. Robert Gibbs believed the classic press briefing would soon be a thing of the past. "My prediction is that in ten years—it may even be five—it will be different from what it is today," he said. "I'm not sure that every day the format that was done in the 1970s and 1980s will survive. A lot has changed about the way this place is covered. What hasn't changed is the message delivery in a lot of ways."

Gibbs believed the briefing was still useful: the clips looped on cable TV all day and helped shape the news. But he saw his daily performance not as a chance to drive a message so much as a chance to rectify and amplify the coverage, like some televised version of a newspaper's corrections and clarifications. "More often than not these days, the media isn't an arbitrator of what is right and wrong. They just cover what happens," he said. "They are just there to cover the fight, whether or not the other person is using facts that can be backed up. Sometimes the briefing becomes a way of saying, 'Wait, wait, wait. The argument that's being made writ large can't be that way because . . .' I read people on the Internet who say I give long answers. Blah, blah, blah. That's the point. It's *my* time. I can take something and broaden it to discuss what I think needs to be contextualized."

You could blame the superficial politicians, or the sensationalist media, or the dysfunctional economics team. But in the end, the public blame for the sluggish economy rested largely with the president. He wasn't in the White House when most of the jobs were lost, and he wasn't able to create jobs on his own. Yet he still struggled to convince voters that he was focusing on jobs, or that he had taken unprecedented measures to save jobs and the overall economy. Obama's concerns for the unemployed, for those without health care, and for those who wanted to reach the middle class were too subtle to combat his opponents and the doubts about economic growth.

As soon as health care was over, the president's aides hoped to shift their focus to jobs and the economy quickly. Their plan was to move on to Wall Street reform, followed by jobs over the summer, then education in the fall, and a final return to the economy as a closing argument before the midterm elections. But the longer that health care dragged on, the more delayed was the message on jobs. Instead of focusing on one issue, they attempted two. As health care continued to inch forward, Obama pushed for a stand-alone jobs bill.

So on a sunny day in early spring, just three days before the final House vote on health care reform, Obama walked into a Rose Garden filled with congressional Democrats, cabinet officials, and his own White House aides. The mood was almost giddy. Secretary of Commerce Gary Locke called over to Peter Orszag for some advice, but not of an economic nature. "Hey, I'm going on the *Daily Show* tonight!" he declared. "Good luck with that," Orszag said wryly, having aced his turn on the show a year earlier. The gathering was to witness the signing of the HIRE Act, a jobs bill that included tax breaks for hiring new workers, especially aimed at small businesses. It included new money for roads and bridges, and easier access to municipal bonds. The bill was a shadow of its original size just three weeks earlier, having started at $85 billion and grown to $150 billion, before ending up at $17.5 billion. Some estimates suggested the bill would help create around 250,000 jobs: the equivalent of what a healthy economy might normally create in a single month. But it represented a rare budding moment of bipartisanship: thirteen Republicans joined with Democrats in the Senate to approve the package.

Standing onstage behind the president's traditional signing desk, Senator Chuck Schumer of New York was mugging for the cameras. He flashed his thumbs-up several times to members of Congress seated below, but he seemed to care more about the media. In case the headline writers were confused, the bill was good news. In the colonnade at the side of the ceremony, Valerie Jarrett and Rahm Emanuel waved and pointed at their friends from the Hill. Larry Summers, looking like he had just woken up, sat in the second row, playing with his BlackBerry and tapping his feet while the president started speaking.

Obama began by praising the Republicans who voted for the bill. "I hope this is a prelude to further cooperation in the days and months to come, as we continue to work on digging our way out of the recession and rebuilding our economy in a way that works for all Americans and not just some Americans," he said. "After all, the jobs bill I'm signing today—and our broader efforts to achieve a recovery—aren't about politics. They're not about Democrat versus Republican. This isn't a game that we're playing here."

At that point, Schumer turned to look at the diminutive Republican congressman Joseph Cao standing next to him. He promptly noticed the cameras closest to him and fixed his gaze on the lenses, his smile tightening as it lingered.

Obama's attention was still trained on the jobs measures he was about to sign into law. He wanted to show he cared about the jobless, and he did so the only way he knew how: by weaving their stories together as part of the shared concerns of a community. "They're about the people in this country who are out of work and looking for a job. They're about all the Americans—of every race and region and age—who've shared their stories with me over the last year. The single mother who's told me she's filled out hundreds of job applications and been on dozens of interviews, but still hasn't found a job. The father whose son told me he started working when he was a teenager, and recently found himself out of a job for the very first time in his life. The children who write to me they're worried about their moms and their dads, worried about what the future holds for their families. That's who I'm thinking about every morning when I enter into the Oval Office. That's who I'm signing this bill for. And that's who I'm going to continue to fight for so long as I am

President of the United States. So with that, let me sign this bill and let's get to work."

He walked over to sign the bill slowly, marking each letter of his name with a new pen. Every member of Congress onstage would get a pen. "Every single person," he said, as if each one was as treasured as a new hire. "All right, everybody," he said, getting ready to mingle with the lawmakers. "Good job." As the members of Congress pressed in to shake Obama's hand, Schumer walked over to Tim Geithner and Christina Romer with some insightful political analysis of the economic impact of the newly signed law.

"Oh man," he said, glancing at the press. "This is going to *move*."

It would prove hard to trace the financial impact of a $17.5 billion measure in an economy worth $14.4 trillion each year. Even in political terms, the act sunk with little trace, as the jobs market struggled to get *moving*. If only the economy were as easy to revive as the spirits of a New York senator in close proximity to the press.

FIVE

SURVIVAL

In the late afternoon of Tuesday, January 12, 2010, some seven hundred miles southeast of Miami—around the same distance that separates South Beach from Atlanta—the earth started to shake and crack. For 240 years, pressure was building along the Enriquillo–Plantain Garden fault line, where the Caribbean tectonic plate meets its bigger North American neighbor. Then, without warning, the fault ruptured with explosive intensity. It took just thirty seconds to destroy the nearest city, Port-au-Prince, home to more than 3 million people. Inside the capital of the poorest country in the hemisphere, the cheap concrete buildings collapsed as quickly as the

National Palace. By the end of the disaster—including the after-shocks and the rescue missions—some 230,000 people had died and 1.5 million were homeless. On any scale of suffering, the Haiti earth-quake was a catastrophe.

Inside the West Wing, the national security team struggled to get hold of reliable news. Denis McDonough, chief of staff to the National Security Council, told Obama about the strength of the quake. "I want a strong response out of the box on this," the president said. McDonough rushed to his young daughter's school play and promptly returned to the White House for a meeting in the Situation Room chaired by Tom Donilon, Obama's ruthlessly efficient deputy national security adviser. "I want to make sure that we are anticipating the scale of this," Donilon said. "We have to anticipate that this is an enormous catastrophe." All they could do was assume the worst, because the facts were hard to pin down. It was five hours after the quake, and night had fallen on a terrified and devastated Port-au-Prince. As news reports began to capture the scale of the death and destruction, Obama was back in the first family's residence when he sent another message to his national security team: "Make sure we are moving fast and aggressively," he said. "I want a full update in the morning."

That was easier said than done, given the devastation on the ground. The next morning Obama woke to order a full gathering of his national security team for later the same day, including the secretaries of state, defense, and homeland security, the chairman of the Joint Chiefs of Staff, and the administrators of FEMA and USAID. In the meantime, his team pieced together what they could. Donilon chaired a meeting of the so-called deputies: the subcabinet officials who could turn policy decisions into real-world action. But McDonough felt something was missing: information. As he sat and talked with other national security officials, he bemoaned the lack of reliable communications with Haiti. A few hours later McDonough talked with Donilon and Ben Rhodes, a deputy national security adviser handling communications, about how they needed someone from the White House to go down to Haiti. They lacked a point man, and they lacked a visible sign that Obama cared. They walked over to see David Axelrod in his office close by the Oval. "You've got to send somebody down," said McDonough, and Axelrod agreed. "I'll go," McDonough volunteered.

That evening in the Situation Room, Obama was impatient. His domestic agenda was stalling, and the polls were pointing toward defeat in the Massachusetts Senate race the following week. But with his national security team, he made it clear he wanted action. Haiti needed to be their top priority across all agencies and departments. "I know this is going to be a tough challenge," he said. "But I don't want to hear any excuses."

It was just the first twenty-four hours of the crisis, but Obama already felt that his government wasn't moving fast enough. "People desperately need our help," he said, as he began to justify why this was such a high priority. "This is an important part of American leadership in the region and the world. We have to have the capacity to respond to disasters like this with competence, and in a coordinated way." Obama argued that superpowers needed to look after their own neighbors. Besides, Haiti was so close to America, it was more than just another country in the same hemisphere: "We have deep ties with Haiti, including a large Haitian American population with friends and family—including thousands of Americans—who are in Haiti."

Just in case they hadn't heard him clearly, Obama repeated himself once again: "I want people to think creatively about how to move resources into Haiti. I won't accept any excuses on this. And I don't want to see any finger-pointing. I won't accept that."

The following evening, McDonough was on the ground in Haiti. A conscientious and efficient staffer, McDonough was not given to excessive displays of emotion other than when he needed to enforce his boss's orders. He had been to Haiti before, in the late 1990s when he worked as a congressional staffer. He was familiar with the poverty and chaos. But this was different. "It was haunting," he said. "You can't help but be moved by some of the stuff you see. Dead people. Knowing that kids are separated from their parents."

He took two other White House staffers who had worked with Obama even longer than he had. Alyssa Mastromonaco had long carried the title of Obama's scheduler, but her influence and capabilities were far broader than that. In addition to her logistical expertise, she was blunt-spoken and trusted enough to deliver unvarnished messages to both Barack and Michelle Obama, as well as their inner circle. She was part of the core group that advised Obama whether to run for president in late 2006, and was a key player in the almost flawless organization of the campaign. Watching the disaster on TV, she asked McDonough if she could help in any way. Joining her was Tommy Vietor from the White House press office, who started work on Obama's communications team as early as the Senate run in 2004. Vietor was a creature of the Obama campaign, having led the press operation in Iowa for almost a year before moving to headquarters in Chicago to work on rapid response.

For five days they slept on the embassy floor, through aftershocks that were deeply unsettling. Mastromonaco coordinated the alphabet soup of agencies in Port-au-Prince, speeding the flow of paperwork that caused gridlock at the overburdened airport. And Vietor reprised his campaign role of sending rapid-fire e-mails, blasting the press with links to reports and even video of Haitians celebrating the work of American rescue teams. After the cumbersome bureaucracy and risk aversion of a year inside the White House, the action and pace of the disaster effort were something of a release. It could also be grim work. They organized the repatriation of bodies and were stunned by the everyday poverty on the island. On one helicopter trip to the hospital ship USNS *Comfort,* Mastromonaco couldn't believe the devastation on the ground. She was even more astonished to hear the area was actually untouched by the quake. "That's what it looked like before; there was no structural damage," she said. "I had really never seen poverty like that before."

To the team back inside the White House, Haiti was a presidential commitment that also served as a political distraction. Obama's attention to Haiti was genuine and compassionate. But it also took him further away from the struggle to keep health care alive and show progress on the economy. "For folks who think everything the White House does is political, this is a perfect example of something that is probably not a political winner," said Dan Pfeiffer. "Competence is good and appreciated, but given the list of concerns of the public, an earthquake in Haiti certainly isn't high up. The president thought it was important, and he has a unique role in being able to get other nations involved by showing it was a U.S. priority so that other nations contribute aid and resources and help generate private donations. But the great challenge of doing communications in the White House is that you have a million things to talk about on any day, and limited days to do it. Every day we talked about Haiti was another day we didn't talk about the economy or health care."

Despite the personal interest of the president—and the personal efforts of his staff—the situation remained overwhelmingly bleak, and the politics began to look just as bad. Haiti represented an insurmountable combination of a massive disaster, captured in an endless loop of shocking TV pictures, with the inability of the White House, or any government, to ease Haiti's suffering. Many in the media likened what was happening in Haiti to Hurricane Katrina, searching for a comparison to one of the defining failures of the Bush presidency. The comparisons underscored the apparent impotence of a commander in chief whose domestic agenda lay in ruins. And they reinforced the centerpiece of perhaps the most common political critique of Obama's young presidency: for all his campaign attacks on President Bush's foreign policy, Obama was little different in office from his predecessor.

Inside the West Wing, Obama's aides indeed made comparisons between their response to Haiti and Bush's approach. But they looked to two other examples, both of them overseas: Bush's response to the 2004 tsunami in Indonesia and the aftermath of the Pakistani earthquake the following year. In both places, the medical and humanitarian aid supplied by the United States helped lift international support for America. "We spend a lot of time around here talking about how we can communicate more effectively to Muslim communities, particularly to Pakistan," said McDonough. "We have studied the good work the last administration did and the U.S. government did around the Pakistan earthquake. And so we talked about that. We did talk about the tsunami, obviously."

Within four days of the Haitian disaster, President Bush himself was standing in the Rose Garden alongside President Clinton and President Obama, leading a new fund for relief and reconstruction. "President Bush led America's response to the Asian tsunami, aid and relief that prevented even greater loss of life in the months after that disaster. And his administration's efforts to fight against HIV/AIDS in Africa treated more than 10 million men, women, and children," Obama said. "As President, Bill Clinton helped restore democracy in Haiti. As a private citizen, he has helped to save the lives of millions of people around the world. And as the United Nations special envoy to Haiti, he understands intimately the daily struggles and needs of the Haitian people." Standing in the weak daylight of a winter's morning in the Rose Garden, you would never know that

Obama had largely built his presidential campaign on opposition to the former presidents beside him.

Obama's relationship to Bush's foreign policy was complicated, both by design and by experience. He campaigned as a full-throated opponent to much of what Bush stood for: a go-it-alone approach that often disdained international agreements and organizations; the politics of fear that sometimes confused Islam with Islamists; the use of torture, secret prisons, and the legal black hole of Guantánamo Bay; above all, the ill-conceived invasion of Iraq and the disastrous occupation that followed. Were it not for his early opposition to the invasion, Obama would never have convinced Democratic voters in the presidential primaries that he represented the Change they could believe in. But his opposition to the war and his outspoken criticism of Bush were only part of Obama's foreign policy. His supporters ignored the Bush-like policies he embraced, such as his aggressive position on counterterrorism and the war in Afghanistan. And candidate Obama had little interest in dwelling on the post-9/11 measures—including widespread surveillance, targeted killings by unmanned drones, and military trials—that liberal activists recoiled from. He could be hawkish against al Qaeda and dovish toward Muslim culture or Iranian history. On the campaign trail, the oppositional clash—with George W. Bush and John McCain—effectively masked the nuances, apparent contradictions, and policy compromises. But once Obama was inside the Oval Office, the tensions grew clearer, and more exposed. President Obama stood in contrast to candidate Obama. Yet there was no neat, simple line between the Revivalist spirit that challenged the orthodoxy of foreign policy and the Survivalist mentality of the real world. Obama was in a state of flux, somewhere between the two.

In the beginning, foreign policy was relatively easy for Obama's team. Their mission was seemingly simple to accomplish: roll back the Bush years. They had spent the best part of two years building their agenda and launching it. During the primaries, the foreign policy attacks had proved extraordinarily effective in an intraparty fight traditionally dominated by domestic politics. "One of my favorite professional periods of time is still July '07 to the Iowa caucus because it was every foreign policy argument that a progressive Democrat could possibly have wanted to make over the course of the Bush administration," said Ben Rhodes. "You could just be clear. It was ending the war in Iraq; it was diplomacy with adversaries; it was closing Guantánamo Bay and prohibiting torture." When Hillary Clinton voted for an aggressive Senate resolution against Iran, they turned their fire on the rival who would later be the face of their own foreign policy. Obama's staffers delighted in the knowledge that the first defensive piece of direct mail from the Clinton campaign in Iowa was a response to their argument about an anti-Iran resolution in the Senate. "We spent a week just ginning it up as indicative of our entire case that she wants to stay in Iraq longer and go to war in Iran—the same kind of habits that let us slide into Iraq," said one senior Obama campaign adviser. "We had this whole intellectual argument about the mind-set that got us into war."

Taking over the White House seemed like a continuation of their campaign mind-set. Now Obama's team could turn their critique into full-fledged foreign policy. "For the first few months we had this ready-made agenda from the campaign," said Rhodes. "And rolling that out was *really* exciting." A month after his inauguration, Obama spoke to the Marines at Camp Lejeune in North Carolina, detailing his campaign plans to withdraw troops from Iraq. A month later he was in the Czech capital, Prague, promising to seek a world without nuclear weapons. For the skeptics, "the voices who tell us that the world cannot change," Obama revived his old campaign slogan. "We have to insist, 'Yes we can.'" Two months later he was standing in Cairo University, at the intellectual heart of the Muslim world. He described himself as a president with the unlikely name of Barack Hussein Obama, and he spoke about the values of Islam and the values of America.

> I have known Islam on three continents before coming to the region where it was first revealed. That experience guides my conviction that partnership between America and Islam must be based on what Islam is, not what it isn't. And I consider it part of my responsibility as President of the United States to fight against negative stereotypes of Islam wherever they appear. But that same principle must apply to Muslim perceptions of America. Just as Muslims do not fit a crude stereotype, America is not the crude stereotype of a self-interested empire. The United States has been one of the greatest sources of progress that the world has ever known. We were born out of revolution against an empire. We were founded upon the ideal that all are created equal, and we have shed blood and struggled for centuries to give meaning to those words—within our borders, and around the world. We are shaped by every culture, drawn from every end of the Earth, and dedicated to a simple concept: E pluribus unum—Out of many, one.

It was the fulfillment of a dream that had started on the campaign trail. In the middle of the primaries, he outlined his message to what he first envisioned as a Muslim summit. "If I had a Muslim summit, I think that I can speak credibly to them about the fact that I respect their culture," he told me, "that I understand their religion, that I have lived in a Muslim country, and as a consequence I know it is possible to reconcile Islam with modernity and respect for human rights and a rejection of violence. And I think I can speak with added credibility."

All three speeches were unthinkable as products of the Bush White House. They were the products of a new Obama White House, where a small staff could turn their campaign spirit into a presidential speech with little hedging and trimming by the cumbersome bureaucracy. "Giving the Prague speech, which was essentially the president's vision, we didn't have a substantial interagency process," said Rhodes. "He had decided he wanted to do all these things on nuclear weapons in the campaign, so he gave a speech saying we're going to do them. It made it an easy speech to write. The president had an agenda and he laid it out. It was a message to our government as well as a message to the world. The Iraq speech, too: we had a review on that, but it was informed by our campaign Iraq policy. Cairo was like that. There were a number of things in the first six months that were very liberating. It was like all these things you talked about in the campaign, just laying them out."

Strong and effective management, combined with a clear vision, was just as important to Obama's foreign policy as correcting Bush's mistakes. Obama could not afford to watch the bureaucracy slow down the rescue effort in Haiti. But that impulse would also take him further away from the campaign spirit and further toward the Survivalist mentality of a Washington insider. He chose as his secretary of state Hillary Clinton, the former rival whose foreign policy and record were such big targets during the primaries. And his secretary of defense, Robert Gates, was a holdover of the Bush administration they so vehemently opposed. "We're the first insurgent campaign to win since Jimmy Carter, which means we come with a different view of the institutions," said one long-standing Obama aide. "People say, why are there so many Clinton people? But what else could we do? It's because they were from Washington. We picked up Gates and others, along with two wars. People don't realize how hard it is to assume management of problems that big." Obama promised change and delivered presidential speeches about change. But he also needed to manage a sprawling national security machine that was more than comfortable with the status quo. He needed to find his own path between challenging the conventional wisdom post-9/11 and managing a post-9/11 world.

The national security debate was shaped by Obama's vision of himself and the world, as well as by what his supporters and critics envisioned of his leadership. Obama saw the power and the challenges of the presidency in almost religious terms—as tests of faith and expressions of doubt—well before he entered the Oval Office. Flying on his campaign plane in July 2008, a month before formally accepting his party's presidential nomination, he explained how Lincoln's experience had demonstrated the kind of moral fortitude needed in a wartime leader.

"My religious influences extend to the founding fathers—and I would include Lincoln in that category—because these were men driven by reason, and were for skepticism and doubt," he told me. "So much so that some of them would be considered—considered themselves—Deists as opposed to strict Christians, as we would call them. But you look at somebody like Lincoln, who starts off, as far as we can tell, deeply skeptical of religion, but a powerfully moral person who, as he finds himself in the midst of history and potential cataclysm, feels it necessary to hang on to a more explicit belief in Providence and faith.

"And so, that resonates with me. I think that there's a place where the more seriously you take the world and the more you find yourself struggling with good and evil, and war—you know, the great moral questions of the day—the more you have to fall back on some sort of North Star. You get lost. Because the kinds of issues that Lincoln confronted are so difficult, the weight he carried was so great, the possibilities of paralysis that Lincoln himself acknowledged sometimes were present, you know, what gets him out of bed is powerful stuff."

The irony was that Obama's predecessor—whose example of wartime leadership he campaigned against so hard and for so long—drew from the same source of inspiration. In late 2005, after the civil war in Iraq spiraled out of control and after Hurricane Katrina, George W. Bush said he spent "a lot of time thinking about Abraham Lincoln." Pointing to a portrait of Lincoln in the Oval Office, he told NBC's Brian Williams that he admired Lincoln's fortitude as the country was tearing itself apart: "Lincoln had this great inner strength and a vision for an America that was united. He worked to achieve that vision as best as he possibly could in the midst of a bloody fight." Even in his final press conference as president, Bush likened his position to Lincoln's. "I've been reading a lot about Abraham Lincoln during my presidency and there was some pretty harsh discord when it came to the 16th president, just like there's been harsh discord for the 43rd president," he told reporters in the White House briefing room.

> Presidents can try to avoid hard decisions, and therefore avoid controversy. That's just not my nature. I'm the kind of person that, you know, is willing to take on hard tasks. And in times of war, people get emotional. I understand that. I've never really spent that much time, frankly, worrying about the loud voices. I of course hear them. But they didn't affect my policy, nor did they affect how I made decisions. President-elect Obama will find this too. He'll get in the Oval Office and there will be a lot of people that are real critical and harsh. And he'll be disappointed, at times, by the tone of the rhetoric. And he's going to

have to do what he thinks is right. And if you don't, then I don't see how you can live with yourself. I don't see how I can get back home in Texas and look in the mirror and be proud of what I see if I allowed the loud voices, the loud critics, to prevent me from doing what I thought was necessary to protect this country.

They grew out of different political beliefs and different levels of eloquence, but on the steps necessary to protect the country against terrorism, the views of Bush at the end of his second term and those of Obama at the end of his first year converged. As a candidate, Obama left the vivid impression that he would reverse his predecessor's approach to civil liberties, suspected terrorist detainees, and international legal standards. His stump speech through the primaries trumpeted that promise out loud. "We are going to lead by example, by maintaining the highest standards of civil liberties and human rights, which is why I will close Guantánamo and restore habeas corpus and say no to torture," he said in February 2008. "Because if you are ready for change, then you can elect a president who has taught the Constitution, and believes in the Constitution, and will obey the Constitution of the United States of America." In a policy fact sheet, his campaign explained that Obama "strongly supports" habeas corpus rights being restored to detainees classified as enemy combatants: "He firmly believes that those who pose a danger to this country should be swiftly tried and brought to justice, but those who do not should have sufficient due process to ensure that we are not wrongfully denying them their liberty."

It took all of five months in office to erode Obama's firm belief in the highest standards of civil liberties and the necessity of swift trials. Without fully abandoning his former positions, he edged away from the terms of his sales pitch under the pressures of politics and national security.

He started out with a serious review of his campaign promise to end torture, beginning even before he moved to the White House. In a secure room inside his transition office in Chicago, the president-elect sat through an extraordinary briefing on the so-called enhanced interrogation techniques approved by his predecessor to apply unbearable pressure on detainees. Inside the federal building in downtown Chicago, there was a Sensitive Compartmented Information Facility (known as a SCIF) where he heard classified briefings in a secure room designed to guard against leaks and spies. But this briefing, with Bush's CIA director, Mike Hayden, and his national intelligence director, Mike McConnell, was unlike any other. With the aid of an assistant, Hayden stood up in the secure room to demonstrate several of the techniques still in use. Of the thirteen most controversial techniques, only a half dozen remained in operation. Waterboarding, which simulates drowning, had ended several years earlier; but sleep deprivation, stress positions, and physical violence were still in use, often in combination with one another.

"There's squaring," said Hayden, as he held the shoulders of his assistant and shook him vigorously. "There's walling," he said as he slammed his assistant into the office wall. The Obama team struggled to maintain their poker-face expressions. "Mike was trying to establish that they weren't as onerous as people thought," said one person present in the secure room. "But I realized I would remember this moment forever."

That sense of shock wasn't enough for Obama. He sent a group of experts to CIA headquarters in Langley, Virginia, including former senators Chuck Hagel and David Boren, for a full day of briefings. The idea was that outsiders—not just campaign insiders—should hear the best case for using the "enhanced" techniques to gather intelligence from terrorists. "We didn't want to move from the campaign to end torture and abolish enhanced interrogation techniques without spending time in due diligence," said one senior Obama aide.

The briefing was unconvincing. On the second day of his presidency, Obama signed three executive orders. One required all interrogations to follow the Army Field Manual, putting an end to the harsh techniques and torture. Another ended the CIA's use of secret prisons. A third set a one-year deadline for the closure of the detention camp at Guantánamo Bay.

Guantánamo Bay rapidly turned into exhibit A of the difficulties in bringing Change to the White House. The Bush administration left the Guantánamo cases in a state of disarray, despite their public statements that they wanted to close the facility. Files were located in three or four different places, and Obama's team created a single electronic database close to CIA headquarters that drew together military and intelligence data about the 248 detainees who were still there. By July, a case-by-case review of each detainee was complete.

The detainees were not the problem; their future home was. Obama's team pinned their hopes on the Saudi government taking custody of almost one hundred Yemenis at the camp, who represented nearly half the detainees. The weak state of the Yemeni government, as well as the rise of al Qaeda in Yemen, made it impossible to send the detainees home. Instead, Obama liked the Saudi rehabilitation program for former terrorists and radicals, which had a relatively low recidivist rate of less than 20 percent. But the Saudis rejected the idea, not least because of the bad publicity from rehab graduates returning to terrorist watch lists. Attempts to start a Yemeni version of the rehab program proved frustratingly slow.

That left one solution beyond the slow trickle of prisoners to other countries around the world: a new prison in the United States. By their second month inside the White House, Obama's aides had identified three possible sites: a state prison in Thomson, Illinois, the Navy brig in Charleston, South Carolina, and the Army's maximum-security prison in Fort Leavenworth, Kansas. Local political opposition killed the Kansas option, while Charleston was close to residential areas. Obama's team knew that if they didn't make a decision within sixty days, there was no way to upgrade Thomson's prison before the one-year deadline.

The politics were shifting all around them. "Everybody made the same miscalculation," said one senior Obama aide. "Bush had come out in favor of closing Guantánamo and McCain had been in favor of closing it. Lindsey Graham and like-minded people had been in favor of closing Guantánamo, and Lindsey even during the transition said he was in favor. So no one anticipated it would be used by the Republicans in the way that it would, and the numbers supporting closing fell drastically. You couldn't find a whole lot of people who supported bringing detainees into the United States. To close Guantánamo within that year, we had to be willing to do that—to process them from the United States and either put them on trial, transfer them to another country, or hold them as law-of-war detainees. It was a political call that the president made. And who could second-guess that? The economy was going over a cliff."

Obama's aides were faced with a stark triage: rescue the global economy or resolve the status of terrorist suspects. In early April, Obama returned from the G-20 summit in London, having jointly committed with other world leaders to a $1.1 trillion package to restore confidence in the global financial system. The International Monetary Fund (IMF), located just a few blocks west of the White House, would need access to hundreds of billions of additional dollars. "The president had to deliver on his commitment of an American increase in appropriations for the IMF, and that wasn't popular in Congress," said one senior aide. "There was a feeling that you could either have your IMF appropriation, or you can have a vote about Guantánamo. You couldn't do both."

By May, the debate was over. The Senate voted overwhelmingly to deny funds for the closing of Guantánamo Bay, stripping the money out of a war spending bill. It was Obama's first significant defeat in Congress. Democrats, including those at the White House, were already more invested in health care reform and did not seem to care that they were leaving the field of terrorism to the other party. "This is neither the time nor the bill to deal with this," said Democratic leader Harry Reid. "Democrats under no circumstances will move forward without a comprehensive, responsible plan from the president. We will never allow terrorists to be released into the United States." The terrorists were never going to be released. What was released was the post-9/11 politics of tough talk and fear-mongering.

At the same time, Obama's approach to the legacies of the Bush era was shifting, too, along with the views of his national security team. By the spring of 2009, the White House faced a court deadline in a long-standing lawsuit over the release of the four most sensitive memos of the Bush administration. The memos spelled out the CIA's methods of torture and harsh interrogation, as well as the Justice Department's legal approval for the techniques, which Obama had already stopped with his executive order. "It was a tough call for him because he didn't want to be perceived as betraying the trust that the president has in the intelligence community," said one senior adviser. "He didn't want to hang out to dry people who had been doing things that the previous administration had asked them to do. But at the same time, he believed in the value of disclosure. He was deeply conflicted about the decision. He was looking for a middle path all the way through this." Obama spoke to intelligence officials at the White House, and he traveled to CIA headquarters in Langley for more debate. Even CIA director Leon Panetta was conflicted. He opposed the Bush detention program and was happy to see the legal analysis released. But he wanted to keep secret any operational details and fought hard to stop any all-out investigation into Bush-era abuses.

Obama finally made his mind up just a few hours before the memos were released. His final rationale was that almost everything was known about the techniques already: from the news media, congressional testimony, and especially a report leaked by the International Red Cross. He found reassurance in the judgment of Attorney General Eric Holder, who argued for the memos' release. Holder believed there was no strong argument to make in court to protect sources and methods when the president had ruled out those same methods. But he also believed that intelligence operatives who stayed within the bounds of the Bush legal advice should not face legal action. "The White House has been very concerned from the beginning, for good reason, about making an enemy out of the CIA," said one senior administration official. "It was a lesson the Bush administration learned in the second term, and this president has tried very hard to avoid doing that."

It did not take long for Obama to shift the line he had only just drawn between national security and disclosure. As with the torture memos, the American Civil Liberties Union had filed a freedom of information lawsuit demanding the release of all photos involving military detention, including detainee abuse at the Abu Ghraib prison in Baghdad. In the final days before the memos' release, Obama met with his senior staff in Rahm Emanuel's large office. White House counsel Greg Craig said the photos were taken as part of the Abu Ghraib investigation, rather than at the time of the abuses. After extensive debate between Justice lawyers and the military, Secretary of Defense Bob Gates and General David Petraeus, commander of U.S. forces in the Middle East, agreed to release the photos.

But the issue of the photos, caught up in the debate about the memos, seemed to blindside Obama. During a secure videoconference in the Situation Room, Obama heard new opposition from his leading general in Iraq, Ray Odierno. The general voiced concerns about the impact of the photos on troops currently serving in Iraq, and Obama was troubled by what he heard. He ordered a full set of options for a new review in the Oval Office, where he abruptly reversed course. The photos were simply not worth the trouble. One senior aide who supported their release said they were "singularly less problematic than Abu Ghraib" because they were part of an investigation that followed the reports of abuse.

The policy shifts, the reliance on bold rhetoric, the messy compromises were all nothing new. In fact, Obama's reversal on the photos mirrored a previous change in the middle of his presidential campaign. Soon after securing his party's nomination, but before the convention in Denver, he shifted his rhetoric and position on President Bush's sweeping program of electronic surveillance. The program involved the tracking of huge volumes of data on telephone calls, Web browsing, text messaging, and e-mails. That surveillance had taken place without court-approved warrants. Rather than opposing the program, Obama agreed to a new compromise that allowed minimal court oversight of the eavesdropping, saying it was not perfect. The compromise also granted immunity to telecom companies that had worked with the Bush administration, against strong opposition from the party's grassroots activists and some prominent Democratic senators. "It is not all that I would want," he said in a statement at the time. "But given the legitimate threats we face, providing effective intelligence collection tools with appropriate safeguards is too important to delay. So I support the compromise, but do so with a firm pledge that as President, I will carefully monitor the program, review the report by the Inspectors General, and work with the Congress to take any additional steps I deem necessary to protect the lives—and the liberty—of the American people." In other words: *trust me*. The court supervision might be limited, but the ultimate safeguard was his character.

The balance between the candidate of Change and the commander in chief was constantly recalibrated, and never truly settled. At the heart of the Guantánamo challenge was how to bring the detainees to justice: whether to use civilian courts, military commissions, or some new hybrid. Obama's campaign position was far more nuanced than his rhetoric suggested. He supported the military court system, but not the version President Bush had tried to create. Even in his early campaign speech in August 2007 on "The War We Need to Win," Obama said he opposed the Military Commissions Act of 2006 (the Supreme Court later struck down as unconstitutional the act's restrictions on habeas corpus rights). But Obama was careful to say he also supported the JAG military lawyers and the Uniform Code of Military Justice in dealing with terrorists—in other words, he supported military commissions themselves. Those aides hoping for more change inside the White House recalled the campaign nuances as a clear warning sign. "The president was from the beginning a pragmatist, and he ran on that. I see this as a virtue," said one senior West Wing aide. "This is not a person who makes a decision on ideological prerequisites. He's looking for solutions, and I think that's a hugely important point to make, especially to independent voters. That's what he's done, and those of us who were hopeful for much more dramatic change have no right to be disappointed, because he gave us fair warning."

The day after the Senate vote on Guantánamo in May 2009, Obama met with the leaders of civil liberties and human rights groups in the Cabinet Room next to the Oval Office. They had broadly supported him as a candidate in 2008 but were now vocal critics of his recent decisions. The conversation was emotional and contentious. Obama bristled as some accused him of simply adopting Bush's policies. He wanted to amend the military commissions to rule out evidence obtained through torture and hearsay, as well as offer detainees more freedom to choose their own lawyers. The civil liberties groups were concerned that Obama might continue with the Bush project to set up a hybrid system of detention without trial. Obama felt there might be a middle ground, allowing long-term detention without trial but with a court review of the detainees' status. It was a shift in principle from the Bush position, but one with minimal differences in practice. "Was it a change from his position in the campaign?" asked one senior aide. "It was a change that he thought would enhance his ability to close Guantánamo."

On one side of Obama were conservative critics, like John Mc-Cain and Joe Lieberman, who opposed terrorist trials in civilian courts. On the other side were the civil liberties activists who opposed terrorist trials in military courts. "In the middle is President Obama dealing in this complicated reality, recognizing the power of the feelings and the complexity of finding a new model for doing this, who has been trying to adapt his campaign and personal commitments to this complex and very hard choice," said a senior West Wing adviser. "It's an execution issue more than anything else." Obama's aides insisted that he "strongly favors" the normal criminal justice courts for terrorists but cannot rule out using military commissions, too. At the same time, he thinks military courts should not just be a dumping ground for cases that cannot reach a successful prosecution elsewhere. "He understands there is a role for military commissions and the question that everyone is struggling with—at least those who don't take a completely binary view of it—is what sort of credible criteria can we apply for determining which is the appropriate forum in particular cases," said one senior Obama adviser.

The day after meeting with civil liberties advocates, Obama

drove to the stately National Archives building to try to give some context to his shifting positions. The symbolism was not subtle: he wanted to remain rooted in American principles and traditions, even as he was rewriting his predecessor's policies and edging away from some of his own campaign language. "I stand here today as someone whose own life was made possible by these documents," he began. "My father came to these shores in search of the promise that they offered. My mother made me rise before dawn to learn their truths when I lived as a child in a foreign land. My own American journey was paved by generations of citizens who gave meaning to those simple words—'to form a more perfect union.' I've studied the Constitution as a student, I've taught it as a teacher, I've been bound by it as a lawyer and a legislator. I took an oath to preserve, protect, and defend the Constitution as Commander-in-Chief, and as a citizen, I know that we must never, ever, turn our back on its enduring principles for expedience sake."

And yet, the speech wrestled publicly with his identity as a scholarly teacher of the Constitution and as a presidential defender of the Constitution. What was the constitutional way to deal with hardened detainees—"people who, in effect, remain at war with the United States"—whose evidence was tainted by torture and who could not be freed? "We must have clear, defensible, and lawful standards for those who fall into this category," he said. "We must have fair procedures so that we don't make mistakes. We must have a thorough process of periodic review, so that any prolonged detention is carefully evaluated and justified." He wanted the power to lock up some detainees indefinitely, but with some checks and balances of "judicial and congressional oversight."

But what Obama really wanted to place in check was the political pressure—the heated debate and emotional torment—that buckled the decisions of presidents and members of Congress: "Now, as our efforts to close Guantánamo move forward, I know that the politics in Congress will be difficult. These are issues that are fodder for 30-second commercials. You can almost picture the direct mail pieces that emerge from any vote on this issue—designed to frighten the population. I get it. But if we continue to make decisions within a climate of fear, we will make more mistakes. And if we refuse to deal with these issues today, then I guarantee you that they will be an albatross around our efforts to combat terrorism in the future."

The debate was not just between politics and principle. It was between the Revivalists of the Obama campaign and the Survivalists of Capitol Hill and the Clinton years. It was a debate that continued back and forth inside the president's mind, as much as among his senior aides. The first casualty was Greg Craig, his White House counsel. A silver-haired former Ted Kennedy staffer, Craig was a foreign policy aide to Secretary of State Madeleine Albright and later entrusted with Bill Clinton's defense in the impeachment trial. Yet in spite of those Clinton credentials, he signed on early to the Obama campaign, traveling through the first primary states as a foreign policy aide and election lawyer. He had not been shy about criticizing Clinton during the primaries, so when Clinton was named secretary of state, there was no place for Craig in the foreign policy ecosystem.

What he didn't realize was that there was little place for him in the White House, either. Craig was a true believer in the campaign ideals and Obama's mission of Change, but that brought him into constant conflict with Rahm Emanuel. "It wasn't a good fit," said one senior West Wing aide. "Rahm has the attention span of a gnat and he doesn't like lawyers. Lawyers create problems, and he doesn't have the patience to work through problems. He is a political animal, and the world revolves around politics for him. And if you don't have the chief of staff working hand in glove with the White House counsel, it's going to be dysfunctional." By the half-year mark, the relationship between the two had broken down. Emanuel blamed Craig for the ambitious deadline for the closure of Guantánamo, and for his personal involvement in the controversial transfer of four Chinese Muslim Uighurs to Bermuda. Craig believed his legal work was superior to that of President Clinton's counsel in his first year. Besides a successful Supreme Court confirmation of Sonia Sotomayor, Craig oversaw the issue of thirty-eight executive orders that survived intact, compared to ten in the first year of the Clinton White House, four of which were withdrawn. Craig decided to leave by the end of the year, and the news leaked almost immediately, leading to several painful months of media speculation about his future.

Even other campaign Revivalists believed that Craig had exposed himself to failure. "Greg is a terrific guy," said one Obama loyalist. "But you can be a terrific person and not be a great manager, and that was the case here. He was ill suited to the job, which involves keeping a million balls in the air. Greg is a wonderful, brilliant guy, and passionate. What he isn't is a details guy. He's not a manager. Managing a lot of different things at once isn't his thing. He's a guy who is used to plunging into a case."

His replacement was Bob Bauer, another Obama loyalist who had served as the campaign's lawyer through 2007 and 2008. Emanuel thought Bauer knew little outside the world of election law. Within weeks, Emanuel conceded that he was wrong. "Bauer is spectacular," said one senior Obama aide. "There's a sense in the White House today that everything is being taken care of and being looked after, that nothing is falling through the cracks. It's a tremendous relief."

To those who traveled with Obama on his epic journey to the White House, the hedging and compromising on terrorism and civil liberties were inevitable with the passage of time. "I don't think his views have changed; I think circumstances have changed," said David Axelrod. "I think he's fundamentally committed to the same things he was always committed to. Our struggle was that we were left with a lot of problems on a range of efforts, including Guantánamo. And the whole war on terror has evolved. We have inflicted a lot of damage on them, and the result is that they are resorting to these smaller, more discrete attacks." But even Axelrod conceded that it wasn't just the external world that had changed; Obama's internal processes had also shifted as he grew into the presidency. "There's no question that he has had to think in much finer detail about how you square fundamental constitutional principles with the realities that he faces as president," he said. "Guantánamo is one, because there are people of indeterminate legal status who undoubtedly represent a threat to the country. You have responsibilities to people in the field, who are doing dangerous things, so the issue of the release of the detainees, what impact it might have on ongoing operations and people in the field—there are a lot of issues one has to confront as president. Throughout he has struggled to do that and reconcile his responsibilities as commander in chief with his oath to preserve, protect, and defend the Constitution."

By the anniversary of his inauguration, Obama knew that the politics had moved decisively against his plans to close Guantánamo Bay. House Democrats voted with Republicans to ban the transfer of detainees to the United States for trial. Elite legal academics on both sides of the partisan divide were just as split as were members of Congress. Foreign policy experts complained about the damage to Obama's international reputation, but European countries were enacting far more draconian laws against Muslims in general and suspected terrorists in particular. There remained a complex debate about where to stage the trial of Khalid Sheikh Mohammed, the most senior al Qaeda detainee, who had murdered the journalist Danny Pearl. But once the entire political leadership of New York opposed plans to hold the trial there, the White House acknowledged it had few options left. "As a practical matter we're at an impasse right now," said one senior Obama aide. "Nobody cares if KSM sits in Guantánamo for the rest of his life, except for people who are totaling up the cost. This is not a place anybody is particularly unhappy about overall. The administration is not happy about it because it's committed to a rational national security policy, which includes the closing of Guantánamo Bay. But why would Americans care if KSM isn't on trial, unless you're the family of one of the victims? So he's in military detention in Guantánamo. He can rot there for the rest of his life. Big deal."

Just one year into his presidency, one of Obama's biggest campaign promises was effectively dead, and the White House—like Congress—seemed not to care.

The climate of fear returned on Christmas Day 2009. It landed in a Northwest Airlines flight from Amsterdam to Detroit, just as Obama was trying to escape from Washington on the first full day of his traditional holiday vacation in Hawaii. There would be no escape once Umar Farouk Abdulmutallab, a twenty-three-year-old Nigerian linked to al Qaeda, tried to detonate explosives hidden in his underwear. All the passengers survived. But the botched attack still posed a potent threat to the political survival of the president. Not least because it tested whether he—and the public—could maintain confidence in his approach to national security. Just like the Haiti disaster that followed, the botched bombing forced a struggling president to question his aides and reproach his own government.

Back in Washington, Obama's most trusted aide on terrorism was preparing Christmas dinner for his family when his phone rang. John Brennan was an improbable home cook: a gruff and grizzly former CIA chief of staff, with cropped hair and curtailed conversation, he was revered inside the West Wing for his relentless pursuit of al Qaeda operatives around the world. He was also an intelligence professional, having joined the agency as a young man after seeing an ad in the *New York Times* while riding the bus into New York City one morning. He spent six years in the Middle East, grew fluent in Arabic, and rose to become station chief in Saudi Arabia. But through the last decade, his career path followed President Bush's journey from the aggressive counterterrorism after 9/11 to the controversies and crises of the war in Iraq. He set up what would become the National Counterterrorism Center, to connect the dots of terrorism threats and tips across an often disjointed government. But he fell out with Bush's team as he opposed their efforts to use intelligence materials to concoct a case for invading Iraq. Some liberal pundits distrusted Brennan for his ties to the Bush era, effectively ending his chances to become CIA director. Yet inside the West Wing he was, if anything, more powerful, as his reach extended from the Oval Office through the intelligence community and the cabinet as Obama's forceful adviser on homeland security and counterterrorism. Brennan worked and spoke with laser-guided precision, an approach that appealed to the president and his inner circle.

As the calls came in from the Situation Room and the FBI on Christmas Day, Brennan immediately reached out to his own team through e-mails and by phone. Within minutes, CNN was reporting problems with a plane landing in Detroit. Half an hour after the first alerts, Brennan abandoned his family dinner and was driving to the White House to gather officials together for a secure videoconference. The first reports suggested that someone was trying to light firecrackers on board the plane, but by the time Brennan arrived at the White House he already knew the name of the Nigerian held at the customs facility in Detroit: that name tracked to a computer record on the U.S. government's central database of people with possible terrorism links, known as TIDE. While FBI officials were interrogating Abdulmutallab, Brennan gathered a half dozen national security staffers at the White House to share facts and ensure all other airplanes were alert to terrorist threats—just in case this was the start of a coordinated series of attacks, like 9/11 and the London bombings in 2005. Two hours later, the FBI was sharing its early information with the team via videoconference: about Abdulmutallab, what he was trying to do, and what he was telling them about his planned attack. The severely burned terrorist rapidly told his interrogators who he was and how he was connected to al Qaeda.

That evening Brennan spoke to Obama twice to update him on the facts known so far and the potential for other attacks that might still be in the pipeline. The president wanted to stay informed, and wanted to know if there was anything he needed to do. But the most obvious omission was already well known. The TIDE record was no random piece of data. It came directly from the terrorist's father, a prominent Nigerian banker, who had grown so alarmed by his son's phone calls that he contacted Nigerian officials. They in turn took the father to the CIA station chief in Abuja, the Nigerian capital, more than a month before his son boarded the flight to Detroit. The intelligence cable that emerged, which formed the basis for the TIDE record, was sketchy. It said the father was concerned about his son associating with extremists in Yemen, not that his son was engaging in terrorism. In fact, the father feared his son was embarking on a suicide mission from Yemen. The CIA in Nigeria produced a draft report with more details but did not share it until after the Christmas Day attack. Other intelligence, gathered separately from surveillance, suggested that al Qaeda in the Arabian Peninsula (AQAP) was preparing to attack western targets, possibly on Christmas Day. The dots had simply not been connected.

Overnight, Brennan and his team pieced together the key facts and wrote a report for the vacationing president. The information only seemed to add up in hindsight, and Brennan was not surprised.

"You could understand why just looking at one piece, the intelligence streams or the TIDE record, there was nothing that let you put Abdulmutallab together with an AQAP plot," he said. "In twenty-twenty hindsight you see when you bring them together that the identity information overlaid on top of the other stuff, the correlation becomes more apparent."

That sense of understanding evaporated the next day, with the discovery of the draft CIA report, which had been kept private in Nigeria until it was too late to do any good. Obama was furious. "He expressed some frustration about the failure to disseminate that information in a timely fashion," said Brennan. "That in itself wasn't dispositive as to why Abdulmutallab got on the plane, as we have intentionally built a system with redundancy. But as we did the review, it was one of many instances where the system did not function as it was designed to work, which understandably concerned and upset the president." In fact, Obama did not express his frustration in a timely fashion, either. The day after his aides learned of the draft report, he spoke to the press for the first time to give some factual information about the attempted attack, to promise a full review, and to threaten the terrorist leaders with a counterattack. "We do not yet have all the answers about this latest attempt, but those who would slaughter innocent men, women and children must know that the United States will do more than simply strengthen our defenses—we will continue to use every element of our national power to disrupt, to dismantle and defeat the violent extremists who threaten us," he said. "Whether they are from Afghanistan or Pakistan, Yemen or Somalia, or anywhere where they are plotting attacks against the U.S. homeland."

It would take another day for Obama to turn his fire on an intelligence system that remained slow, bureaucratic, and stovepiped. "When our government has information on a known extremist and that information is not shared and acted upon as it should have been, so that this extremist boards a plane with dangerous explosives that could cost nearly 300 lives, a systemic failure has occurred," he told reporters gathered at the Kaneohe Bay Marine Base in Hawaii. "And I consider that totally unacceptable. The reviews I've ordered will surely tell us more. But what already is apparent is that there was a mix of human and systemic failures that contributed to this potential catastrophic breach of security. We need to learn from this episode and act quickly to fix the flaws in our system, because our security is at stake and lives are at stake."

Obama was determined to maintain the pressure on his own intelligence and homeland security team. But within a week of the terrorist attempt, the CIA suffered a devastating attack near the Afghan border with Pakistan. A suicide bomber, who was supposedly being groomed as an al Qaeda spy, detonated his vest and killed at least seven CIA officers. Obama issued a rare public statement about CIA casualties, expressing his sympathy and admiration for the agency. "Because of your service, plots have been disrupted, American lives have been saved, and our Allies and partners have been more secure," he said, making no reference to the plot that was not disrupted on Christmas Day. "Your triumphs and even your names may be unknown to your fellow Americans, but your service is deeply appreciated. Indeed, I know firsthand the excellent quality of your work because I rely on it every day."

Would the Afghan attack weaken the president's will to reform a failed system to defend the homeland? He seemed to veer between challenging the intelligence community and threatening the terrorists. On one hand, Obama's openness about his intelligence failings was extraordinary in the post-9/11 era: the antithesis of Bush's bravado. But he also wanted and expected a team that worked together, not apart, to target and kill terrorists. The review he ordered was already threatening to degenerate into an endless round of finger-pointing, which made him even more frustrated. "That's a factor of being president," said David Axelrod. "You don't want to see this kind of thing, and when it happens it makes him angry."

On his return to the White House, Obama called for a full session of his homeland security and national security teams in the Situation Room. There he berated them for their failures and the likely blame game, even as the officials in the room kept their finger-pointing out of view. "This was a screwup that could have been disastrous," Obama told them. "We dodged a bullet, but just barely. It was averted by brave individuals, not because the system worked. And that is not acceptable. While there will be a tendency for finger-pointing, I will not tolerate it." The most recent example of bureaucratic buck-passing had taken place within the last twenty-four hours, as Brennan finalized his review. The agencies and departments challenged his characterizations and his facts. They questioned his view that Abdulmutallab should have been placed on the no-fly list, not just the TIDE list. They wanted caveats and softer language.

In the end, the softer public language came from the president himself. In Hawaii, he judged that the information was not shared as it should have been. In Washington, he toned that down, at least in front of the cameras. "In sum, the U.S. government had the information—scattered throughout the system—to potentially uncover this plot and disrupt the attack," he told reporters in the State Dining Room inside the Executive Mansion. "Rather than a failure to collect or share intelligence, this was a failure to connect and understand the intelligence that we already had." Obama wanted to do more than identify a culprit. He wanted to challenge his team's assumptions and force them all to raise their game.

Terrorism posed not just an existential threat to Americans but also a political threat to the president. In two traumatic elections—2002 and 2004—Republicans had deployed what Obama called the politics of fear to weaken the image of Democrats and gain political power.

Now in power, he could not simply ignore the politics of fear. He wanted to defend the country more professionally, and he wanted to defend himself more politically. He was always exposed to the charge of being weak against terrorism, based on his extensive criticism of Bush's policies as well as his outreach to the Muslim world. But the reality was vastly different. In the first year of his presidency, there were fifty-three airstrikes by unmanned drone airplanes on suspected terrorist targets in Pakistan. Following the suicide attack on the CIA, there were another twelve drone strikes in the space of three weeks. In 2008 under President Bush, there had been just thirty-four such attacks. It was hard to verify whether the drones were hitting terrorist targets as well as civilians nearby. But it was clear that Obama was more aggressive in ordering such strikes than his predecessor. The White House official overseeing the so-called capture-kill program was John Brennan.

That record mattered little in the days and weeks after the failed attack. Pundits and political opponents questioned why Obama stayed on vacation and why he delayed speaking to the press for three days. The charge was led by an old foe. Dick Cheney waited just four days after Christmas to accuse Obama of weakness, naïveté, and delusional behavior. "As I've watched the events of the last few days it is clear once again that President Obama is trying to pretend we are not at war," he said in a statement. "He seems to think if he has a low-key response to an attempt to blow up an airliner and kill hundreds of people, we won't be at war. He seems to think if he gives terrorists the rights of Americans, lets them lawyer up and reads them their Miranda rights, we won't be at war . . . He seems to think if he closes Guantanamo and releases the hard-core Al Qaeda-trained terrorists still there, we won't be at war. He seems to think if he gets rid of the words, 'war on terror,' we won't be at war. But we are at war and when President Obama pretends we aren't, it makes us less safe."

Cheney's dismissive and inflammatory comments opened the door for Republican officials to do the same.

As much as they caricatured and distorted Obama's record, Cheney's comments reflected a political shift in Washington and exploited a certain ambivalence inside the White House. On the campaign trail, it had been much easier to take a tough stand against Bush's approach to terrorism. Democrats were united in their opposition to Bush, and even Republicans had been critical of detention and interrogation abuses. But from the West Wing, with Republicans turning their fire on Obama, the challenges of multiple terrorist threats made Obama even more risk-averse than normal. So when he sat down with his national security team to review their mistakes, Obama drilled down on the circumstances of Abdulmutallab's interrogation. The wannabe terrorist had spoken freely to the FBI initially, then clammed up for several hours after undergoing surgery for his burns. He was read the Miranda rights that affirm his right to silence, but it was not clear if the rights or the surgery prompted him to stop talking. He later resumed answering questions after his family's intervention to persuade him.

Still, Obama wanted to know why the Miranda rights were read at that point. The FBI could delay reading those rights for reasons of public safety, as they had done initially. But why not wait longer? Even the man who taught constitutional law at the University of Chicago was challenging the basic approach of law enforcement. Had an unthinking officialdom made a bad situation worse, exposing the country to security threats and exposing him to political attacks? He pushed Attorney General Eric Holder to explain and defend what had taken place. Holder was tasked with making a presentation about the arrest and the interrogation, and fielded Obama's follow-up questions. Obama said he thought they had ultimately reached the right outcome on Christmas Day once Abdulmutallab was detained, but he wanted to know what the thinking was behind the timing of the Miranda rights. "I think it's true that he wanted to know the process by which all decisions were made," said David Axelrod. "More than anything, the president wants to make sure that whatever is done, is done with all factors considered, and in a consistent and consistently conceived way. I don't think he had a quibble that Abdulmutallab was due his Miranda rights. But he wanted to make sure we got what we could get." Obama asked Holder to take another look at the FBI procedures, to make sure they were gathering all the intelligence they could, while not jeopardizing the chance of a successful prosecution.

It wasn't a choice between counterterrorism and legal rights; Obama wanted both. In more lofty terms, in his inaugural speech, he declared, "We reject as false the choice between our safety and our ideals." Now in the privacy of the Situation Room and the prosaic aftermath of security screwups, the rhetoric was facing its toughest reality check. Defense secretary Robert Gates was unhappy with the timing of the Miranda rights. But he told the president and cabinet that Abdulmutallab should be detained, prosecuted, and interrogated in the civilian courts. "We don't have any tools available to us that the Justice Department doesn't have in terms of interrogation," he observed. Even the former CIA officials inside the White House believed the question about Miranda rights was faulty. "Embedded in the question is the idea that an alternative path would have led to a treasure trove of information," said Brennan. "*Let the military get them.* As if putting them in the brig in South Carolina would get reams and reams of data. Instantaneously. That is operating under a totally unrealistic sense of what works and what doesn't." Still, for all the defensive pushback, the White House quietly agreed to a new approach just one month after the botched attack. Mobile teams of interrogators—from the FBI, CIA, and Pentagon—would now question suspects to gather intelligence while also building a legal case.

Cheney's attacks proved ironically helpful to an embattled president, for they pointed to a path of political revival, a way to step beyond the intelligence stumbles and the complex choices of counterterrorism. Instead of debating themselves, Obama's aides could fire back at an old enemy, whose extreme language appeared out of the mainstream. Dan Pfeiffer accused Cheney of playing politics and failing to finish off al Qaeda. "Seven years of bellicose rhetoric failed to reduce the threat from al Qaeda and succeeded in dividing this country," he wrote on the White House blog. "And it seems strangely off-key now, at a time when our country is under attack, for the architect of those policies to be attacking the president." The day after Obama grilled his attorney general on Miranda rights, Republican senator Kit Bond—the senior GOP figure on the Senate Intelligence Committee—echoed Cheney's attacks. "We must treat these terrorists as what they are—not common criminals, but enemy combatants in a war," he said in a statement. His words dismayed Brennan, who had briefed members of the committee and Congress in general and found nobody raised the question of Miranda rights. Soon Brennan joined the fray, writing an op-ed in USA Today. "Politically motivated criticism and unfounded fear-mongering only serve the goals of al-Qaeda," he wrote. "Terrorists are not 100-feet tall. Nor do they deserve the abject fear they seek to instill. They will, however, be dismantled and destroyed, by our military, our intelligence services and our law enforcement community. And the notion that America's counterterrorism professionals and America's system of justice are unable to handle these murderous miscreants is absurd." As if to underscore the point, at the same time as the op-ed appeared in print, Brennan was helping to oversee the capture of Mullah Abdul Ghani Baradar, the Taliban's top military commander, in Karachi, Pakistan.

Obama needed something more than a botched al Qaeda attack to spark his political revival on national security. He needed the political foil of his old opponents. "Frankly, the Cheney stuff helps," said Ben Rhodes. "Some people think, 'Oh you must be really annoyed when Dick Cheney hits you.' Well, actually no. Because it reminds people what the other course was. It gives us the contrast which helps explain what we're doing. I think there's no coincidence that our poll numbers have gone up on terrorism since Cheney started unloading after Christmas."

For all its intensity, the ideological squabble over detention and trials was less emotional and meaningful for Obama than the real life-and-death battle in Afghanistan. Shortly before dawn on Saturday, February 13, five thousand U.S. Marines and Afghan troops swooped into the fields outside the southern Afghan town of Marja. Using mine-clearing vehicles and mobile bridges, they slowly moved to take control of a Taliban stronghold. It was the first real test of Obama's new strategy, finalized in December, to send more troops to the battlefield and refocus the Afghan effort on reconstruction and handover to Afghan control. Marja was close to the spiritual home of the Taliban in Kandahar, and would provide a springboard for a bigger operation later in the year, if this one was successful. Back in Washington, the president was alone in the White House as Operation Moshtarak—meaning "together" in the Dari language—got under way. His wife and daughters were at Camp David enjoying the record snowfall, as he received multiple updates from the Situation Room about the troops' progress.

Obama made little public show of his management of the Afghan war, even as he risked thousands of troops' lives—and his own presidency—on his new strategy there. Behind the scenes, he was characteristically bloodless and single-minded about the mission. The reporting flow was extensive. His daily security briefing included an Afghan section, complete with bullet points on the latest action and charts showing the movement of forces and clashes with insurgents. Each week there was a written memo solely on Afghanistan, and Afghanistan dominated his weekly sessions with Secretary Gates and the chairman of the Joint Chiefs of Staff, Admiral Mike Mullen. There were Afghan updates on the diplomatic side from Secretary of State Hillary Clinton in her weekly meetings with the president. Each month Obama chaired a lengthy National Security Council meeting that included, by secure videoconference, his Afghan commander, General Stanley McChrystal, and the Afghan ambassador, Karl Eikenberry. "That's what he wants: rigorous process," said Ben Rhodes. "Making sure that there's regular updates to him and regular interagency coordination. The strategy that he put in place isn't just left there. He wants to make sure we're following up on it. But he's not the kind of guy that wants to manage the Marja operation." Instead, Obama would probe on one or two elements of what he considered the weakest parts of the reports. Was the Afghan police force improving its performance? What else could they do to encourage less corruption inside the Afghan government?

Obama was far less interested in the military tactics than in what followed. His repeated advice to military leaders sounded like a simple restatement of the long-standing principles from the successful strategy in Iraq: clear, hold, and build. But Obama's new strategy added one more element that he believed was most critical: transfer. Of the four elements, Obama made it clear he was most concerned about the last two. "Don't clear and hold what you can't build and transfer," he would often say. That was the endgame of his new approach—the transfer of control to Afghan leaders and forces, and the drawdown of American troops, starting in just eighteen months' time. After two exhaustive reviews, Obama had tripled the number of troops in Afghanistan, but he also wanted his military leaders to know there was a broader purpose that did not involve military force alone. "This wasn't about providing a bunch of resources to carry out a campaign," Rhodes explained. "It was very deliberately a process of evaluating how these military resources are one piece of a broader strategy. It has a diplomatic component and a Pakistan component. That's why he'll probe on the police training. Because if the strategy is that these guys are going to clear a bunch of areas that the Afghans are then going to have to hold, then you need to test that there's something to back that up." Obama also pushed hard on the question of civilian casualties. If there was going to be a successful transfer—and if they could ever truly secure an area from Taliban control—they needed to keep civilians on their side and avoid indiscriminate killing. On the second day of the Marja operation, the limits of that approach were already clear: an errant rocket hit a crowded compound, killing at least ten people, half of whom were children.

Despite all his efforts, the building and transferring stages were frustratingly difficult to accomplish. "We struggled with this since the beginning of the Afghan strategy," said Denis McDonough. "If the building and transferring were easy, the whole strategy would be easy. That's a tough nut. We take it for granted that the whole thing is hard, but the building and transferring is a very difficult piece of the puzzle. Everyone from Gates to McChrystal to Clinton will tell you that."

The Afghan review in the last few months of 2009 had been protracted and fraught with political risk. It exposed internal divisions with the military leadership and opened Obama to Republican accusations that he was dithering about a final decision concerning the troops. Over the course of ten sessions, from September to early December, Obama grew increasingly frustrated with the military leadership. Just one week after their first session, a secret McChrystal report on the deteriorating situation in Afghanistan—and the need for more troops to avoid "failure"—was leaked to Bob Woodward at the *Wash-*

ington Post. Obama's aides were furious about the leak, suspecting that McChrystal and the Joint Chiefs were trying to box in the president before the review began in earnest. They believed that the generals were using Woodward—who rarely wrote for the newspaper—to test the president's authority. If true, the strategy backfired. Obama asked for a copy of his first strategy review, completed just six months earlier, as an interim position before the Afghan presidential elections in August. Obama's conclusion was damning: key elements of his first strategy had not been implemented or followed through. The next day, McChrystal delivered a speech in London in which he flatly rejected the notion of a narrowly focused mission of counterterrorism against al Qaeda. "The short answer," the general said, "is no."

The Afghan review lingered in large part because the generals were dragging their feet as Obama explored his options. "He was frustrated by the length of time to elicit everything he needed from the military," said one senior White House adviser. "McChrystal was an initial problem." McChrystal was a blunt-spoken former commander of special operations forces—including the Army's Delta Force and Navy SEALs—with a record of hunting down al Qaeda leaders in Iraq. Washington politics and diplomacy were not his forte. McChrystal offered Obama three options for more troops: 80,000 for counterinsurgency across the country, 40,000 for counterinsurgency in the Taliban strongholds of the south and east, or 15,000 to train Afghan forces.

Obama's approach was an effort to move beyond a simple yes or no to more troops. He believed his role as president involved weighing factors other than purely military concerns. Were they fighting the right war? Could the country afford a lengthy deployment of thousands more troops? He had clashed with McChrystal's boss, David Petraeus, over the same questions about withdrawing from Iraq. On his first trip to Iraq, in the middle of his presidential campaign, Obama came under pressure to defend his plans for a sixteen-month withdrawal. Petraeus wanted more flexibility, but Obama insisted he had a different perspective. "If I were in his shoes, I'd probably feel the same way," he said shortly after meeting Petraeus. "But my job as a candidate for president and a potential commander in chief extends beyond Iraq." Obama wanted to focus attention on al Qaeda and Afghanistan, and had done so since one of his earliest foreign policy speeches of the election, to the Chicago Council on Global Affairs in April 2007. There he said he wanted to withdraw from Iraq so he could focus on the Middle East, Iran, and Afghanistan, "where more American forces are needed to battle al Qaeda, track down Osama bin Laden, and stop that country from backsliding toward instability." Two and a half years later, he was still trying to refocus attention on those goals.

His ally was the man who had largely ignored and dismissed him on foreign policy when they were both senators. Joe Biden used to chair the meetings of the Senate Foreign Relations Committee where Obama tried to get his voice heard. Now it was Obama who ran the sessions, and he wanted Biden to speak up. The vice president believed that nation-building in Afghanistan was not in line with America's national security interests. "The issue was al Qaeda, and it's not in Afghanistan. It's in Pakistan," said one senior White House official. "Stabilizing Afghanistan and preventing the government from being toppled was only a means to an end to stabilize Pakistan and get to al Qaeda. Why do we spend $30 in Afghanistan for every dollar in Pakistan? Do you really need 100,000 troops to kill one hundred people in Afghanistan?" McChrystal's focus on Afghanistan was understandable, but Obama needed to have a broader outlook, just as he had in Iraq.

Biden focused on the central question of Hamid Karzai, the struggling Afghan president, who was tainted by corruption. If American forces were dying to prop up Karzai, was he worth it? Would the likely Taliban takeover mean that al Qaeda would return? Would Karzai's fall actually help gain Pakistani support, since they distrusted Karzai and could help the United States more directly in rounding up what was left of al Qaeda's leadership? Biden won support from the intelligence community to question the conventional wisdom on Karzai. "The last time the Taliban government hosted al Qaeda, they got the shit kicked out of them," said one senior White House official. "The Afghan Taliban don't like us, but they are not a threat to us directly. He wasn't alone in the room to say that it doesn't necessarily follow that Taliban control of more of Afghanistan would result in al Qaeda relocating in Afghanistan." Given the choice, Biden would likely have taken McChrystal's lower figure of fifteen thousand extra troops to build up Afghan police and soldiers. Still, even Biden acknowledged that the small risk of al Qaeda's return was too great to bear, especially when combined with the likely civilian casualties of a chaotic civil war.

Obama's decision in December 2009 was to create a hybrid that combined his campaign principles with his commander-in-chief priorities. He was both the anti-Bush, setting down a clear timeline for withdrawal beginning in July 2011, and the über-Bush, adding another 30,000 troops to make a total of almost 100,000 American soldiers in Afghanistan. His predecessor's open-ended commitment to spreading democracy and freedom was gone. "After eighteen months, our troops will begin to come home," he said to West Point's cadets as he announced his new strategy. "These are the resources that we need to seize the initiative, while building the Afghan capacity that can allow for a responsible transition of our forces out of Afghanistan." To Biden, and to Democrats in general, the promise of withdrawal was key. Biden vouched for Obama's sincerity about beginning to pull out of Afghanistan in 2011. The day before the West Point speech, at a meeting between Obama and congressional leaders, some Democrats turned to Biden for support as they asked for withdrawal now. "Just so everyone knows," said Biden, "I'm not for drawing down the troops."

Marja would be the first real test of the strategy, even before the additional troops arrived, and Obama wanted to make sure he was getting ground truth from the region. He prided himself on his sense of realism about the war, and he valued information that was not filtered by the uniformed leadership. The man tasked with obtaining something close to the real story was himself a retired Marine Corps general: James Jones, Obama's national security adviser. The former commander of NATO forces in Europe, Jones filled the role of a national security principal, not a staffer. Obama's team scorned his work ethic, saying he operated on "retired general time." In return, his aloof manner and military bearing gave little hint that he cared about the scuttlebutt. When asked why Jones kept such a low profile inside the White House and on the foreign policy team, one senior Obama aide simply shrugged. "Er, he has his own style," he ventured.

Jones had never been a part of the Obama campaign; indeed, he was personally and professionally close to John McCain, their election opponent. He had worked for McCain in the Marines' Senate liaison office thirty years earlier, and the two had been friends ever since. But two weeks before the election, Obama asked Jones to consider becoming his national security adviser, and they discussed how to restore the National Security Council after the Bush years of disarray. For Jones, the conversations with McCain's archrival were strange, but he believed this was a vital time in the nation's history for him to work on the many foreign policy challenges facing the new president. Still, when he called McCain after the election to let him know about the new job, the conversation was difficult. "I think in the aftermath of the election there are not many people who know what it's like to lose a presidential election, or win one for that matter," Jones said.

"I'm sure it was a very difficult time for him, and he knows that my willingness to serve in this capacity wasn't a political statement."

Jones created an NSC in Obama's image: one that worked by consensus from the bottom up, concentrating on strategy and oversight of the president's decisions. "The key word is strategy," said Jones. "It has been my observation over the years that when the White House in any form tries to get into an operational direction of anything, we generally don't do it well." At their first meeting with the president-elect in Chicago, the new NSC members, including Clinton and Gates, were told their presence was required at meetings if they were in Washington; they told Jones they expected him to represent their views fairly to Obama. In fact, Jones delegated much of the management of policy to his deputy, Tom Donilon, a workaholic former Biden adviser who had served as chief of staff in the Clinton State Department. While Donilon managed the NSC process, Jones traveled the world, meeting with leaders, building relationships, and gathering insight. "One of my functions, and that of the NSC, is to periodically go out and see what's going on and report back to the president," Jones said. "It's a different set of eyes. We work very closely with all the other agencies. But I think we have to be careful that we don't become victims of drinking our own Kool-Aid."

Just before the Marja operation, Jones traveled to Pakistan and Afghanistan, a region he knew well from his days as NATO commander. He had grown alarmed at the downward spiral in Afghanistan when he left NATO three years earlier, as the alliance struggled to exert control outside Kabul. His later visits only confirmed his fears: the country was deteriorating. However, this time around he observed something different. Karzai seemed to be more serious about corruption. Economic development was starting to move, together with security operations and good governance. Jones felt hopeful that the different strands of the new strategy might just be coming together. On the other side of the border, in Pakistan, he witnessed something more striking. In the Swat Valley previously controlled by the Taliban, as well as in the North-West Frontier Province close to Afghanistan, Jones believed there was a transformed attitude among the Pakistani leaders. There was more cooperation between NATO forces and the Pakistani army in dislodging terrorists. And he saw evidence that locals were rejecting the Taliban on their side of the border. "I saw firsthand film footage of the atrocities committed by the occupiers of the Swat Valley during the time of Sharia law: public beheadings, beating of women, public examples of cruelty," he said. The videos explained why the Army had moved into the valley, and how they had tried not to harm civilians or the infrastructure. "Now the challenge is rebuilding a place like the Swat Valley so it becomes economically viable and secure with local authorities controlling their destiny," Jones explained. "Until then, the army has to stay there." It was as if the Pakistanis had developed their own policy of clear, hold, build, and transfer.

There were obvious dangers from these kinds of reports: Obama's team might fall for their own wishful thinking, or try to oversell incremental changes to a skeptical public. "The president said recently that there might be a little more pessimism than is warranted. He thought that he was doing the right thing when he did his strategy review, but he's more confident now," said Axelrod as the Marja offensive began. "But like Vietnam, we have to be careful not to believe our own bullshit." The best way to guard against an overly sunny disposition was to recall what happened to their predecessors in Iraq. Each glimmer of good news was exaggerated into a turning point that proved transitory. "Our view is that the long-term success is more important than a short-term story," said Dan Pfeiffer. "There are going to be moments of success and moments of tragedy in any conflict like this, and we need to be very careful not to overplay the points of short-term success. When the long-term results of the last administration didn't match up to the short-term hype, it hurt them for many years."

If Obama kept some distance from the generals, he felt the need to get closer to the troops whose lives he was placing at risk. Like Bush, he was honored to be their commander in chief and felt inspired by their sense of service, their performance on the battlefield, and their spirit in the face of casualties. Unlike Bush, he wanted to see for himself the cost of war even as he was deciding to escalate. Midway through his Afghan review, Obama took a midnight trip to Dover Air Force Base in Delaware to see eighteen bodies return to the United States. They were the remains of fifteen soldiers and three drug enforcement agents who died two days earlier, in two separate incidents: one helicopter crash and one vehicle struck by an improvised bomb. He walked on board the cargo plane holding the caskets and took part in prayers over the remains. Then he joined other officials standing outside to salute the fallen as they were carried away.

His interest in the real experience of war was not new. Through the long presidential campaign he secretly arranged regular meetings with young Army and Marine Corps officers who had served in Afghanistan and Iraq. Out of public view, the roundtable sessions helped test Obama's thinking, and he never mentioned the meetings to the media. "They pushed back on him and he liked that. He liked hearing different sides of the debate," said an Obama foreign policy staffer. Sometimes the conversations revolved around his Iraq policy; at other times Obama wanted to hear more about counterinsurgency strategies. Obama's aides believed the candidate wanted to prepare himself early on about the culture and challenges of military life, in readiness for the responsibilities of commander in chief. He also wanted to hear what life was like on the front lines. An Obama foreign policy adviser who had served in

Afghanistan told how one of his soldiers had been killed in an ambush along the border, and Obama wanted to know what it felt like to lose one of his own men. "The hardest thing wasn't getting through the firefight," the adviser said. "Your training prepares you for that. But training doesn't prepare you for the grief and fear and weight of responsibility. Going back on patrol, walking the same ground, you needed resilience. After being hit like that, there are two ways a platoon can go as an organization. It can dissolve into finger-pointing or it can actually strengthen the organization."

Across the Potomac River from the White House, Obama marked Veterans Day at Arlington National Cemetery, less than two weeks after his trip to Dover Air Force Base. He delivered traditional remarks at the cemetery's memorial amphitheater, then he embarked on something untraditional. He took his motorcade to Section 60, where fresh graves mark the resting place of those who died in Iraq and Afghanistan. He and his wife walked among the headstones, speaking to families visiting at the same time. He stopped at the headstone of a Medal of Honor recipient, Specialist Ross A. McGinnis, and bent down to his grave to leave a presidential coin.

He returned to the White House Situation Room that day with a new determination to send more troops into Afghanistan quickly—and bring them home quickly, too. For a commander in chief who could be coldly analytical in policy discussions, the Afghan decision had become deeply personal. The way he translated that into action was not, in itself, emotional. But his focus on follow-through, his interest in process, was nonetheless an expression of keeping his commitment—just as much as praying over the caskets at Dover or walking among the headstones at Arlington. "I don't think you ever put the issue of troops' lives aside," he told me in the Oval Office as the Marja operation dragged on two months after its launch. "It haunts you every day. I'm getting daily reports of our casualties.

When I was in Afghanistan, I visited the hospital there and there were some young men who had been grievously injured. See, that never goes away. Having committed ourselves to a strategy, though, the best way I could serve those soldiers is to make sure that it's executed effectively."

There was a template for Obama's complex approach to Afghanistan, with its mix of military pressure, intense politics, and planned withdrawal. It lay at the heart of his presidential campaign, yet it was all too often ignored once the election was over. Throughout the election, Obama promised that he would give the military a new mission on the first day of his presidency: to end the war in Iraq. Sure enough, on his first full day in office he gathered his national security team, including his military leaders, to plan for what he called "a responsible military drawdown from Iraq." The result was three options: withdrawal of combat troops in sixteen months (with most risk), twenty-three months (with most flexibility), and nineteen months (something in between). One month later, at Camp Lejeune, he detailed the plans in a speech that promised the end of the combat mission in nineteen months, by the end of August 2010, reducing the number of troops from more than 140,000 to less than 50,000. The transitional force that remained would be gone by the end of 2011. A year after his inauguration, Obama had withdrawn enough troops to bring down the total to below 100,000 for the first time since the war began. Obama had been careful to allow himself enough wiggle room in the election to be flexible about the number of troops left behind. "He did an extraordinary job in the campaign of appearing dogmatic on Iraq while building in enough flexibility to govern—and we did that on purpose," said one of the Obama campaign's national security advisers.

The goal was the transfer of power and responsibility to Iraq's politicians: that the ethnic and sectarian factions should solve their disagreements through debates, arguments, and deal making rather than through militias and the cycles of revenge. That had long been the hope of the Bush administration, too, but the formal transfer of sovereignty in mid-2004 proved hopelessly premature and superficial. Almost five years later, Obama's view was that the Iraqis remained too reliant on the United States. "We were determined to take them seriously about restoration of sovereignty," said Tony Blinken, Biden's national security adviser. "We needed to cut the umbilical cord; otherwise you have a never-ending dependency. The fact is the Iraqis were becoming increasingly capable militarily, and their leaders were using the political process, not violence, to secure their interests."

The job of mentoring and overseeing the Iraqi transition was too great for Obama. Swamped with an economy in a deep recession and an Afghan war spiraling out of control, the president made a snap decision. Not long after his speech at Camp Lejeune, he was sitting in his daily security briefing when he turned to his vice president.

"Joe, I think it would be great if you would take this on. This needs to have sustained focus from the White House. You're the guy to do it. You've spent more time in Iraq than anyone. You know the players. You just do Iraq."

"Whoa, Mr. President," said Biden, taken aback. Biden liked the idea, both for the substance of the mission and for the recognition of his expertise. The rest of the national security team approved, and Biden agreed. "Sign me up," he said. In fact, Biden should not have been so surprised. Obama had sent him to Iraq and Afghanistan before the inauguration to get a baseline sense of the conditions in both countries. And Biden enjoyed extensive relationships with Iraq's politicians, especially Kurdish leaders, having led the Democrats on Senate trips for many years. It was in that capacity that he proposed a radical plan in mid-2006, as the civil war raged in Iraq, to turn the country into a loose federation with three autonomous regions under Kurdish, Sunni, and Shia control. Now he was tasked with helping to turn a more peaceful Iraq into a more tightly knit country.

At the start of 2010, Biden's attention was on the Iraqi elections in March. He had already carved out much of his weekly schedule for Iraq and was chairing the kind of strategy review that Obama had led on Afghanistan. The challenge was to intervene with the Iraqis behind the scenes, without making a public show of American interference. "It was important not to be overtly heavy-handed," said Tony Blinken, "but for us to weigh in quietly when it looked like things were going off the rails. Compare that to the much more blatant Iranian efforts. Iraqis don't want other countries to decide their future for them." Biden helped to convince the Kurds to abandon a referendum on their own constitution, including disputed boundaries, which could have destabilized the entire country. And he urged the ruling government to be careful to act openly and fairly in using laws designed to exclude the old Baathist party of Saddam Hussein.

The White House was in some ways the victim of Iraq's success. Turnout for the election was high, in spite of an uptick in violence, and the result was exceptionally close. Prime Minister Nouri al-Maliki, who expected to win outright, narrowly lost to the former prime minister, Ayad Allawi. The resulting mess—including fraud allegations—delayed the already complex process of forming a coalition government. Biden found himself in the middle of the negotiations and was ready to mediate between the rival parties as well as the Kurds. "I think they're very close to the kind of power-sharing arrangement that is needed," he told me in his West Wing office. "The message I've been delivering uniformly is that the government has to reflect the election." Biden held out some explicit incentives for the new government—as long as the Iraqis created one responsibly. The United States was ready with aid and expertise to help the new Baghdad administration succeed. There were Treasury officials ready to stay in Iraq to help set up a new budget process and prepare them for dealing with the International Monetary Fund. There were agricultural officials who could help them improve their farming industry. "They all understand they can get their ticket punched for their country if in fact we stay engaged as we draw down our forces," he said.

But it all rested on Biden's vision of power-sharing, which revolved around the two main jobs: the prime minister and the president. Biden believed the jobs could be split between the two largest rivals: with al-Maliki keeping his job as prime minister, and Allawi taking the job of president. Both jobs would need to be reconfigured slightly, with some power shifting from the prime minister to the president. But there was an added complication: since 2005, Iraq's president had been the Kurdish leader Jalal Talabani, and the Kurds needed concessions to their long-standing desire for autonomy to relinquish the position. That would mean a significant U.S. consulate in the Kurdish government center of Erbil, as well as a continued security presence—of American, Iraqi, and Kurdish troops—along the disputed boundaries of the Kurdish region. Biden's strength was his personality and his political longevity. He could connect with the Iraqi politicians as someone who had experienced the highs and lows of elected life, including the loss of the Democratic primaries to Barack Obama. "He can get on the phone and really engage them as someone who has been through elections and understands the political pressures on politicians themselves. He can talk to them in a way that military leaders and diplomats just can't get to," said Biden's chief of staff, Ron Klain. "Managing Iraq has largely been about managing this process of political reconciliation."

For Obama, who was so often accused of misleading voters or

betraying his election spirit, Iraq was a promise kept. And not just any old promise, but the biggest single factor driving his campaign for most of the first eighteen months: to end the war in Iraq, which he had opposed from the outset. In an Oval Office address marking the end of combat operations in Iraq at the end of August, Obama praised the troops and even President Bush. There was no sense of triumph or mission accomplished; only sacrifice, perseverance, and responsibility. The irony was that the people he relied on to end the war were two former Democratic rivals in the 2008 campaign—Biden and Hillary Clinton—and his predecessor's defense secretary, Robert Gates.

For many of Obama's most loyal campaign aides, Clinton and Gates represented something complex in their boss. The two cabinet secretaries were a betrayal of the campaign spirit to bring fundamental Change to Washington. At the same time, Obama claimed they represented a Lincoln-style, "Team of Rivals" approach to bridging differences in a hyperpartisan era.

Gates endeared himself to Obama's team early on, with a quiet, efficient, and practical demeanor that matched the president's. "He's Yoda," declared one cabinet official early on, referring to the diminutive Jedi master in the *Star Wars* movies. Gates seemed to share Obama's nonideological and highly pragmatic approach to foreign policy and national security, and their relationship was as close as a professional bond could be. "There's a lot of mutual respect," said Denis McDonough. "They are both very levelheaded and calm decision makers. They are busy and impatient to get things done. So it's a very businesslike relationship, in a good way, which means they have a lot of trust in each other's judgment and commitment to do what they say they will do." Obama had little contact with Gates before winning the election. As a senator on the Foreign Relations Committee, he had no reason to be close to the defense secretary. Their real contact began as the election drew to a close. But once inside the Obama cabinet, Gates thrived. "No one is more valued and trusted by the president on the national security team than Gates," said one campaign aide and current national security staffer. "The Afghan review went in the direction of Gates's position."

The relationship between Obama and Hillary Clinton was far more fraught. The two had barely concealed their disdain and bitterness for each other through the long primaries, and that sentiment lingered among their aides inside the administration. Obama's aides described a polite, deferential relationship where it was obvious who was following the leader. "She is certainly respectful and he is respectful of her. He was her biggest booster for the job, and his feeling was that we had an economic crisis and he needed a strong secretary of state to carry a big load. He believed that she could do it," said one Obama confidant. "But I think it's fair to say the president is the conceptual architect of his own foreign policy. He does that with the advice of those around him, and she is effectively executing it." Indeed, some aides believed their working relationship was itself helpful as a practical lesson in politics to other countries. "I think one of the great stories of the administration is that it's a great thing for the world to see two rivals join together the way they have," said one senior aide. "It's a great affirmation of our democracy."

Some of their own aides seemed to believe that the contest was still playing out. West Wing officials disliked dealing with Clinton's loyalists at the State Department, especially the former White House lawyer Cheryl Mills. Mills was known for her combative style and had proved difficult to negotiate with as the two campaigns came together once the primaries ended in mid-2008. Mills was now Clinton's chief of staff at the State Department, and there were several early disputes over the control and allegiances of key appointments, including ambassadors and assistant secretaries. "The relationship, especially with Cheryl Mills, is bad," said one senior Obama aide. "She behaved as if Obama is illegitimate. They think we're screwing them, when we're not, by having our own people over there." At the State Department, officials said the disputes had eased over time, as the debate moved from personnel to policy. "Cheryl vigorously represents the secretary of state in the inter-agency process," said one senior State Department official. "There were some tensions earlier but we are largely past that." Such tensions and suspicions seemed more like the remnants of 2008 than a harbinger of things to come, and Obama's senior staffers dismissed speculation about Clinton running for president again. "I don't think she will run for president," said one close Obama aide. "It takes a lot out of you. It's a brutal, brutal thing. Anyone who has been through it will not undertake it again lightly. By the time he's done, she's going to be almost seventy years old."

Still, there were some rare moments of warmth. The day after health care passed through the House, Clinton and Obama were in the Situation Room together for a national security meeting. Clinton smiled and threw her arms around him, before hugging others in the room. "I'm *so* happy," she said simply. Her former rival had managed to achieve what she failed to accomplish in her husband's White House. "It was a genuinely moving moment," said one observer in the room. "It was a great moment. I don't think it was obsequious. It was a genuine expression of her own feelings."

Obama could delegate entire regions and combat zones to his cabinet. But he also made personal choices to stay involved in the kind of foreign affairs that he had enjoyed as a candidate, senator, and student. During the doldrums of his presidential campaign, he asked for more private policy briefings with his foreign policy team to give him some respite from a political contest that had stalled. Now, as the politics of health care—and his presidency—were limping along, he devoted himself to some of the most arcane details of diplomacy. The tension between the two sides of his job, and his personality, was the cause of continuous disagreement inside the West Wing. Rahm Emanuel would regularly complain about the hours Obama would dedicate to international affairs at a time when his domestic agenda was in crisis. "Obama spends about half his time on foreign affairs, which drives Rahm crazy," said one senior national security aide in early 2010. The truth was that Obama wanted to spend more, not less, time on foreign policy, an ambition that sometimes drove his schedule to the breaking point.

By the time he approached the anniversary of his inauguration, Obama had been toiling for months on an agreement that returned to one of his first interests as a student at Columbia University: nuclear arms control. The arms treaty known as START was set to expire at the end of December 2009, and any replacement would be measured against at least two milestones in his brief presidency to date. First there was his speech in Prague in April, when he had pledged to seek peace and security without nuclear weapons. Then there was his Nobel Peace Prize, which he had accepted just three weeks before the START treaty deadline. Could he live up to those ideals, and would the Russians try to exploit those stated goals? By the spring of 2010, he was working toward three targets for his nuclear policy. In addition to the Russian treaty, Obama had ordered a rewriting of America's nuclear strategy to redefine when and how the country would develop and deploy its most devastating weapons. Moreover, Obama was planning to stage a nuclear conference of world leaders in April 2010, which would be the biggest such gathering on American soil since the creation of the United Nations in 1945.

Nuclear treaties had long been an opportunity for American presidents to take the measure of their Russian counterparts and demonstrate their negotiating and diplomatic skills. And while such talks were immeasurably more tense during the Cold War, Obama was starting his presidency at a low point for recent relations between Washington and Moscow. His predecessor had started off bonding with Vladimir Putin by looking into his eye and getting a sense of his soul. Bush and Putin agreed on the brief Moscow Treaty to limit their nuclear arsenals, but their relationship declined rapidly as the United States pushed ahead with its missile defense plans and Russia sought to extend its influence over former Soviet countries. Obama told his transition officials that he wanted to reset relations with Russia, and he wanted to avoid personalizing the diplomacy by analyzing the soul of Putin's successor, Dmitri Medvedev.

The original START treaty took nine years to negotiate. The process began under Reagan, and it was signed by President George H. W. Bush and Mikhail Gorbachev just months before the collapse of the Soviet Union. In contrast, Obama started negotiating the successor to START just eight months before it was due to expire. The last treaty with Putin was 3 pages long; Obama and Medvedev were working on an agreement that would run to 180 pages.

Besides the traditional disagreements over defense between two former enemies, there was a simple clash of strategy in the negotiations. "The Russians kind of figured out that we were in a hurry," said Michael McFaul, Obama's senior Russia adviser inside the White House. The Russians hated the inspections regime, which the Americans valued highly. "For the Russians, the old START was a terrible treaty. It was awful, because it was signed at a time of weakness for them. For us, it was a hurry to try to get the follow-on treaty agreed as soon as possible, because we didn't want the gap, especially in terms of inspections. They miscalculated. They thought they would just hold to their hard-line positions, because we're going to be in such a hurry to get this thing done—because Obama is Mr. Nuclear-Free World. And, by the way, the Nobel Prize did not help. They thought [the award] added another pressure on us to get it done, because there was some talk of signing it on the sidelines of that."

The pressure inside the White House was intense. Rahm Emanuel goaded the team to get a deal—as long as it was a good one. "Did you guys get the fucking treaty done yet?" he would ask. When the White House experts answered no, his reply captured the split personality of the moment. "Well, don't get too horny for a deal. But get the fucking treaty done."

Instead, the deadline lapsed, and the treaty expired. The real work began in Moscow on the day after the anniversary of Obama's inauguration. Two planeloads of U.S. military and civilian officials arrived to hammer out the details of the treaty, and the talks went so well that the team ended up celebrating with beers in the bar of the Ritz-Carlton hotel. They agreed to unique identifying numbers on all missiles, on a regime of inspections of nuclear weapons, on the number of launchers, and on telemetry for tracking missiles. James Jones called Obama on Air Force One to share the good news: the deal was done.

They should have known the deal would unravel. Their plane broke down as they tried to return to Washington. Then the Russian government went on its traditional, extended New Year break and halted all work on the treaty. Two weeks later, the Romanian president revealed that his country would take part in a new American missile defense system. In public, the White House welcomed the unplanned announcement, but in private the treaty negotiators were in trouble. The Russians used the news to reopen talks on limiting American plans for missile defense.

The parallels with Obama's domestic agenda were uncomfortably close. As with health care, the White House had been on the verge of a landmark achievement against all the odds—only to find the entire project reduced to rubble. The combination of both collapses placed unbearable pressures on the foreign policy team.

Obama was already negotiating in greater detail—about unique missile identifiers and telemetry to track missiles—than other presidents had done. That was partly because Medvedev needed to assert his authority in Moscow. But Obama's engagement was also the result of his fascination with the details of nuclear arms and treaties. He had made a personal commitment in Prague and was close to delivering on part of his vision. Yet the treaty seemed to be dying just when he was struggling to keep his domestic agenda alive. As Emanuel would often say at the time, they weren't landing any planes. The nuclear treaty was one more delayed flight circling ominously overhead. "It was very tense when we would walk into the suite yet again, needing an hour of the president's time to talk telemetry again," said McFaul. "Especially when they needed to talk health care."

Obama was impatient and overburdened. He had already phoned Medvedev in January to hail the nuclear deal agreed by their teams in Moscow. Now he had to call again and he was pissed. As McFaul walked into the Oval Office to prep him before he spoke to Medvedev, Obama was reading his briefing memo.

"I thought we were done with this, guys," he said.

The memo explained that he had to get tough with Medvedev and shut down the Russian efforts because the Russians believed the Americans were prepared to buckle. Russian pundits speculated that Obama was weak because of the defeat in Massachusetts and the apparent collapse of health care reform.

"Look, Dmitri," Obama said, "I can't do this. If you're going to continue to do this, we're not going to get a treaty."

The call with Medvedev did not end positively or negatively. It was unclear which way the Russians would go, and Obama's team was left uncertain about the outcome. Either the deal would be done in two weeks, or not for another year. "We were at a very pivotal moment," said McFaul.

Two weeks later, in mid-March—a week before the final House vote on health care—Medvedev called Obama and sounded upbeat about the unresolved items that separated them. After Obama put the phone down, he and his aides realized the finish line was in sight. "All right, the deal is sealed," said Obama. "That's it." Less than a month later, Obama traveled to Prague once again to sign the new START treaty with Medvedev. It was a year, almost to the day, since he promised to work toward a nuclear-free world.

Obama could not grasp everything he reached for on the world stage. As the health care debate reached its critical point, Obama was scheduled to travel with his family on formal state visits to Australia and Indonesia. It was the week after sealing the deal with Medvedev, and Obama was looking forward to returning to Indonesia, where he had spent part of his childhood and where he finished writing his memoir, *Dreams from My Father*. The anticipation in impoverished Indonesia, which claimed Obama as one of its own, was even greater. And the Australian prime minister, Kevin Rudd, was planning to spend quality time with the Obamas, including at a family barbecue at his residence. For Obama, the trip was personally and diplomatically important. The two countries were important Asian allies, and his family was looking forward to a trip that coincided with his daughters' spring break. With the girls along for the journey, the pace would be more relaxed than his usual breakneck schedule, and there would be time to explore the cultural side of the host countries.

But the trip also clashed with the final push for votes in the House to pass health care reform, leaving Obama and his inner circle with a fraught decision. The president wanted to do both: to secure the votes for health care and stick to his international schedule. As the vote neared, his team debated whether or not his departure would serve as a deadline to concentrate the minds of congressional Democrats. They scaled back his trip, but the extra days in Washington were not enough. As the White House made its final preparations, the House plans pointed toward a final vote on the day of Obama's departure.

These were no ordinary preparations. When the White House travels, it deploys several huge C-17 transport planes to carry motorcade vehicles, including the president's armored limousines. Marine One, the president's helicopter, and its backups are dismantled and placed on board, to be reassembled on the other side. By midweek before the planned departure—and the House vote—a team of eighty volunteers was already in place in both countries to handle preparations on the ground.

For Alyssa Mastromonaco, Obama's scheduler, the trip looked like a disaster. The C-17s would need to be pulled over from the wars in Iraq and Afghanistan. Transporting the cars and helicopters would cost millions of dollars. As the week before the trip passed by without a final decision, she was faced with a bill for $100,000 just to lock down the venue for Obama's speech in Jakarta, where security was set to bring gridlock to the Indonesian capital.

Obama had an unpleasant choice. Canceling the trip meant offending allies; going on the trip meant jeopardizing health care and his party's fate. "What if someone were coming to visit us?" asked Mastromonaco, as she forced the president's inner circle to realize what the delays meant. A later cancellation would simply waste more money and annoy more allies overseas. "This is too much. These are real relationships and this is real money. We can't spend this kind of money if there's a good chance we can't go." During the campaign she had been careful not to waste cash, and she saw no reason to stop now, even though the White House congressional team believed they might have health care finished by the weekend.

The White House finally canceled the trip just three days before Obama's scheduled departure, on the day of his final rally for health care reform, as the undecided House votes on health care started to fall into place.

Determination and endurance might help to revive a president's fortunes at home, but overseas those qualities were insufficient. That was especially true in the Middle East, where the White House was dealing with allies as well as hostile forces. Israel triggered more anguish than any other alliance for Obama and his inner circle. More than all the frustrations and reversals with Moscow, more than the protracted and delicate talks with Baghdad's politicians, the relationship with Jerusalem was an anxiety-ridden cycle of courtship and breakup. By his first anniversary inside the White House, Obama's interchange with the Israeli government was lukewarm at best and distrustful at worst.

In the beginning, the omens were not good. The Clinton campaign started raising questions in the primaries about Obama's commitment to Israel, and the doubts continued to spread through the general election. Joe Lieberman, perhaps the most prominent Jewish senator and a former Democrat, campaigned with his Republican friend John McCain and wondered out loud why Hamas supported Obama's candidacy. Lieberman attacked Obama's positions on Iran and Israel, despite Obama's professions of an unbreakable bond between Israel and the United States. There were anonymous e-mails claiming to prove that he was a Muslim who went to a madrassa in Indonesia. And there was the inconvenient fact that his given names were Barack and Hussein, reflecting his paternal grandfather's conversion to Islam. It made no difference that Obama had never known his grandfather and barely knew his father, who was apparently an atheist. It made no difference that he condemned Hamas, was a practicing Christian, and had never attended a madrassa. It made no difference that his chief of staff was the son of an Israeli-born father, went to summer camp in Israel, and volunteered as a civilian engineer for the Israeli Defense Force during the Gulf War. In his first run for Congress in 2000, Obama was distrusted by African Americans for being too close to the Jewish liberal elite of Chicago. Eight years later, as he ran for president, he was distrusted by Jewish and Israeli conservatives for being too close to pro-Palestinian liberals, African American anti-Semites, and Muslim relatives he barely knew.

Obama entered the Oval Office determined to make progress on a peace process between the Israelis and Palestinians, after the collapse of the last process during the Bush years. But the facts on the ground were little short of disastrous. Israel finished its military campaign in Gaza just two days before Obama's inauguration. Two months later, Benjamin Netanyahu became prime minister, leading a Likud party and coalition that opposed surrendering territory to the Palestinians. The Palestinian territories were divided physically and politically between a West Bank under the control of the Fatah-led Palestinian Authority, and Gaza under the control of the terrorist movement Hamas. With nothing worthy of the title of a peace process, Obama needed to build from the ground up. Bush's approach started with the Palestinians taking credible steps toward security. After the bloodshed and destruction in Gaza, Obama started by demanding the Israelis take credible steps to stop the growth of settlements, and ease economic restrictions in both Gaza and the West Bank.

By the one-year mark of his presidency, Obama and his aides admitted their approach had largely failed, even as the need for a solution had grown. The Israelis agreed to a ten-month freeze on settlements in the West Bank, but excluded Jerusalem. The move, while significant, was not enough for the Palestinians or their Arab neighbors. "The president's own words are that he's disappointed with where we ended up at the end of 2009," said James Jones. "We had high expectations—maybe too high—but we are clear-eyed about what we achieved and didn't achieve, and this is one where we felt we underachieved. But that doesn't mean that the problem is any less significant in 2010 than it was in 2009; in fact, to the contrary."

Israel's security and the stability of the region were now tied up with the advance of Iran's nuclear program. The Palestinian conflict was not just a moral and historic challenge; it was a stumbling block to a far greater existential threat to Israel and the Sunni Arab powers nearby. Even before Iran might become a declared nuclear power, it could try to destabilize the region through its proxies in Lebanon, Syria, or Yemen—especially as the United States was talking once again about the prospect of "crippling" sanctions against Tehran. "We now have in the region an emerging Iran reality that we're going to face in the next few months," Jones explained in the spring of 2010. "So it's not just about the Middle East peace process now. It's about the whole stability of the region and the threat of a nuclear arms race in the Persian Gulf—proliferation and the threat of a nuclear-armed Iran and what that means."

Obama had fulfilled his campaign vision by reaching out to the Muslim world in Cairo and extending an offer of talks to Iran's leaders. But the Israelis felt slighted by the Cairo speech, and Iran continued to develop its nuclear program. Obama's aides found themselves making the complex argument that their approach to Iran was more successful than Bush's belligerent rhetoric, because their outreach had helped unify world opinion behind tougher sanctions. Still, the results were not encouraging, and they started their second year in office with a scaled-back approach to the peace process. Instead of pursuing direct talks, they had spent months setting the stage for indirect proximity talks through Obama's Middle East special envoy George Mitchell, the former senator and mediator of the peace talks in Northern Ireland. Those indirect talks would be a first step toward reviving the peace process, but they would not be enough.

Inside the West Wing in January, Obama's national security team knew they had to improve their own position with the Israeli government. Mitchell was on the cusp of announcing four months of proximity talks between the two sides. But the Israelis lacked confidence in Obama's approach. Vice President Joe Biden, among others, believed they needed to hear directly from the administration. "Things got off to a little shaky start. I had been urging that we had to engage the Israelis in Israel," said Biden. "I wasn't alone. I may have been the first or one of the initial people to raise it, but it was the general consensus. Things were sort of getting cattywamped." Biden himself was tapped to go to Israel, not least because he had known "Bibi" Netanyahu since his days at the Israeli embassy in Washington in the early 1980s. The Israelis saw Biden as the most pro-Israel senior official inside the West Wing, making him a natural choice to straighten them out.

Biden had a relatively simple goal as he traveled to Israel in early March: to reaffirm the unique relationship with Israel and to boost prospects for the proximity talks, which were announced the day before he arrived. Biden had just toured the Yad Vashem Holocaust museum and was returning to his hotel when his aides' Black-Berrys started to buzz. His national security adviser, Tony Blinken, showed him his e-mail: the interior ministry had just announced it was moving ahead with approval for 1,600 new housing units in

East Jerusalem. The proximity talks, along with Biden's visit, were in jeopardy before they had a chance to begin.

The news was perplexing to Biden. Earlier in the day, he had held a press conference with Netanyahu, who had praised the Obama administration for its exceptional support for Israel's security. The Bidens were even scheduled to have dinner with the Netanyahus at the prime minister's residence that evening. "I believed from the beginning that it was not a crisis of Bibi's making," said Biden. "That was my overwhelming instinct. There was no rationale to do this. It just made no sense for it to happen."

Back in Biden's hotel suite at the luxury David Citadel hotel in Jerusalem, his aides established the facts and set about deciding what to do next. Dinner would go ahead as planned. But they needed to issue a statement as soon as possible. They sat around a laptop in Biden's suite drafting the words that would convey enough formal disapproval to give the Palestinians some political cover to stick with the new talks. They made an intensive series of phone calls to George Mitchell and deputy national security adviser Tom Donilon, as well as to Biden's chief of staff, Ron Klain, and Rahm Emanuel. The collective conclusion: to issue an unprecedented condemnation of Israel while on Israeli soil.

After spending the day affirming the unshakable bond with Israel, Biden ended the day condemning America's closest ally in the region. Biden called Netanyahu to tell him about the statement.

"Is this already out?" asked Netanyahu. "Can we negotiate?"

"No, this is it," said Biden. The statement was already out, and he was now late for their dinner by ninety minutes.

When the Bidens finally showed up, Netanyahu apologized profusely for the settlement news. "You don't owe me an apology," said Biden, who brushed aside the notion that he was snubbed by the announcement. "But you've got to clarify this, man. You've got to get this done," he said. Biden suggested that the prime minister put out his own statement, explaining that Netanyahu had only just learned of the news himself.

The statements were not enough to revive the talks. As Biden met with the Palestinian leaders the next day, it was clear they needed more political cover. By the end of the week, Hillary Clinton was calling Netanyahu to repeat the condemnation and urging him to demonstrate his commitment to the peace process. But as they attempted to help the Palestinians, Obama's aides found they were exposing themselves to accusations of being too tough on the Israelis. Clinton's strong suggestions became demands and ultimatums, as they were filtered through news reports and conservative critics. "That isn't what we intended at all," said one senior White House official. "It created a reaction from the community here and some Israelis who were interested in making more of a crisis than existed, and things spiraled down."

Obama had increased U.S. military cooperation with Israel over and above Bush's close ties. He sided with Israel in condemning the UN's Goldstone Report, which accused the Israelis and some Palestinians of war crimes in the Gaza conflict. But it would take more time to repair the damage from their first year's approach to the Israeli-Palestinian conflict. "I think we raised the bar too high on Netanyahu," said one of Obama's senior national security aides. "We asked him to do things he couldn't possibly do, and ironically the Palestinians weren't even asking for a total settlement freeze. We created the dynamic where we raised the bar so high, the Palestinians couldn't lower it: 'The U.S. has demanded it; how can we expect anything less?' In retrospect, that wasn't the best way to proceed." Instead of reviving the peace process, Obama's team started its second year struggling to keep any kind of process alive.

Biden's trip exposed how little control Netanyahu had over his own government, especially in a coalition with parties that vehemently opposed any kind of peace process. It would take another crisis—this one largely of Israel's making—to shift the dynamic two months later. On May 31, Israeli commandos killed nine activists on a Turkish flotilla trying to break the blockade of the Palestinians in Gaza. The ensuing international condemnation led Israel to ease the blockade as it sought to repair relations with Turkey, its biggest regional ally. Biden continued to stay in close contact with Netanyahu and believed the prime minister was in a position to move forward with talks. "I think that Bibi's hand is strengthened quite frankly now in his own coalition," Biden said. "I can assure you that Bibi is ready for direct talks. For practical reasons, political necessity, and long-term Israeli security, he has reached the point where he's ready to pull the trigger, if there's a deal that can be made." That would mean a realignment in Israeli politics. For Netanyahu to pull the trigger, he would need to include some of his right-of-center rivals from the Kadima party in his cabinet to replace the support he would surely lose from the ultra-Orthodox and nationalist parties. "In order to ultimately make a deal, it's probable he will have to broaden his government," Biden said.

Sitting in the Oval Office, Obama dismissed the talk about a permanent rift between Washington and Jerusalem. "I've always considered this an argument among friends," he told me. "I don't think we were all that hard on the follow-up. If you think about it, we have been adamant about maintaining all the bilateral elements of our relationship that are needed to preserve Israel's security. I've said repeatedly that Israel's security is sacrosanct."

Obama preferred to see the struggling peace process as a challenge of mutual understanding, as if the dispute could only be solved with empathy—not just borders, security, and settlements. "What I think happened was that there's just been a legitimate difference of opinion in terms of how to approach the peace process," he explained. "I think the view of the Netanyahu government is that the settlement issue is tangential to those discussions. And what we've been trying to suggest is that from the perspective of the Palestinians and the Arab states, they're central. And if negotiations are going to move forward, then each side has to take into account the other side's concerns and sensitivities. The Arab states and the Palestinians have to take into account Israel's legitimate concerns about security, and not dismiss those."

Direct talks began in Washington in September, with the support of Egypt and Jordan. But the White House had very low expectations of a breakthrough any time soon. While both sides seemed cordial in the talks, Obama's hopes for sensitivity seemed a long way from becoming real.

The day after Biden's so-called snub in Israel—and the apparent collapse of any hopes for peace—the White House staged a celebration of an extraordinary revival. On a warm, sunny afternoon in mid-March, Obama's staffers arranged two sets of flags behind two podiums in the Rose Garden. Chairs surrounded three sides of the stage, close to the bulbs that were just beginning to show through the flower beds. It was almost two months since the devastation of the earthquake in Haiti, and Obama wanted to thank the people, including his own staff, who had volunteered to help.

In the depths of his own far less dire crisis—with health care still out of reach, a struggling economy, and a toxic political atmosphere—Obama also wanted to revive his team and the nation. "The president asked us specifically to find an opportunity for an event where we could bring together all of the people who worked on this," said Ben Rhodes. "His view is that at a time of so much negativity, here's something where everyone did something really good. He wanted to lift it up and not be forgotten." So Obama welcomed President René Préval of Haiti to the White House, along with dozens of rescue workers, military personnel, charity groups, and elected officials who had scrambled to help after the earthquake. He had chaired a meeting in the Situation Room a day earlier, where his national security team debated a PowerPoint presentation by Clinton's State Department officials titled "From Natural Disaster to Economic Opportunity." As priorities for recovery, it identified jobs growth and an end to politics as usual in Haiti. Even in the face of a catastrophe and a painfully slow recovery, Obama's team did not lack ambition.

For now, he wanted to remind his fellow Americans of the scale of the tragedy, and the scale of their response. "It's as if the United States, in a terrible instant, lost nearly 8 million people; or it's as if one-third of our country—100 million Americans—suddenly had no home, no food, or water. That gives you a sense of, relative to the populations, what has happened in Haiti. No nation could respond to such a catastrophe alone. It would require a global response. And that's exactly what we have seen these past two months."

Then he praised his own government officials: "our heroic embassy staff" and "our disaster response teams," "our military personnel" and "our search and rescue teams." And especially "all our men and women in uniform . . . our remarkable soldiers, sailors, airmen, Marines and Coast Guardsmen." He celebrated their work opening airports, pulling people out of the rubble, treating casualties, and distributing food, water, and medicine. And he praised the American people for donating so much money at a time of such economic distress back home. In the first week after the earthquake, the Text Haiti campaign raised a record $24 million for the Red Cross rescue efforts.

But above all, Obama celebrated the spirit of the survivors themselves. The spirit of a people who could endure the worst and carry on; who could struggle through grief to rebuild their lives; who could inspire the world with their story of revival. "In the face of devastation that shocked the world, the people of Haiti responded with resolve and faith that inspired the world—in song and in prayer, and in the determination to carry on," he explained, as he turned to the president standing next to him. "As you declared during last month's national day of mourning, it is time to wipe away the tears; it is time for Haiti to rebuild."

It wasn't historic legislation or an election victory. It was barely the beginning for an impoverished and devastated neighbor. But it was a confident statement from a new president who was in the midst of rebuilding his own edifice. Haiti was not Katrina; Afghanistan was not Vietnam; and Obamacare was not Hillarycare. The political cycle of disaster and recovery would surely return, as it had so many times during the long presidential election. Obama had now served as president for fourteen months, which was still only two-thirds of the time he spent campaigning for the job. He was already a war president utterly unlike George W. Bush and a health care president utterly unlike Bill Clinton. He aspired to have the impact of a Reagan and avoid the fate of a Carter. He wound down a war like a Nixon but hoped to inspire like a Kennedy. There would be many cruel months ahead, but he had stumbled his way through the wasteland. This was the season of his revival.

SIX

DEADLOCK

itting in a dimly lit pub, picking at a plate of half-cooked fries, David Axelrod was splitting his attention between the NBA finals on the flat screen over his shoulder and a baseball game streaming on his brand-new iPad. Axelrod's love of the perennially doomed Chicago Cubs was a daily distraction, but it seemed to have little bearing on the fate of his candidates or his ability to track a conversation. During one of the prep sessions for Obama's presidential debates against John McCain, Axelrod was watching a game on his laptop but forgot to turn the sound off. When the Cubs hit a home run, the announcer started shouting, the fans went wild, and the candidate wondered what the hell was going on in the darkened room. In his rush to turn the sound off, Axelrod slammed the laptop shut and knocked it to the floor. The candidate and the laptop survived.

As he half-watched another ballgame by the Lovable Losers almost two years later, Axelrod was resigned to defeat—and not just in baseball. It was four months before the midterm congressional elections, and the White House was publicly insisting that they had a viable strategy to maintain control of Congress: the economy was improving, health care was done, financial reform was on the way. Democrats had a positive agenda of change; Republicans had a negative agenda to block change. But in private Axelrod's mood was like the droopy, pale fries on his plate. "We have people in office now whose elections were completely improbable," he reasoned. "They got dragged in by a high tide. And now the tide is going out, and a bunch of folks are going to get washed up on the beach."

The losing members of Congress were not the only ones who would get punished. Axelrod knew that the White House, especially its political and communications operation, would take much of the blame—even as they tried to mitigate the damage. "I am sobered by the knowledge that until there's real improvement in the economy that people can feel, until jobs are growing and home prices are rising, and people feel a greater sense of security, we're the governing party and we're going to bear some of the brunt of that. I think structurally we're set up for a difficult election. It's axiomatic," he said. That suggested there was little they could do to affect the overall trend of the midterms as long as unemployment remained high. However, Axelrod believed they could still help at the margins. "I think we can affect this to some degree through the messaging that we do, through the campaigning that we do," he said hopefully. "I believe there are some districts where we can go in and through hand-to-hand combat we can save those seats, and that has to be our goal."

Inside the White House, the blame game was well under way, no matter what the results in November. Axelrod's fellow aides were feeling the political pressure of the midterm elections, and they were more than ready to point fingers at the political and communications teams. "It's mismanagement, that's what it is," said one senior White House official. "None of the people at the top have ever run *anything*. They need to fire people. In politics and in communications, this White House has been terrible. The irony is that in terms of substance, we have achieved a huge amount, a historic amount. But in terms of the politics, it's been a disaster." Two months before the midterms, Change was already coming to the White House. Emanuel quit in order to run for mayor of Chicago; David Plouffe was preparing to join the West Wing full-time; and Axelrod was looking forward to leaving Washington.

Some believed the political team was too focused on independent voters, who had been drifting away from Obama and back to the Republican Party that was their first home since the first months of his presidency. Instead, those aides believed they needed to tend to the old base of the party—not the liberal antiwar activists, but the old Democrats of the Rust Belt. "We're losing the Democratic blue-collar, non-college-educated white male voter," said another senior aide. "It's because of jobs and the economy. It's the people who voted for Hillary in the primary in Pennsylvania, and for us over McCain in the general election, because of jobs. They're harder to get back. There's been all this focus on independents, and that's important. But if we don't get the base back, the independents aren't going to deliver for us."

Some pundits speculated that Obama would be happy to govern with a Republican-controlled Congress. It would serve as a foil, allowing him to position himself as the moderate, bipartisan figure he had campaigned as in 2008. That sounded like fantasy to Obama's senior aides. The prospect of working with a Republican House (none of them believed they would lose the Senate) was awful. "I think it's disastrous and that's what we have to stop," said one senior aide concerned about a wave of subpoenas and investigations similar to the Clintons' experience in the 1990s. "Obama is worried about the election, especially that unemployment isn't coming down substantially. But by 2012, we'll be fine, barring something unforeseen." In the meantime, the notion of working with the GOP was growing ever more distant. Rahm Emanuel believed that Republicans had morphed into a party of extremists, with no mature leader to deal with. "This is a different breed of Republicans. Show me the Bob Dole leader of this generation," he told me. "My point to every CEO who asks for bipartisanship is I say, 'Okay, do you know that Ronald Reagan could not be nominated by today's Republican Party? He would be seen as too liberal. He raised taxes as governor of California and signed a no-fault divorce policy. Ronald Reagan as a governor could not be nominated today to lead the ticket.' Their icon. This is a different Republican Party from ten years ago, fifteen years ago, twenty years ago, or thirty years ago. Who is the George Herbert Walker Bush of this contemporary Republican Party?"

What Obama's aides relished was not the GOP in power but an opposition locked in the same obstructionist posture. "If we beat expectations in terms of losses—if we're down to fifty-four in the Senate and in the House we lose twenty-five, instead of worse—I don't know if they can sustain another two years of blocking everything and slowing things down."

The tensions and finger-pointing—which were far less visible through the presidential campaign of 2008—were worsened by at least two challenges in addition to the struggling economy. Both were intractable stories that were only distantly under the president's influence, but both were directly capable of inflicting political damage.

One was BP's gushing oil well far below the seafloor of the Gulf of Mexico. Soon after the Deepwater Horizon oil rig exploded and sank in mid-April, Obama and his inner circle knew they were probably facing an unprecedented environmental disaster. Carol Browner, director of the White House Office of Energy and Climate Change Policy, warned Obama in late April that capping a well at such depths had never been done before. They ought to expect an oil spill that would continue until the drilling of a relief well was completed in August. From the beginning, Obama's senior team approached the spill with a sense of fatalism that stemmed in part from the initially bleak prognosis. After two months of failed attempts to cap the well, and up to sixty thousand barrels of oil gushing into the Gulf each day, Obama faced intense pressure—from his own Democrats as well as from elected officials in the Gulf—to look like he was taking charge. The Oval Office address that followed was the first of his presidency, and it earned poor reviews from the pundits. But when he met face-to-face with BP's executives at the White House the next day, and the company agreed to a $20 billion compensation fund, Obama's aides believed they had effectively capped their own gusher. "There's a view internally that we didn't demonstrate he was involved and on top of all of this early enough," said one long-standing aide. "Even something as relatively minor as never meeting with [BP CEO] Tony Hayward raised the suggestion that he wasn't really interested or involved." Other senior aides believed their mistake lay in appearing to take too much responsibility, not too little, for the disaster. "Here's where I think we made a mistake," said one senior Obama official. "They owned the rig. We owned the recovery. By saying the buck stops with me, all of a sudden you co-opted the rig. And we shouldn't have done that. But that's in retrospect and that's a messaging issue. It took us a while to get BP to get their act together. Nobody had had this happen before. In the United States, there had not been a major well blowout in deep water."

Besides looking engaged or sounding tough, there was one new approach largely overlooked by the media that the White House valued above all others—at least until the well was sealed in early August. The $20 billion commitment would fund not just short-term compensation for Gulf businesses but also the long-term recovery of a region still struggling to rebuild after Hurricane Katrina in 2005. "That was a big turning point," said another senior aide. "What's going to make or break it is how we do recovery and restoration. That's something arguably we're responsible for. If you can get the money out of BP, we can actually do something. We didn't have the money to deal with the post-Katrina situation, but here's the one chance to hopefully do it right."

For BP, the encounter at the White House was not as confrontational as Obama's aides suggested. The session began with the president recounting his trips to the Gulf and the stories of suffering and destruction that he heard and saw. BP chairman Carl-Henric Svanberg assured Obama that the company was committed to meeting its obligations and would not attempt to dodge its responsibilities. Obama wanted BP's assurance that small businesses would not be shortchanged, and the executives agreed. They even said they would improve the claims process so that small businesses could obtain compensation ahead of losses rather than afterward. Obama left the executives to work on the details of the $20 billion fund for the next three and a half hours with Browner and White House counsel Bob Bauer. BP's priority was to end the uncertainty that threatened to destroy the company's share price. Just a week earlier, stock market rumors of a BP bankruptcy had pushed its shares down to around half their value before the blowout. "What BP needed to have was support and statements that the United States wanted BP to be a viable, successful company to meet its commitments and emerge down the road a stronger company," said Bob Dudley, who would later replace Hayward as BP's CEO. The executives left the West Wing satisfied they had found agreement with the White House and could reassure BP's partners and investors that it would survive. But their satisfaction was short-lived. On the driveway outside the West Wing lobby, the Swedish-born Svanberg described Obama's focus of interest—the small businesses—as "the small people." Dudley insisted the phrase was a mistranslation: "He gave a heartfelt speech to a large gathering of reporters outside the White House and he meant to say small businesses. He didn't even realize he said it. Unfortunately English isn't his language."

In many ways Obama was helped by such trip-ups. No matter how much he was struggling with events out of his control, the gaffes of others always made him look more in charge.

However, looking back, after the well was capped and the oil flow ceased, Obama's aides blamed the blowout in large part for halting their momentum after health care. "History will be different than the contemporary writing," said Rahm Emanuel, sitting on his West Wing patio in midsummer. "The history will be that it was actually a successful federal response. It was the private sector response that was inadequate." Still, the gusher had a lasting political impact. "On March 23, the president signs his health care bill," said Emanuel. "In April, there's a very good jobs number, 100,000 north of expectations. And then all of a sudden we got hit by the G-force. Greece became upended; Europe went into economic turmoil. And we got hit by the problems in the Gulf."

Obama needed to look in control overseas as well as at home. Even after the exhaustive strategy review of late 2009, Afghanistan was adrift—caught between the delays in deploying more troops and the continued momentum of the insurgents. Obama's position was essentially wait-and-see, and he had little to show to the American people in terms of progress on the ground. So when Stanley McChrystal, the commander of U.S. forces in Afghanistan, unwisely cooperated with a *Rolling Stone* profile, the president could rapidly assert himself as commander in chief in ways not readily available to him on the battlefield. McChrystal was described mocking the vice president, disdaining a French cabinet minister, and trashing the U.S. ambassador in Kabul. McChrystal's aides dismissed the president as intimidated by the military and blew off Obama's special envoy to Afghanistan and Pakistan.

The reaction inside the West Wing was clear. "He had to go. There wasn't any choice," said Biden. "I was the most absolutist about that from the front end. And the reason is, it wasn't about McChrystal. I literally spoke to six four-stars. I said, 'Guys, cut through all the bullshit; what is the deal here? Can you have unity of command if this thing goes?' And the answer was 'No. Period.'" Others inside Obama's inner circle were astonished at the article's suggestion that the president was unready for his first meeting with McChrystal. "The one thing Obama never looks is unsure," said one senior aide. "Lack of confidence isn't his deal." Like the rest of Obama's senior aides, defense secretary Robert Gates was conflicted. He preferred to keep McChrystal in place to maintain the new Afghan strategy. Some senior Pentagon officials believed McChrystal was the victim of his opponents in the White House (such as Biden) who lost the debate about sending more troops to Afghanistan. But Gates soon embraced Obama and Biden's idea of replacing him with David Petraeus, McChrystal's boss and the architect of the counterinsurgency strategy. It was a perfect solution that both won immediate Republican support and underscored Obama's authority as commander in chief. "He turned it around and maintained civilian control," the senior aide said. "He turned it into a sort of character moment and passed the test."

Dealing with McChrystal would be a lot easier than dealing with Afghanistan, where the Marja offensive had stalled and the early promise of the new strategy seemed to be fading away. The bigger effort to take control of Kandahar, the spiritual home of the Taliban, was further delayed. McChrystal had stated from the outset that he would install "a government in a box"—consisting of local Afghan officials—as soon as his forces cleared the way. But several months later, the box was only partly open. Many of the stalls in the Marja bazaar returned, but the only baker fled when his son was kidnapped. The Afghan government representatives emerged from their box but preferred to spend their time twenty miles away in the provincial capital of Lashkar Gah. Obama and his inner circle did not seem surprised by the slow progress of a strategy that was designed to move quickly before the planned drawdown of troops began in 2011. When asked how he thought the operation in Marja had progressed, Joe Biden said, "To be blunt with you, exactly like I thought it would. And like the president thought it would." He explained that the full surge of troops and trainers had not yet materialized: "Neither the president nor I ever wondered about our ability to clear and hold. The question was: Could we build and transfer? And Marja is a tough case, as is Kandahar—a bigger tough case. I think there's a tendency on the part of warriors—the thing that makes them great warriors is their confidence in success. Remember McChrystal saying there was going to be government in a box? Well, we didn't see any box."

Biden believed a box would ultimately turn up, and he was not ready to dismiss the strategy or to say that it had run out of time. "It doesn't mean it won't happen. It just means it's in progress," he explained. "I think the time does exist. Here's the deal. To use the phrase the military kept using . . . we've been there a long time and proof of concept is not going to take forever. And so I think that by December—the date they picked, not the president—we're going to have a pretty clear idea whether this concept of counterinsurgency with a strong dose of counterterrorism is working, is going to work."

Standing in the Map Room, where FDR followed the course of World War II, President Obama was getting ready to meet the press in late July with the new British prime minister, David Cameron. Two years earlier, they had met and chatted warmly when both were merely candidates for high office, during Obama's foreign trip in the middle of the presidential campaign. Cameron was a conservative and a son of Eton, the most aristocratic of Britain's private schools; Obama was a liberal and a son of Hawaii. Yet Cameron's election borrowed some of Obama's presidential themes, and Obama admired Cameron's energy and style. For all their ideological and personal differences, they agreed on the new Afghan strategy, as well as on BP's duty to pay its full share of the cleanup. And they spoke freely to one another. "I like [Cameron's] style. He's not nearly as circumspect about how he wants to talk," said Biden. "He's pretty direct. It was interesting to watch him and Barack. Barack was more direct with him as well. I felt good about it."

As the two leaders prepped for their joint press conference inside the Executive Mansion, they felt good enough about their new bond that they indulged in something rare for Obama: small talk.

"Do you have an iPad?" ventured Cameron.

"No," deadpanned Obama. "I have an iReggie."

There were perks to being president, and having a body man like Reggie Love attend to his every need ranked near the top—whether Reggie was shooting hoops with the boss, keeping well-wishers at a reasonable distance, or carrying his bags. Obama's Chicago friends marveled at the gilded nature of the cage he lived in. "You're living in a bubble," said Marty Nesbitt, as he looked around the White House movie theater. "But your bubble has some nice stuff in it."

But the bubble offered only temporary shelter, and even served to increase the distance from the political realities outside. Cameron was a fiscal hawk who made a virtue out of his sweeping plans for spending cuts; Obama still believed in the power of stimulus spending, while his own fiscal commission struggled to find common ground between Republicans and Democrats. The two leaders diplomatically agreed to disagree, citing differences between the sizes of their economies. Still, Obama's aides believed there were signs that the politics of spending was shifting in Washington. Claire McCaskill, the Missouri Democratic senator who was an early endorser of the Obama campaign, joined forces with Jeff Sessions, the conservative Alabama Republican, to push for spending caps. "It's a problem but it also reflects where Congress is going," said one senior Obama aide. "We have got to deal with this, but Democrats never want to deal with spending in an election year, so you have to do it early."

There was a clear tension between Obama's attempt to both spend money on the short-term stimulus and cut spending for the long-term deficit. "Short-term, you gotta do what you gotta do," said Rahm Emanuel. "Medium- to long-term, we've got to address the fiscal health of the country that was also one of the legacies of the Bush gift bag. In the gift bag from George W. Bush and his team was an automobile industry that was on its back, a country that had almost doubled the national debt on his watch, an economy that was now experiencing the deepest recession in history since the Great Depression, and a financial system that was in its worst contraction in more than fifty years. That is exactly the gift bag that was left."

No matter how he felt about the presents from his predecessor, at some point Obama had to switch from spending to cutting. The question of the timing and seriousness of that switch caused friction with Peter Orszag, his budget director, who left the administration three months before the midterms. But that was not Orszag's only reason for leaving: he had clashed too many times with Larry Summers, Obama's chief economic adviser, and was burned out. "He was worried about deficits and felt we weren't pushing hard enough. He wasn't getting his way on deficits as much as he would like and was a little bit concerned that would tarnish his reputation," said a senior White House official. "But more importantly, he and Larry weren't talking anymore. Plus he's tired and getting married. And he was just worn down . . . by both the nature of the job and the internal dynamic. The tough thing about Larry is that he's hard to fight with because he doesn't even know he's fighting." Orszag's replacement was Jack Lew, a budget office veteran from the Clinton years who had balanced the budget in the late 1990s and earlier worked on the reform of Social Security. West Wing staffers believed that Lew was the seed of a new economics team that would surely work more smoothly than the original group. Less than a month later, Christina Romer announced that she too would quit. Six weeks later, Summers also quit, completing an overhaul of Obama's White House economic team. Obama's closest aides, who had wanted to push Summers out for several months, said he was still bitter that he had been passed over for the job of chairman of the Federal Reserve.

Instead of fading away, the politics of the stimulus were about to become more interesting. Many of the biggest Recovery Act projects were only beginning in the summer before the midterm elections, and the spending would continue through to the spring of 2011, just as the Republican presidential candidates were lining up for the start of their race. "The act was designed to make sure—to use a phrase of one of the economists round here—we didn't hit an air pocket," said Biden in midsummer. "The signature programs are just kicking in now. So people are actually seeing stimulative impact. There's another $300 billion . . . going . . . into the economy between now and April." One of the biggest beneficiaries of that cash: the governors whose states would be shedding jobs without federal assistance. Among them were at least two GOP presidential hopefuls: Haley Barbour of Mississippi and Bobby Jindal of Louisiana. The hypocrisy of some Republican officials never ceased to surprise and amuse several senior Obama aides. "You have . . . Republican governors who repeatedly and profusely thank me," said Biden. "Everybody profusely thanks me, from Haley Barbour to even Jindal. Yet at home in their states, no one there is talking about the reason why you have over 300,000 teachers in the classroom, [who] wouldn't have been there otherwise, is because of Barack Obama's Recovery Act."

Reviving the economy was not enough for Obama, no matter how tough it was to lower unemployment. His ambition was to move ahead with big legislation on two pieces of unfinished business: energy and immigration. That drive to do more—after the Recovery Act, health care reform, and financial regulation—was the cause of a new round of battles between the Revivalists and the Survivalists. "He believes immigration reform is the right thing to do as a matter of policy, both economically and in terms of making the border safer," said one senior Obama aide. "He actually believes it's like health care reform. He thinks it's important not just because it's a moral issue but practically he sees the situation as untenable. But Rahm is adamantly opposed to it. He calls it political malfeasance. He thinks it's too volatile and runs the risk of losing seats in the Southwest, and that we ought to just focus on the border." For his part, Emanuel saw his position as being far more realistic about the politics of immigration. "I'm the son of an immigrant and the grandson of an immigrant. I believe you need to have a comprehensive immigration policy," he explained.

The dispute simmered as Obama prepared to deliver a speech at

American University in Washington on July 1. His aides had framed the immigration debate as a matter of personal responsibility, but Obama saw the issue in broader terms. "I don't like this," he said of the draft speech, before staying up until 4:30 in the morning to rewrite the speech the night before the event.

The dispute was all the more emotional because American University held a special place in Obama's campaign memory. Obama had last spoken there at a dramatic turning point in his presidential campaign, when Ted Kennedy, along with Caroline and Patrick Kennedy, endorsed him early in the primaries. For many inside and outside the campaign, it was a symbolic moment of the torch passing from the Kennedys to a new generation. Ted Kennedy himself likened Obama to his brother, and the crowd of students roared. To White House aides, the model of JFK remained uppermost in Obama's mind. "The president he admires most and draws most inspiration from is Lincoln," said David Axelrod. "But the president he is the most similar to, in terms of his style and principle, is JFK. No question about it."

Behind the stocky presidential podium and two teleprompter screens, Obama began his speech by recalling Ted Kennedy's presence and his legacy. But he also cited that moment in the campaign, and the arguments he spelled out for Change. "I was a candidate for President that day, and some may recall I argued that our country had reached a tipping point; that after years in which we had deferred our most pressing problems, and too often yielded to the politics of the moment, we now faced a choice: We could squarely confront our challenges with honesty and determination, or we could consign ourselves and our children to a future less prosperous and less secure," he explained.

Yes, he was tough on border security and employers hiring illegal workers. Yes, he offered a path for illegal immigrants to come out of the shadows and obtain citizenship. But what he really wanted was to take on the toughest political challenges he could find. His friends liked to say he was a restless spirit before winning the presidency. The truth was that he remained a restless spirit inside the West Wing. "Yes, this is an emotional question, and one that lends itself to demagoguery," he said. "Time and again, this issue has been used to divide and inflame—and to demonize people. And so the understandable, the natural impulse among those who run for office is to turn away and defer this question for another day, or another year, or another administration. Despite the courageous leadership in the past shown by many Democrats and some Republicans—including, by the way, my predecessor, President Bush—this has been the custom. That is why a broken and dangerous system that offends our most basic American values is still in place. But I believe we can put politics aside and finally have an immigration system that's accountable. I believe we can appeal not to people's fears but to their hopes, to their highest ideals, because that's who we are as Americans."

That's also who he was as a candidate and who he wanted to be as a president. Inside the West Wing, he liked to say that he would rather do big things in one term than small things in two terms. Of course, he wanted to win, and he was readying for a reelection campaign that returned to his roots in Chicago. Survival was essential, but it was not enough. Against the hard realities of a weak economy, against the poor poll numbers and the prospect of lost seats in Congress, against the advice of his own trusted aides, Obama was a true believer in his own revival.

SEVEN

RETURNS

They gathered on election night in the West Wing office that was spiritually and physically closest to Obama's Oval. David Axelrod's workplace was a rectangular shrine to Chicago and the 2008 campaign, where the president's senior strategist shuffled polling data, while juggling his two BlackBerrys and tracking a single TV screen at the edge of a small, deflated sofa. Through the long night of November 2, a half dozen of the president's best political brains walked in and out, trading news of dismal midterm races and gaming out their prospects for the next cycle, surrounded by snapshots of happier times: an inaugural ticket autographed by the new president, a blue-and-white Obama campaign sign in Hebrew script, and a photo of their beloved deli in Chicago. Two years ago they were rushing from the expansive boiler room in campaign headquarters to Grant Park to celebrate a victory that exceeded all expectations. Now they tracked across the empty West Wing hallways from office to office in search of any data or contest that might defy all expectations.

The president was gone, preferring to watch the results alone with his family in the White House residence, less than a minute's walk away. His closest adviser, Valerie Jarrett, sat on a sofa in her Georgetown condo preparing for the worst with the First Lady's friend and chief of staff, Susan Sher. The West Wing was left to the spirits of campaigns past and future. David Plouffe, the driving force behind the '08 victory, planted himself in Axelrod's office, where he would soon take over the chief strategist's job when Axelrod returned to Chicago in the new year. Alongside him was Joel Benenson, the president's trusted pollster. Jim Messina, readying to manage the reelection campaign, paced across the hallway from the closet-sized office of the deputy chief of staff. Communications director Dan Pfeiffer and press secretary Robert Gibbs shuttled back and forth past the Roosevelt Room to their more comfortable offices close to the briefing room. Nobody was ready or willing to brief the press that night, much less the next day.

They knew they were going to lose; the only question was how badly. Even in their best year, they could expect to lose thirty House seats from the high-water mark of 2008, according to projections by Sean Sweeney, a political aide to the former chief of staff Rahm Emanuel. Just one month earlier, some eternal optimists inside the West Wing believed they could hang on to a sliver of the Democrats' seventy-seven-strong majority in the House by picking up a handful of Republican seats to offset their own deep losses. But as October dragged on with little to change the political dynamic, the sense of looming failure was inescapable. The remaining glimmers of hope lay in the Senate, where Tea Party supporters had replaced viable Republican candidates with politically extreme neophytes in Colorado, Nevada, and Delaware.

For a couple of hours after the first polls closed, Obama's inner circle could almost believe the optimists. In Kentucky, Democrats John Yarmuth and Ben Chandler managed to survive the GOP wave, if only narrowly: the latter winning with just 50.1 percent of the vote. But those hopes were destroyed by the next results in southern Virginia, where Rick Boucher and Tom Perriello were wiped out. Even in the northern Virginia suburbs of Washington, D.C., Gerry Connolly was barely hanging on to a seat he had won by a double-digit margin two years ago. "At that point, we knew it was the sign we were in big trouble," said Dan Pfeiffer. By 10:00 p.m. in Washington, an hour before voting ended in the western states, Obama's confidants knew they were watching a political demolition.

For another five hours they stayed on the scene, long after the president and his closest friends had gone to bed. They were cheered by the early call of victory for Senate leader Harry Reid in Nevada. But the race they felt more invested in, and more concerned about, was that of an appointed senator in Colorado running in his first general election: Michael Bennet. A former schools superintendent in Denver, Bennet was an early Obama supporter in 2007 who had become a friend of Axelrod's. Bennet had survived a primary challenger backed by former president Bill Clinton, in a sign of the enduring rivalry of the 2008 presidential primaries. Then he faced an intense onslaught of hostile advertising from outside donors, including those organized by Karl Rove, the GOP strategist who was Axelrod's counterpart in the George W. Bush White House.

Bennet was the kind of untraditional and pragmatic politician who appealed to Obama and his inner circle. A victory for Bennet would give them a little breathing room in the Senate, rather than having to rely on unpredictable votes belonging to the independent Joe Lieberman or West Virginia's Joe Manchin. It would also give them reason to hope. Denver was the site of Obama's 2008 convention, and Colorado was one of a bloc of western states that served as a new battleground in presidential politics. "Colorado is an important state for us and the notion that he could resist the relentless pounding he took from the Rove forces—and they really targeted him as they did Harry Reid, unmercifully—was encouraging to me, looking forward," said Axelrod. "The fact that he was able to withstand that was encouraging to me for 2012. I believe Colorado is very much in play." They left the West Wing at three in the morning, as Colorado seemed to be heading the same way as other western victories in California and Washington State: a rare glimmer on a dark night.

Three hours later, Dan Pfeiffer was roused from sleep by his cell phone, which he had forgotten to power down. It was ABC's Jake Tapper, asking him to spin the unspinnable. There was little he, or anyone, could say to make the results sound better. He hauled himself to the Oval Office for the regular early morning meeting for senior staff, delayed by one hour following their miserably late night. After his absence and isolation the night before, President Obama led the session with a simple pep talk to his downbeat team. "Obviously this is going to be a rough period for us," he acknowledged. "In the never-ending cycle of idiocy and genius, we're going to be idiots again." He just wanted them to remember all the work they had done together; all that they could be proud of achieving through the last two years—and all the work still ahead of them, starting today. Someone asked, tentatively, if it might be a good idea to stage a press conference today. "Of course," Obama said. "Absolutely."

On a day when his aides were grinding through stories about their failures and imminent staff shake-ups, Obama walked into the East Room—where he had signed health care reform into law just eight months earlier—to state the obvious. It felt bad to lose so many allies in Congress, he said. When a Reuters reporter asked whether he was out of touch and would change his leadership style, Obama admitted that he had traveled a long way since the 2008 campaign. In Iowa, nobody questioned his leadership or his ability to connect. But perhaps now he needed to reconnect with people outside the White House. He said he was often heartbroken or inspired by the letters he read every night from regular Americans. But he acknowledged that nobody filmed him reading them, so how could voters know what he was feeling?

Even as Obama conceded a lack of public emotion, he stepped out of body to analyze his situation from afar. He ended his press conference by noting that Reagan and Clinton, two great communicators, had faced the same questions two years into their presidencies. "This is something that I think every President needs to go through because the responsibilities of this office are so enormous and so many people are depending on what we do, and in the rush of activity, sometimes we lose track of the ways that we connected with folks that got us here in the first place," he admitted. "Now, I'm not recommending for every future President that they take a shellacking like I did last night. I'm sure there are easier ways to learn these lessons. But I do think that this is a growth process and an evolution. And the relationship that I've had with the American people is one that built slowly, peaked at this incredible high, and then during the course of the last two years, as we've, together, gone through some very difficult times, has gotten rockier and tougher. And it's going to, I'm sure, have some more ups and downs during the course of me being in this office."

His closest staff felt the admissions of mistakes, the humbling talk of shellackings, were the release they all needed. "He just said what was floating in the air," said Valerie Jarrett. "His willingness to say it was a nice punctuation." Instead of going home to catch up on sleep, several senior staffers joined Axelrod that evening at his favorite Thai restaurant to commiserate. They had no idea how quickly the cycle of ups and downs, idiocy and genius, would turn once again.

Over the next two months Obama and his inner circle would revive their fortunes in dramatic fashion. It was not their first revival by any means, but it was one of the most rapid and least expected. They had revived themselves before—not just during the 2008 election, but more recently in the White House. After the near-death experience of losing the Massachusetts Senate seat in January, Democrats lined up with Republicans and journalists to declare the presidency—and its biggest domestic project, health care reform—finished. Two months later, Obama signed health care reform into law, enacting the most sweeping legislation in a generation or more. Many of the same critics now blamed health care for Obama's shellacking, writing once again the early obituaries of the presidency. But over the course of the next two months, the Obama White House would secure a sweeping set of legislative victories, in part by reviving the themes and approaches of candidate Obama in 2008. By the early new year, instead of marveling at the revival of the Republican Party, Washington's political insiders were astonished at the revival of a president who was rebounding in the opinion polls as quickly as he had fallen in his first summer in office. This revival would chart a course for Obama and his team through the 2012 reelection campaign, not least in starting to restore the support of independent voters who had abandoned the Democrats over the last two years. The period would reshape Obama's inner circle and rebalance the debate between the Revivalists and the Survivalists—the campaign's true believers and the Washington insiders. And while the president himself still liked to straddle the divide between the two, the revival of late 2010 was also the result of the stubborn, strategic, and unconventional politics that were the hallmarks of his Renegade election.

In the days before and after his shellacking, Barack Obama was hardly a portrait in confident, upbeat leadership. In fact, according to several close aides, he was moping and downbeat. Not so much about his own fate, since his position was secure for two more years, but about the House Democrats he had come to admire: the ones in conservative districts who had had the courage to vote for health care reform; the ones who had followed his lead and were now facing defeat. Some of his advisers urged him to shake off his gloom and rejoin the fight against the GOP. They were too late: even before the election, he was obsessing about those destined to lose for him and his party. He traveled to some of the doomed districts where he expressed his admiration for struggling Democrats like Tom Perriello in Virginia, John Boccieri in Ohio, Betsy Markey in Colorado, and Patrick Murphy in Pennsylvania. He phoned them the weekend before their losses and in the days afterward. But instead of lifting their spirits, he found the defeated Democrats lifting his own a little. "Many of the people who lost said they wouldn't have changed their vote on health care and he found that heartening," said Jarrett. Maybe they would have lost with or without health care reform or 10 percent unemployment. But then again, maybe not. "The people he felt worst about were these very promising Democrats," said Axelrod. "He was grieving."

He was also plotting for the final weeks of a Congress in which he still commanded big Democratic majorities—at least until January. He was leaving Washington for a presidential trip across Asia just three days after the election, but decided to keep his key staffers behind in the White House rather than accompany him as usual. The challenge was both ridiculously ambitious and organizationally mundane. "OK, what do we do now?" he asked his senior staff. "I've got a number of things I want to get done," he said before rattling off his wish list: some form of extension for the Bush-era tax cuts, extending unemployment insurance beyond the end of the year, ratification of his START nuclear treaty with Russia, and the repeal of Don't Ask Don't Tell, the Pentagon's policy on gays serving in the military. That's a pretty audacious list, thought Axelrod, who felt dubious about accomplishing anything close to Obama's full agenda.

The strategy lay in the hands of a quiet Senate veteran with little desire for a public profile and even less appetite for partisan battles. Pete Rouse was an avuncular, easygoing confidant of Obama's since his first days as a senator. Constantly toying with the idea of retirement, Rouse cared little for face time with either the president or the press. Preferring to write long strategic memos and to nurture the careers of much younger staffers, he watched the traditional infighting with a mixture of bemusement and dismay. He had won Obama's trust and admiration as he set up the new senator's office and then stuck around to run the place. A senior adviser in the White House, he was the antithesis of chief of staff Rahm Emanuel: unflappable, low-key, unambitious, and a long-range thinker. When Emanuel quit the West Wing to run for mayor of Chicago just one month before the congressional elections, Rouse stepped in as a stopgap chief of staff. The contrast in political style was as great as the contrast in character.

Rouse was already working on a long-term reorganization of the West Wing when Emanuel left for Chicago. Reflecting the president's frustrations, he focused on the struggling communications and press operations. Now he needed to set aside the grand vision for something far more pressing: how to stop the defeated congressional Democrats from going home. Even a quick review of history suggested the prospects were grim. "In 1994 there was all this talk about Democrats passing all these big things in the lame duck after the election, their last gasp of power," said communications director Dan Pfeiffer. "But they passed the GATT agreement [General Agreement on Tariffs and Trade] and went home in something like three days. It's really hard because the House members lose their offices after a while and they end up working out of the cafeteria."

Obama himself was working out of Air Force One and presidential hotel suites, having escaped Washington on a ten-day Asian tour. Back in the West Wing, Rouse performed some triage alongside legislative director Phil Schiliro. If they didn't deal with taxes first, there would be nothing to follow. The Republicans were looking for any reason not to vote on the START treaty and Don't Ask Don't Tell. The only path was to remove any excuse for inaction and build momentum quickly. Rouse urged the staffers in Washington to sketch the contours of a tax deal while Obama toured Asia. There were two priorities beyond simply getting a deal done: stop taxes from rising on those earning lower and middle incomes, and extend unemployment insurance. But they faced an unexpected challenge: Democratic senator Chuck Schumer was a vocal advocate of extending the tax fight into the new year to force Republicans to argue for the needs of the wealthy. Schumer especially liked the idea of a millionaire's tax, but Obama's aides believed that idea would forever define the wealthy as those earning vast sums of cash, instead of the merely large sums above $250,000 a year. In the meantime, taxes would go up for everybody—not least middle-class voters— and the White House's chief economist Larry Summers warned that the impact on the sluggish recovery would be devastating.

Their internal polling suggested the politics would be devastating, too. Nobody wanted their own taxes to go up for any reason. Liberals who supported tax hikes for the wealthy were just as adamant that their own taxes should stay where they were. Their outrage over the Bush tax rates seemed, to Obama's aides, to be manufactured. While Obama was in Asia, Axelrod spoke to *The Huffington Post* about the tax debate, saying blandly, "We have to deal with the world as we find it." That statement of the obvious prompted the headline: "White House Gives In on Bush Tax Cuts." Axelrod went to a Chicago Bulls basketball game that evening convinced he had made no news. The next morning, Obama's staffers awoke to dozens of angry e-mails from their counterparts traveling with the president in Asia, who had already started their day by reading the screaming headline. "We knew we're going to take tremendous crap from the left," said one senior White House official. "The whole world exploded with *The Huffington Post*. It set the left off in a furor."

For the first time in two years, Obama and his inner circle believed they faced the same dynamic as Republican leaders: neither side wanted to deal with its own party's extremes, or with the incoming Congress and its Tea Party–backed newcomers, many of whom had never held elected office before. The new rapport was partly the result of two White House insiders: between Rouse and Vice President Biden, the White House could count on decades of experience in Senate deal making. Rouse handled the Democratic leaders while Biden concentrated on Mitch McConnell, the Republican leader in the Senate, who had proved such a masterful opponent over the last two years. Biden insisted that, despite McConnell's determined and disciplined obstructionism, he could now be trusted. "If Mitch gives me his word, I believe him," Biden told Obama's aides. "I don't know a lot of things. But one thing I do know is the United States Senate."

The best way to keep them in Washington was to go for the whole wish list, which Republican leaders desperately wanted to avoid. Soon after the elections, McConnell approached Biden with a deal. His members hated the prospect of voting on two issues that might be used against them in future elections: Don't Ask Don't Tell and the Dream Act, which offered legal status to the children of illegal immigrants. McConnell offered to get Obama the votes on his treasured START treaty as long as he could dodge the controversial votes on gay rights and immigration. Obama's response was "no": those votes could go to the back of the queue, but he refused to kill them.

For many in Obama's inner circle, this position would have been unthinkable if Rahm Emanuel had still been chief of staff. As the leading advocate of the Survivalist group of Washington insiders, Emanuel cared little for Obama's campaign commitments on civil rights to either gays or Latinos. "Rahm would have made that deal," said one senior Obama adviser. "He would have wanted to give up Don't Ask Don't Tell for START. He would have made deals earlier than we should have made them. And, given his history on health care and everything else, even if the president had held firm, God knows what he'd have been telling the press about the vote numbers. In this case we were helped by Rahm not being there to negotiate these things. Because Rahm would have freaked out at losing the House."

Obama's aides were stunned to find out that McConnell was so desperate for a tax deal for the wealthy that he was prepared to sweeten the agreement on a wide range of Democratic tax priorities. The cost of extending tax cuts for the super-wealthy and cutting the estate tax for two years amounted to $114 billion. In exchange, the White House extended unemployment insurance, initiated a payroll tax holiday, and extended tax credits from the Recovery Act that helped lower-income families and those with children. The Democratic priorities amounted to more than twice the value of the GOP's tax breaks: $238 billion. In effect, the Republicans agreed to extend the life of the very stimulus spending they had campaigned against so robustly and successfully for the last two years.

Such calculations meant little to Obama's liberal supporters in Congress and beyond the Beltway. The outrage was as loud as it was short-lived. Senator Tom Harkin of Iowa suggested to reporters that a tax deal would weaken Obama in 2012 to the point where almost any Republican would beat him. "He would then just be hoping and praying that Sarah Palin gets the nomination," Harkin said. The normally loyal activist group MoveOn.org aired a TV ad of supporters disappointed with the tax deal, including one woman who asked: "What's happened to that bold, progressive man we elected President in 2008?" Keith Olbermann, the flame-throwing MSNBC anchor, taped one of his infamous "special comments" excoriating Obama for being "goddamned wrong" and for his "foot-dragging on Don't Ask Don't Tell." Olbermann even predicted that, barring some change of course, "he will not only not be re-elected, he may not even be re-nominated." Olbermann's rant struck a chord even with Obama loyalists; one major fund-raiser e-mailed friends afterward to say: "I'm truly done with Obama. Maybe I'll come back by voting for him in a primary, but if there's a better choice, I'll actively support another candidate."

Inside the White House there was a sense of disbelief at the excessive outrage, a frustration that Democrats could not see how disastrous the alternatives were for the economy and for all Democrats. Taxes would rise for middle-class families and the estate tax might disappear altogether, as several Democratic senators threatened to vote with the GOP to eliminate it. Instead of tax hikes, the deal amounted to a second stimulus for the economy, adding as much as a full percentage point to economic growth in 2011, according to Wall Street economists. Besides, for all the angry rhetoric about capitulation, the war was far from over: the two-year deal guaranteed a long debate about taxes and spending in the 2012 presidential election. "Despite all the shit that Biden and the president had to take, particularly from the House liberals, it passed with eighty-one votes in the Senate," said one senior Obama adviser. "Those guys in the House still bitch about it, but if we hadn't done it, they'd have gone home with a lot worse or a $4,000 tax increase on the middle class in January. Then they'd have been bitching about that."

Instead of worrying about their liberal critics, Obama's aides believed they had reconnected with the identity and spirit of 2008. The economic revival was a campaign revival, too: a return to the days when Obama promised to unite red and blue America, instead of the last two years of intense partisan battles. "We loved this period," said Pfeiffer. "We were doing what we had run to do, which was work with Republicans and Democrats together to solve tough problems, and there wasn't that much partisanship. There was legislative wrangling but it wasn't partisan. It was the Obama of Springfield, of the United States Senate and the campaign trail. Only we were doing it as president, and we hadn't had the opportunity to do that really."

The political audience they cared about was not, in fact, the Democratic activists who felt so betrayed by the tax deal. The target audience was the independent and moderate voters who had turned away from Democrats in the last two years. In 2008, independent voters backed Obama over John McCain by eight points. In 2010, independent voters reversed themselves, backing Republicans over Democrats by nineteen points. By their nature, independent voters have little interest in partisan battles and had initially warmed to Obama's original mission of bringing the two parties together. The lame-duck revival proved that the first mission was still alive. "There was something fairly invigorating about it in the White House because it was kind of like throwing caution to the wind," said David Plouffe. "You just got this big electoral setback, and a common belief that these things can't get done. Senators were calling every day saying they can't get things done. So it was really meaningful for the American people because for the first time in a long time they saw a good amount of people coming together from both parties. And that's what they hunger for more than anything else. They are hungering for it now." For Plouffe there was a lasting political benefit for Obama in the revival of late 2010. "Look at the president compared to other political figures and ask questions like does he look for common ground, is he willing to work with the other side, does he play politics, or does he try and solve problems? He has very good ratings on all of these things," Plouffe said. "They were pretty good before the lame duck, and they strengthened after the lame duck." Those ratings were undoubtedly lifted by the president's measured reaction to the mass shooting in Tucson, Arizona, in early January, which left six dead and critically wounded Gabrielle Giffords, the district's Democratic member of Congress. Obama refrained from seeking political advantage, despite the heated and personal rhetoric on both sides of the spectrum. And his upbeat memorial speech was widely praised by Democrats and Republicans as a uniquely presidential moment of national unity. By the spring of 2011, Obama had recovered much of the lost ground among independents, but still had some way to return to his support from 2008. In some polls, he had moved into positive territory for job approval by independents; in others, he was running level with the Republican front-runners for the nonpartisan vote.

For many Washington insiders, this seemed like a familiar script. Obama was finally fitting into the Clinton template: after a leftward tilt in the first years and a midterm electoral defeat, he would now return to the center and restore his political standing. He was triangulating between Republicans and Democrats, and moving toward the middle.

There was just one small problem with that old script. What followed in the lame-duck session was more liberal, not less. The issue of gays in the military was one of the biggest progressive priorities for two decades, including Bill Clinton's 1993 effort: Don't Ask Don't Tell. Repealing that flawed compromise, and allowing gays to serve openly in the military, became a landmark promise from candidate Obama in the 2008 campaign. Yet gay rights groups came to believe that President Obama was delaying action repeatedly to the point where nothing would change during his first term. With the support of the Joint Chiefs of Staff—but not the top officers of the U.S. Army and Marines—the White House and its congressional allies pushed ahead in early December, little more than a month after the midterm elections.

Even then, advocacy groups were not convinced Obama would follow through. "He had given his word, but people didn't really believe he was sincere," said Valerie Jarrett. When several groups met with White House officials in the Eisenhower Executive Office Building next to the West Wing, Obama called them over for an impromptu session in the Roosevelt Room next to the Oval Office. "Often it's darkest just before the dawn," he told the gathering of skeptics. "I'm telling you, I'm going to get this done." The first attempt, as part of the Defense spending bill, failed. At the second attempt, as a stand-alone bill, the repeal passed with sixty-five votes in the Senate.

Obama signed the bill into law in the Interior Department's auditorium, where he had hailed the signing of health care reform nine months earlier. As he walked on stage, the audience turned his campaign chant into a raucous celebration of the power of governing: "Yes We Did!" "We are not a nation that says, 'Don't ask, don't tell,'" he told them just before signing the repeal into law. "We are a nation that says, 'Out of many, we are one.' We are a nation that welcomes the service of every patriot. We are a nation that believes that all men and women are created equal." Of all the laws passed in the rush of the post-election revival—more than the tax deal or the START treaty, more than the new food safety law or health care for the 9/11 responders—the repeal of Don't Ask Don't Tell stood out. Its passage made up for the failure of the immigration vote on the Dream Act. It was his biggest contribution to civil rights since his election, and one of his personal highs of his presidency. And like health care reform, it just happened to be one of those moments when Obama was cleaning up after Bill Clinton: taking a long-held

Democratic dream and bringing it into reality the right way. "The idea that we could pass Don't Ask Don't Tell through Congress was a pipe dream at best, even in the euphoric days right after the election," said Pfeiffer. "We got it done through a slow, deliberate process that brought all the appropriate stakeholders on board. Anybody who saw the president's remarks at the signing could tell that he knew this was a very big deal."

A few hours after signing the repeal into law, Obama faced the press for one last time before the new year, and the arrival of a Republican-dominated House. "A lot of folks in this town predicted that after the midterm elections, Washington would be headed for more partisanship and more gridlock. And instead, this has been a season of progress for the American people," he told reporters in the temporary auditorium of the Eisenhower Executive Office Building, which was still in the midst of a lengthy remodeling. He was not just talking about Washington's political fortune. He was explaining his own revived fortunes: how he had achieved much more than the pundits' predictions by returning to the kind of strategic, pragmatic compromises that he promised throughout the presidential election. "If there's any lesson to draw from these past few weeks, it's that we are not doomed to endless gridlock," he said. "We've shown, in the wake of the November elections, that we have the capacity not only to make progress, but to make progress together. And I'm not naïve. I know there will be tough fights in the months ahead. But my hope heading into the New Year is that we can continue to heed the message of the American people and hold to a spirit of common purpose in 2011 and beyond."

By the new year, with his approval ratings back above the symbolically important mark of 50 percent, Obama moved ahead with sweeping staff changes that would help shift the balance back to the campaign style of 2008. In his reorganization memos, Rouse identified three big course corrections for the president and his senior staff. First, the inner circle needed to expand to include more outside people and more Cabinet voices. The president's world was simply too insular. Second, the whole operation was too tactical and not strategic enough. Third, the White House deployed Obama far too much: he was everywhere and nowhere, and he complained repeatedly about the burden of being his own spokesperson. "Some of that is true," said one senior Obama aide, "but some of that is that he just doesn't want to do it. And on our side, he's better at it than anybody else. But I think this does morph into being too tactical and not strategic enough. He became a sort of prime minister negotiating with Congress, cutting deals, which ran against coming to change Washington. He became part of Washington to get three quarters, or even 60 percent of the loaf." There was a recognition at the highest levels that Obama had become too much of an insider, a Survivalist, and drifted too far from his campaign identity as an outsider.

The changes to Obama's inner circle reflected those corrections. Early in 2011, Bill Daley took over as chief of staff from Rouse, who made it plain he did not want the job and did not have the skills required for two critical parts of the newly defined position: to go on TV as the president's surrogate and to find common ground with the business community. Daley was a consummate political insider, the son and brother of two legendary Chicago mayors, as well as a Washington expert, having served as commerce secretary under President Clinton and as Al Gore's campaign chairman. But unlike Emanuel, he was not seen as a sharply partisan figure by Republicans. Moreover, Obama's critics among business leaders respected Daley, not least because he had spent much of the Bush years working as a banking executive at JP Morgan Chase.

However, that did not make him a perfect fit. Daley had no prior relationship with the president, and in late December 2010 Obama still remained uncomfortable with expanding his inner circle. "I think that's fair," he told one senior adviser who said he needed to bring in fresh people. "I'm more comfortable with people I know. I don't like breaking out of that comfort zone. Quite frankly, that's one of the reasons I'm not sure about this. I don't know Bill. I know Rahm and David like him, and I know him, but I don't know how this is going to work."

At this point in his presidency, Obama felt confident that he could navigate Washington without the help of an Emanuel-style figure. So he found it easier to push back when Daley suggested he should take over the management of the West Wing. When Daley asked if he could bring in his own team with him, Obama limited Daley's entourage to two people. "My management team is here and it's staying," the president said. "I've got Valerie, Bob Bauer, Pete Rouse, and David Plouffe. That's my management team." When Daley insisted that he did not want to be a figurehead, Obama brushed aside his concerns. "Look, the chief of staff is the chief of staff," he said. "The buck ends with him and you have the final say. But this is my team." Obama envisaged Daley as the CEO of his West Wing, with Rouse staying on as his chief operating officer. If Daley didn't work out, Rouse would still be there. Still, Daley had business credentials—a connection to the outside world—that his management team could never replicate.

Obama knew he needed to work to improve business sentiment: not only were CEOs strongly supportive of the Chamber of Commerce (and its TV campaign against the administration), but he could hardly urge them to create jobs while there was such a high level of distrust. To Obama, their sense of victimhood seemed hard to understand. He had been critical of only the financial sector, and even then his words were mild compared to the public hatred of Wall Street and the bank bailouts. At the end of an Oval Office meeting with one CEO, Obama asked why his comments about reckless bankers were taken as such a broad attack on all businesses. "Come on," Obama said. "If you're critical of politicians and say they are terrible, I don't assume you're talking about me. But if I say something about a business leader, why do you impute that I'm talking about you? I'm not. You're terrific. You're great. You're hiring. You're paying people good wages. You're investing in your community. So if I make a comment about one segment of one part of one industry, why do you assume it's directed at you? Why do you take it personally?" The answer, as Obama knew well, was that life was different for a president. Business leaders seized on his every word as they tried to interpret what kind of leader he was, and how he viewed the private sector. Daley's role was to speak to them as a known quantity, as a member of their club. "He's served in both the public sector and the private sector, so he gets both worlds," said Valerie Jarrett. "I think that helped signal that the president doesn't vilify bankers. Bill is a banker. It sent a message that he's willing to have at the top of his administration someone who understands their world."

He also needed to understand the world of the people who got him elected. Daley's arrival was an attempt to play the inside game among the elite power brokers: to neutralize opponents and live within the political realities of Washington. His counterbalance was David Plouffe, the disciplined and driven former campaign manager. Plouffe's early return, as Axelrod accelerated his departure, was the clearest sign of Obama's campaign-style revival. The hallmarks of the 2008 effort were Plouffe's priorities: strategic planning, a focus on the grassroots, and disciplined messaging. Inside the West Wing, the stylistic difference between the two strategists was immediately clear. "Plouffe is laser focused on whatever strategy we decide," said one senior Obama aide. "Almost too much. We don't have a lot of vacillating, relitigating, thinking about it that you had with David Axelrod. You have a much more crisp execution. Plouffe is much more focused: this is the message, and this is how we're going to execute it. David Axelrod was a great wordsmith and has a more out-of-the-box thinking, but that's part of the problem. He thinks very fast about a lot of things, but that can slow the process down." Plouffe's problem was that he could take pride in stubbornly ignoring opportunities or responding slowly to developing challenges. He represented the antithesis of both Axelrod's indecision and Emanuel's hyperactivity.

Other senior staff changes reinforced the shift away from a team of rivals to a group of lower-ego teammates. The affable Gene Sperling took over the National Economic Council, after the turbulent and backstabbing atmosphere under Larry Summers. Press secretary Robert Gibbs left when it became obvious that Plouffe's arrival meant there was no vacancy for another senior strategist. His replacement, the former journalist Jay Carney, was a mix of a White House insider and outsider; the short list for the job had included internal candidates in communications and press, as well as four external contenders: among them, the Democratic strategists Karen Finney and Doug Hattaway. Carney, who was previously Biden's communications director, emerged ahead of the pack in part because of his expertise in having reported on two White Houses.

Unlike during the Gibbs era, strategic messaging lay not in the press secretary's hands but in Plouffe's. He began to relentlessly focus on independent voters, whom the campaign courted diligently and to great effect in 2007 and 2008. Plouffe believed the electorate was evenly divided between Democratic and Republican support, with just 20 percent up for grabs in between. He saw a clear opening: it was Democrats who cared about the independent 20 percent of voters, while Republicans cared mostly about their Tea Party–driven base. "I think the Republican Party rented independent voters for one night in 2010," said Plouffe. "That's all it was. I think independent voters have put both parties on probation. And whichever party seems to be more honest about solving problems, is more focused on their needs, is going to earn their support. The Republican Party have completely overplayed their hand in states like Wisconsin. But even here, what people want is compromise and common sense. My sense is that the Republican leaders on Capitol Hill understand that. I'm not sure their members do."

That was the backdrop for the defining debate of 2011, if not 2012: the size and scope of the federal government, as measured by its budget. Through at least four separate clashes—over the 2011 budget, the 2012 budget, the national debt ceiling, and the expiration of the Bush-era tax cuts at the end of 2012—the question of rightsizing the government was the central front in the war between both parties. Obama's aides believed they were playing a long game of chess, and waited to make their moves sequentially, over several months. It was not enough to focus on one set of negotiations, such as how to avoid a government shutdown. They needed to know what to offer—and what to demand—in the next round. So they ignored the advice of Democratic senators to reject out of hand any attempt to reform vastly expensive social programs such as Medicare, Medicaid, and Social Security. Many Democrats believed the GOP's readiness to cut benefits gave the White House all the ammunition it needed to scare older voters back into the arms of the Democratic Party in time for 2012. "That's why we never solve problems," said Plouffe. "Sure, that's an approach. But it's not our approach. If there's a way in the context of this discussion to do something on Social Security that will strengthen it for the long term, that is done in a balanced way, then he would be open to it. I don't know how you could not take that opportunity if it doesn't affect any current or near-term retirees, or slash benefits." For Obama's inner circle, the readiness to deal with spending and taxation was the reasonable—and characteristic—approach for someone at the center of American politics.

But beyond a desire to look reasonable, there was little agreement on the scope of negotiations among Obama's advisers. The economic team wanted to focus purely on the question of raising the debt limit and avoiding the disastrous prospect of the United States defaulting on its debt. The political team wanted to maintain the electoral advantage of attacking Republicans for proposing deep cuts to Medicare and Medicaid while also offering tax cuts to the wealthy. However, those closest to the president realized there was no way to deal with the deficit debate without opening up a broader discussion with the GOP over the so-called entitlement spending of the social safety net. Their goal was to publicly test the Republicans' seriousness—their opponents' desire both to deal with deficits and to manage the finances of the federal government. "Let's sit down for the first time and talk seriously about entitlements with some ground rules and raise the debt limit," said one senior Obama aide. "Let's see if they're serious and can make some progress on entitlements. If we can't, we'll have a fight. Nobody wants to govern in an economy that is tanking. If the government defaults, McConnell and Boehner will look terrible because the responsibility is on them, too." There was more than a little realpolitik in this strategy. Obama's advisers knew this was a negotiation that they could not avoid because there were a handful of Democratic senators who wanted to join the deficit debate themselves. And they also knew they had to offer up some new concession to Republicans after cutting deeply into their 2011 budget to avert a government shutdown. They just hoped and believed that the offer of serious talks would be enough to avert a possible default on America's debts.

Other crises were harder to game out through 2011 and beyond. Above all, that was true about the sweeping series of protests, revolutions, and rebellions across the Arab world. When the wave spread from Tunisia to Egypt in late January, the administration was deadlocked between the Survivalist group of Washington insiders—notably Defense Secretary Robert Gates and Secretary of State Hillary Clinton—and the Revivalist group of campaign veterans, especially United Nations ambassador Susan Rice, as well as Samantha Power, Michael McFaul, and Ben Rhodes at the National Security Council. The Washington insiders were deeply troubled by the notion of dumping a key regional ally like Egypt's president Hosni Mubarak, not least because of the impact on other surviving allies in the Middle East. But the campaign veterans were determined to keep their historic and unconventional president on what they believed was the right side of history: with the protesters.

Three days after the Egyptian revolution began in Cairo and Alexandria, Obama's national security team was meeting in the Situation Room to debate how they should handle the uprising. Under siege from the world's media, the White House press office was struggling to respond and urged the president to speak out. But the national security team was deadlocked. Denis McDonough, Obama's deputy national security adviser and a campaign veteran himself, walked into the Oval Office to tell the president that the group's advice was for him to say nothing. Obama's communications team thought that was crazy: an untenable position for the leader of the free world. Obama agreed and walked down to the Situation Room to talk to the national security team himself. "I want to go out and make a statement," he told them. The group promptly reversed its advice. A few hours later, Obama's aides hastily assembled the press pool of reporters and cameras in the State Dining Room for a four-minute statement. The president warned the Egyptian authorities to refrain from violence, and he promised that the United

States would "stand up for" the universal human rights of the protesters. It was a clear sign that the White House was ready to break with its longest-serving Arab ally. "Had some people got their way, the only time the president would have spoken was the day Mubarak stepped down," said one senior Obama aide.

The deep internal schism inside Obama's national security team led the president to use a little subterfuge in siding with his campaign-era aides. Four days after his first public statement, Obama met with his senior advisers in the Situation Room again. As they met, President Mubarak took to Egyptian state television to deliver what was expected to be his concession speech to the protesters. Instead, he offered a vague promise of reforms, which he would oversee himself. Susan Rice argued that the administration needed to be more critical of Mubarak in public to urge him to step down, but Clinton and Gates insisted on a more careful approach, with measured tones in public and more pressure behind the scenes. After two hours of deliberation, Obama decided to make a public statement in the Grand Foyer of the White House mansion that evening. "I think I know where we ought to be," he told his security team, "but I don't think the differences are as deep as they sound." Obama spoke to Mubarak on the phone for thirty minutes, and made a public statement that sounded measured. "What I indicated tonight to President Mubarak," he told the cameras, "is my belief that an orderly transition must be meaningful, it must be peaceful, and it must begin now."

He returned to the Oval Office to discuss the next steps with his inner circle. Gibbs asked him how he should brief selected reporters about the phone call with Mubarak. His order: make it sound tougher than the public comments. The next day, Secretary Clinton complained bitterly to the president about Gibbs and his political team taking risks with a volatile situation, and she urged him to rein them in. "The State Department wanted us to say nothing," said one senior Obama adviser. "They were freaked out by everything to do with Egypt." Yet Gibbs was not freelancing; he was merely following orders. Obama wanted to send a message indirectly to the Egyptians, and to an increasingly critical audience at home, that he was on the side of the protesters. White House officials were later wryly amused by press accounts detailing how the State Department was at the forefront of promoting protests across the Arab world, and instrumental in pushing Obama to speak out more forcefully on behalf of the rebels.

Ten days after Obama's public criticism of the Egyptian president, Mubarak was forced out of office by his own military. That news came too late for the cover of *Newsweek* magazine, which purported to tell the story of "How Obama Blew It." For all their improvisation and internal squabbling, Obama's aides believed the end result vindicated their cautious approach. "Plouffe always says the key is landing the plane; it doesn't matter how much turbulence there is getting there," said one senior Obama aide. "Egypt was one of those. We knew that our goal was to be in a place where we would have an orderly and peaceful transition with minimum violence and bloodshed on the path there. If we were going to get beat up on the path to that, for not being strong enough, we knew that was going to happen because it required some measured words to achieve that goal. So it was fitting when *Newsweek* came out with their cover. That to us was the perfect validation of our choosing a strategy over a series of tactics, and not tying our decisions to the news cycle."

Other revolutions were less swift and less readily shaped by American pressure. When the protests and rebellions began in Libya, the administration was even slower to respond than it had been in Egypt. Faced with intense public criticism, the White House was reluctant to condemn Muammar Gadhafi's violent suppression of the protests in his country. Obama's senior national security aides were afraid that U.S. citizens would be targeted by Gadhafi's forces, and spent the early days of the Libyan uprising in an increasingly desperate attempt to get Americans out of the country. Denis McDonough grew so alarmed by the need to move Americans out of Libya that he was working at one in the morning to coordinate the rental of a boat to ferry people to safety. As the Libyan rebellion dragged on, despite an intense NATO air campaign against Gadhafi's forces, some White House officials admitted they had no real sense of what lay ahead. "We've got a tiger by the tail," said one senior Obama adviser. "I don't know how it's going to evolve." Even those focused on Obama's reelection conceded they could not predict how the events in the Middle East might impact the president's political fortunes. "The presidency is defined not by things you can plan, but by the things you can't plan on," said Axelrod. "And this whole Middle East set of developments is plainly one of those things. I don't know what it will mean. I don't where it will go. But whether it is definitional in the election, I think it's far too early to say. If you go back not too many months when people said the oil spill was definitional and would define the Obama presidency—how many people are talking about that now?"

What would they be talking about as Obama tried to revive himself in time for the 2012 elections? Not the partisan battles that consumed Washington or the most vocal activists on both sides of the aisle—at least not in the view of Obama's inner circle. In their analysis, the very quality that annoyed Obama's partisan supporters—his readiness to compromise with Republicans—was one of the key factors that appealed most to the voters who lifted him to his historic victory in 2008. "You have to understand what made Barack Obama different from most presidential candidates was that 50 percent of the people that got involved in his campaign had never done so before in politics," said Plouffe. "For many people this will be their only engagement. What they signed up for *was* the reasonableness, was the 'no red states, no blue states.' The ideological purists are actually fairly small in number. They are loud in voice and small in number. The vast majority of Americans, and the vast majority of people involved in the Obama campaign, are more interested in finding common ground rather than making a political point." That perspective heartened Obama's advisers as they watched Republican leaders in Congress expand the debate over deficits to include abortion rights, Planned Parenthood, and the Environmental Protection Agency. Obama was trying to talk to a group of moderate, less ideological voters ignored by both the Republican and the Democratic leadership in Congress.

Beyond the style and tone of politics, Obama's political advisers were counting on something more fundamental for the president's reelection: demographics. Even at their low point in 2010, they watched states like North Carolina—which would be hosting the Democratic convention in two years—run surprisingly close. Republican senator Richard Burr won with 55 percent of the vote in a state that Obama won by less than half a point two years earlier. "We'd win that today," said Plouffe with unbridled confidence. "I'll make the case right now. It will be close, as it was last time, but North Carolina and Virginia will be central battlegrounds. People need to get their heads out of 2000. It's not just Florida and Ohio. Those are still going to be critical battlegrounds. But Virginia and North Carolina—along with those western states of Colorado and New Mexico, Arizona and Nevada—are all going to be critical, too. Why? Because of the demographics. Burr's race wasn't seen to be that competitive. It shows you there's a pretty low Republican ceiling there. With young voters, African American voters, and the tech community there, it's a rapidly, rapidly changing state. It's much more favorable for us demographically than it was even two years ago." When you can no longer campaign on a platform of Hope and Change—when the promise of a campaign turns into the reality of governing—there is a certain hope in demographics.

Obama's team also hoped that an untested, ideological Republican challenger would be too much Change in 2012. By the start of their third year in office, Obama's senior aides were enjoying the return to the themes and style of the 2008 campaign. But they were also looking forward to the contrasts they could offer to some of their own disappointed supporters in 2012: a contrast between Obama's original reassuring formula of Change, and the Republicans' unnerving, extreme version. "This is no longer going to be a referendum on Barack Obama. It's going to be a choice," said David Axelrod. "I think anybody who cares about progressive causes, moving the country forward, is going to see the stark choice between some candidate who will, in order to win the Republican nomination, essentially pledge to turn the clock back, and Obama. I think that will be stimulative to our supporters." Obama's senior aides were praying for a polarizing, erratic opponent like Sarah Palin or Donald Trump, but they were planning for a more reliable, centrist foe like Mitt Romney or Jon Huntsman. In case of a Palin or a Trump, they figured they could simply step aside and watch the train wreck. If they faced a Romney or a Huntsman, they were preparing to remind voters (including Republicans in the primaries, if necessary) how their candidate's politics were close to those of the very president they wanted to unseat. Romney's health care plan in Massachusetts served as a model for Obama's health care reform; Huntsman served as Obama's ambassador to China.

However, no amount of political strategy could match the combination of character, calculated risk taking, and good fortune that was the foundation for Obama's first presidential campaign and for his landmark achievements as president. Obama's signature moments as a candidate and president were Renegade ones: unconventional, high-profile, high-stakes gambles that made him look like the embodiment of his Secret Service codename. Yet he was also a careful decision maker with a meticulous approach to the risks he was prepared to take on.

He would take few greater gambles than the top-secret mission to capture or kill Osama bin Laden. Throughout the period of the midterm shellacking, and the post-election revival, Obama was closely monitoring and managing the final hunt for America's nemesis. Just three months before his shellacking at the polls, Obama learned of the intelligence breakthrough that would lead the CIA to the Pakistani lair of bin Laden. Four months after shaking up his senior staff, in the midst of an intense debate over government shutdowns and debt defaults, he was ordering the mission to kill the mastermind behind the 9/11 murders. His trusted senior aides, along with his family and friends, knew nothing of his work until he told the rest of the world. "It's inhuman," said one close friend of Obama's cool demeanor under the private pressure of the bin Laden mission. "It's just unbelievable, even to me." Even Obama's understated counterterrorism official John Brennan—whose work was dedicated to killing al Qaeda figures in the Afghan border region—could not resist a moment of gushing. Speaking to reporters the day after the news broke, Brennan called Obama's decision to order up the commando mission "one of the most gutsiest calls of any president in recent memory."

Obama was given the choice between the relative safety of a massive aerial strike and an extremely risk-laden commando raid on bin Laden's suspected hideout in Abbottabad, a highly secure garrison city an hour's drive from the Pakistani capital of Islamabad. Despite all his critics' efforts to compare him to Jimmy Carter, he set aside the very real prospect of a failed commando raid, like the botched hostage rescue of Operation Eagle Claw. The certain success of a bombing raid would have left women and children dead, destroyed priceless intelligence on the ground, and made it impossible to confirm bin Laden's presence. Instead he chose to gamble with the lives of the Navy SEALs and with his own political survival as president and commander in chief. Success meant delivering on one of his biggest promises as a presidential candidate: In addition to improving America's standing in the world, ending combat operations in Iraq and boosting the war in Afghanistan, Obama pledged repeatedly that he would hunt down bin Laden. As a campaign promise, it ranked somewhere between desirable and a dream to many involved in his campaign. As a presidential reality, bin Laden's death prompted late-night celebrations in the streets outside the White House and lifted the spirits of a nation wearied by wars, terror threats, and recession. It also lifted his struggling job approval numbers by almost 10 points.

Obama's cool exterior only broke after the event, as Washington digested the extraordinary end of bin Laden and what the mission said about the commander in chief. One column by the liberal writer E. J. Dionne in the *Washington Post* provoked Obama to a more extended outburst than the moments after bin Laden's death. Under the headline "Who Is Obama? Now We Know," Dionne wrote that the president was "not the man many Americans thought he was." He could be "bold at an operational level, even as he remains cautious at a philosophical level." Obama could barely contain himself. "What was health care? What was the Recovery Act? What was sending more troops to Afghanistan?" he asked his confidants in disbelief. "That wasn't bold enough?" The notion that he was unknown, or unambitious, seemed preposterous to a president who felt he had gambled his career repeatedly over the last two and a half years. The best consolation was to get out of Washington and visit Ground Zero in lower Manhattan, where the streets were crowded with supporters cheering his visit and waving flags. "We should do more days like this," joked one senior aide as they left New York to return to the nation's capital.

Over the last four years, since he started running for president, each successive revival in Obama's fortunes was followed quickly by yet another desperate struggle for survival. The cycle of genius and idiocy rarely ceased. At the heart of the cycle was a president who emerged from analytical contemplation to make his moves frustratingly late, testing the confidence of his staff and supporters alike. It took a historic shellacking to force him—or allow him—to revive the campaign spirit of compromise and reform. Perhaps, after two years in the Oval Office, he was less reliant on the Washington insiders who had cautiously guided his path as president. Much like Dick Cheney, whose influence on President George W. Bush waned after the invasion of Iraq, the Survivalists no longer held the same kind of sway over President Obama after the 2010 defeat.

There was an alternative explanation: that a pragmatic and competitive president was simply shifting toward his own reelection at a time when the country still hungered for Change. Obama would always try to straddle both camps: as an insider and an outsider, he could maintain his elusive quest to be all things to all people for at least one more election. The balance between Survivalist caution and Revivalist risk taking was shifting once again. He had now reached a midpoint between campaigning and governing: after life as a candidate for twenty-one months, he had served just as many months as president by the time of the Democrats' midterm defeat. In another twenty-one months he would accept his party's nomination for the last time. Until then—and until the end of his term—he would be his own work in progress, caught somewhere between his two roles: as Barack Hussein Obama, the candidate and political outsider who advocates for more change, and as the forty-fourth president of the United States, the commander in chief who wants to stay the course. He was stuck somewhere between his political revival and his professional survival.

ACKNOWLEDGMENTS

This book tries to answer what sounds like a straightforward question, first asked by a great journalist friend. On reading the manuscript of *Renegade* in the spring of 2009, she wondered simply, "What I really want to know is: How has he changed?" It was, and remains, a great question. Obama's journey did not end on election day, and he remains far from his destination. But the Obama team traveled so far in such a short period that it was all too easy to lose perspective in the daily whirlpool of political news. So how had life in the West Wing changed the candidate and his team? To answer that question, I needed to draw on the experience of covering the Obama campaign for twenty-one months. But I also needed to lean on the sources who made *Renegade* possible, as well as the team who turned the book into reality.

Revival relies, like its predecessor, on a rolling conversation with its central characters and those associated with them. I am enormously grateful to all those inside and outside the White House who gave their time so generously, and shared their thoughts so freely, to make this book possible. President Obama and Vice President Biden top the list for many reasons, but especially for their forthright and frank interviews. Just as essential was the extensive time spared by the overworked inner circle of David Axelrod, Rahm Emanuel, Robert Gibbs, Valerie Jarrett, and Pete Rouse. I owe a big debt of thanks to the following: on the national security team—John Brennan, James Jones, Denis McDonough, Mike McFaul, and Ben Rhodes; on the political and domestic side— Melody Barnes, Nancy-Ann DeParle, Linda Douglass, and Patrick Gaspard; on the economic team—Ken Baer, Jared Bernstein, Austan Goolsbee, Peter Orszag, Christina Romer, Larry Summers, and Matt Vogel; on the First Lady's team—Camille Johnson, Sam Kass, Katie McCormick Lelyveld, Susan Sher, Semonti Stephens, and Melissa Winter; around the Oval Office—Katie Johnson, Reggie Love, and Brian Mosteller; on the road—Emmett Beliveau, Ben Finkenbinder, Katie Hogan, Katie Lillie, Alyssa Mastromonaco, and Marvin Nicholson; in speechwriting—Jon Favreau and Adam Frankel; in the vice president's office—Tony Blinken, Jay Carney, and Ron Klain; in the West Wing—Kate Herbek, Eric Lesser, Caitlin Naidoff, Darienne Page, and Molly Tranbaugh; on the press team— Amy Brundage, Bill Burton, Reid Cherlin, Josh Earnest, Sarah Feinberg, Marissa Hopkins, Caroline Hughes, Ben LaBolt, Kevin Lewis, Nick Shapiro, Priya Singh, Lauren Thorbjornsen, Tommy Vietor, and Meridith Webster; in the outside world—Joel Benenson, Jim Margolis, and David Plouffe. This book would not have been possible without the support and insights of the communications gurus Anita Dunn, Dan Pfeiffer, and Jen Psaki. My extra-special thanks go to the tirelessly efficient and endlessly patient Lauren Paige.

Outside the White House, I am very grateful to P.J. Crowley at State, Geoff Morrell at Defense, Brendan Daly in Speaker Pelosi's office, and Jill Kozeny in Senator Grassley's office. Several sources asked not to be named in this book, but I am still hugely grateful to them for sharing their insights.

This was the first book I wrote as my main day-to-day occupation, as opposed to squeezing it alongside a full-time job. The book, and its pressing deadlines, were undoubtedly better for that. But I could not have managed professionally or personally without the support and friendship of my surrogate family at MSNBC and NBC. I am honored to be part of the NBC team and deeply grateful to the following: Phil Griffin and Mark Whitaker; Steve Capus and David McCormick; Keith Olbermann and the *Countdown* team, especially Gregg Cockrell, Katy Ramirez Karp, Greg Kordick, Izzy Povich, Amy Shuster, and Rich Stockwell; Chris Matthews and the *Hardball* team, especially Brooke Brower, Colleen King, Ann Klenk, Connie Patsalos, Querry Robinson, and Tina Urbanski; David Gregory and his unrivaled *Meet the Press* team, especially Betsy Fischer and Shelby Poduch; the extraordinary D.C. bureau, especially Andrea Mitchell, Kelly O'Donnell, Norah O'Donnell, Antoine Sanfuentes, Mike Viqueira, and Pete Williams, and the bureau's unsung heroes, especially Vicky Blooston, Patrick Chung, Scott Foster, Alicia Jennings, France Latremoliere, Libby Leist, Alicia Majeed, Domenico Montanaro, Mark Murray, Rose Procopio, Sharon Spurrier, Adam Verdugo, and Bob Witten; the truly dynamic duo of Chuck Todd and Savannah Guthrie, and the White House team of Dennis Gaffney, Athena Jones, Gil Solorzano, and Ali Weinberg; the booking team at 30 Rock, including Sheara Braun, Shanta Covington, Michele Loschiavo, and Lisa Nelson.

At the rollicking Daily Beast, enormous thanks go to Tina Brown, Edward Felsenthal, Jane Frye, and my old Yorkshire pud Tom Watson.

I am very grateful to my friends at Public Strategies, who were hugely supportive and understanding when I walked out the door to write another book, especially Jack Martin, Dan Bartlett, Jeff Eller, Bob Ludke, Mark McKinnon, and Miguel Romano.

My book-writing career would never have begun, never mind gotten this far, without the support, wisdom, talent, and friendship of Kris Dahl at ICM. For her judgment and energy, for her sanity and her humor, for being true and for believing, I will always be grateful beyond measure. A huge thanks also to Laura Neely for going above and beyond the call of duty.

This is the second book I have published with Crown and my superb editor, Sean Desmond. In addition to being a real gentleman and an all-around great guy, Sean is simply the best editor I've ever worked with. From his vision for the book to its thematic shape, he guided me expertly and under intense time pressures. His criticism and edits always improved my work, whether they involved chapter flows or word choices. It was once again an honor and delight to work with him, as well as the entire team at Crown, especially Tina Constable, Julie Cepler, Stephanie Chan, Kelly Gildea, John McElroy, and Campbell Wharton. A special thanks to my outstanding copy editor, Maureen Clark. (To those Amazon reviewers who suggested that the faults of *Renegade* were because of my editors, I have an admission: the faults were all mine.)

In Washington, our friends have been enormously supportive, encouraging, and understanding, despite the added pressures—and absences—that book-writing brings. This book could not have happened without the friendship of Julie Diaz-Asper and Tom Young, Linda Douglass and John Phillips, Tichi Fernandez de la Cruz and José Andrés, Nathalie Goldfarb and José Bassat, Jamie and Edward Hull, Gwen Ifill, Sarah Jessup and James Bennet, Cindy and Todd Klein, Karen Kornbluh and Jim Halpert, Anne Kornblut and Jon Cohen, John McCarthy, Michele Norris and Broderick Johnson, Na-Rae Ohm Petro and Lee Petro, Eser Ozdeger and Tim Schaffer, Monica Pampell, Analia Porras and Charlie Bruetman, Susan Rice and Ian Cameron, John Rice and his basketball gang, Mira Saxena and Miles Fawcett, Katharine Weymouth, Beth Wilkinson and David Gregory, Pary Williamson and Quinn Bradlee, and my ever-optimistic pool sharks. Many thanks to the outstanding faculty at Maret for all their support and guidance, especially Tim Emerson, Holly Hinderlie, Bryan Jones, Julia Lipton, Kathy Sweeney-Hammond, and Marjo Talbott. A special thanks to Tati Espinoza Alfaro and Betty Valdez Beltran for saving us at home.

I cannot thank our families enough for all the love and support they have given so freely for so long. There isn't enough space here to say a full thank-you to all the Wolffes and all the Cuellos, so please know that I love you, admire you, and miss you.

I really don't deserve the love and understanding of my family. When I'm writing, I'm mostly silent, often grumpy, frequently self-absorbed, and almost always distracted. It's not clear I'm much better before or after the writing is done. And yet I could never write, or serve any other useful purpose, without their laughter and tears, their kisses and hugs, their hopes and fears, their stories and spirit. To my monkeys, who can't wait for this to be finished so I can read better books with them; and to Paula, who never thought twice about supporting yet another book, despite her starting a new job: I love you.

SOURCE NOTES

This book is based on my contemporaneous notes of White House events from January to March 2010. It is also based on my notes of covering the Obama campaign from its launch in February 2007 to election night in November 2008. This volume draws heavily on exclusive interviews with several dozen White House officials, congressional staffers, administration officials, and Obama advisers and friends, using a variety of ground rules: on the record, on background, and off the record. Many were kind enough to endure several hours of interviews in multiple sessions, and several showed me copies of notes, memos, e-mails, and presentations that were relevant. Exclusive comments from President Obama include several drawn from interviews during the presidential election, as well as two Oval Office sessions, one of which was dedicated to the subject of this book, on April 22, 2010. My interview with Vice President Biden was held in his West Wing office on July 21, 2010.

In addition, I drew on the following published and broadcast sources in each chapter:

ONE

DESTINATION

Matt Viser, "Rep. Kennedy to Bow Out, Spelling End to Family Era," *Boston Globe*, 2/12/10; Biden speech, San Francisco, 10/18/08, via Politifact.com; John McCormick, "Obama's Mother in New Ad," *Chicago Tribune*, 9/20/07; White House transcript of Remarks by the President in an AARP Tele-Town Hall on Health Care Reform, AARP Headquarters, Washington, D.C., 7/28/09; Sheryl Gay Stolberg and Robert Pear, "Obama Signs Health Care Overhaul Bill, with a Flourish," *New York Times*, 3/23/10; Martin Luther King Jr., edited by James M. Washington, *I Have a Dream: Writings and Speeches That Changed the World* (Harper San Francisco, 1992: pp. 110, 151); Barack Obama, *Dreams from My Father* (Three Rivers Press, 2004: pp. 134–35, 228–30); White House transcript of Remarks by the President at the Acceptance of the Nobel Peace Prize, Oslo City Hall, Oslo, Norway, 12/10/09; Sarah Palin Keynote Speech at National Tea Party Convention, C-SPAN video, 2/6/10; Presidential Proclamation: National African American History Month, 2/1/10.

TWO

TERMINAL

"Different People, Same Message" commercial by Scott Brown campaign, 12/30/09; "Hey, Dad" commercial by Scott Brown campaign, 1/4/10; David Filipov, "In Short Race, Coakley Picks Targets Carefully," *Boston Globe*, 1/13/10; Washington Wire, "Foul Ball: Coakley Calls Schilling 'Another Yankee Fan,'" *Wall Street Journal*, 1/16/10; Dan Balz and Haynes Johnson, *The Battle for America 2008* (Viking, 2009: pp. 30–32); *Morning Joe*, MSNBC, 1/19/10; Reid Wilson, "Frank: Health Care Compromise 'Dead,'" *Hotline*, 1/20/10; Federal News Service transcript, Press Conference with Senate Minority Leader Mitch McConnell, Senator John Cornyn, Senator Judd Gregg, Senator Lisa Murkowski,

1/20/10; *Hardball with Chris Matthews*, MSNBC, 1/19/10; Fred Barnes, "The Health Care Bill Is Dead," *The Weekly Standard*, 1/20/10; White House transcript, Remarks by the President in Town Hall Meeting on Health Care, 6/11/09; White House video, *The Urgency of Reform—Laura in Green Bay*, 9/9/09; David D. Kirkpatrick, "Drug Industry to Run Ads Favoring White House Plan," *New York Times*, 8/8/09; Anne Kornblut, "For Obama's Political Knots, He's the 'Fixer,'" *Washington Post*, 2/21/09; Jeffrey Young, "Baucus, Kennedy to Huddle on Healthcare," *The Hill*, 11/17/08; David M. Herszenhorn and Robert Pear, "Health Policy Is Carved Out at Table for 6," *New York Times*, 7/29/09; *Morning Edition*, National Public Radio transcript, 7/29/09; Carl Hulse and Adam Nagourney, "Senate GOP Leader Finds Weapon in Unity," *New York Times*, 3/16/10; Peter Baker, "What Happened? The Limits of Rahmism," *New York Times*, 3/14/10; Baird Helgeson and Michelle Bearden, "Senator Set to Intensify Investigation of Ministries," *Tampa Tribune*, 2/8/08; Jason Hancock, "Grassley: Government Shouldn't 'Decide When to Pull the Plug on Grandma,'" *Iowa Independent*, 8/12/09; White House transcript, Remarks by the President to a Joint Session of Congress on Health Care, 9/9/09; White House, Guest List for the First Lady's Box at Tonight's Joint Session of Congress, 9/9/09; Jessica Van Sack, "Martha's Fall Blamed on 'Ignorant' Respite," *Boston Herald*, 1/15/10; Lori Montgomery and Michael D. Shear, "White House Nears Deal on Health Care," *Washington Post*, 1/15/10.

THREE
REDEMPTION

White House transcript, Remarks by the President at Signing of Memorandum on Childhood Obesity, 2/9/10; White House transcript, Remarks by the President Before Meeting with Bipartisan Leaders of the House and Senate, 2/9/10; White House transcript, News Conference by the President, 2/9/10; Ryan Lizza, "The Gatekeeper; Rahm Emanuel on the Job," *The New Yorker*,

3/2/09; David Plouffe, *The Audacity to Win* (Viking, 2009: pp. 22–24, 103, 321–22, 382); White House transcripts of Bipartisan Meeting on Health Care Reform, 2/25/10; transcript of press conference by Nancy Pelosi, 2/26/10; White House release of Text of the Letter from Natoma Canfield to President Obama and the President's Response, 3/4/10; White House transcript, Remarks by the President on Health Care Reform, 3/3/10; White House transcript, Remarks by the President on Health Insurance Reform, 3/8/10; White House transcript, Remarks by the President on Health Insurance Reform in Fairfax, Virginia, 3/19/10; Kendra Marr, "Obama recalled Laura Klitzka, others," Politico, 3/22/10; White House transcript, Remarks by the President at Grassroots Fundraising Reception for Senator McCaskill, 3/10/10; Robert Wang, "Boccieri Skips Obama's Health Care Speech in Ohio," *Canton Repository*, 3/15/10; White House transcript, Remarks by the President on Health Insurance Reform, 3/15/10; Rick Klein and Byron Wolf, "Kucinich a 'Yes' on Health Care; First Dem to Switch from 'No,'" ABCNews.com, 3/17/10; David Herszenhorn and Robert Pear, "Obama Delays Trip as Report Aids Final Push on Health Care," *New York Times*, 3/17/10; Alan Fram and Ricardo Alonso-Zaldivar, "Obama's Health Care Plan Picks up Support," Associated Press, 3/17/10; David Herszenhorn, "Boccieri to Vote Yes," *New York Times*, 3/19/10; CNN coverage of John Boccieri press conference, 3/19/10; The American Presidency Project (University of California, Santa Barbara), "Ronald Reagan: Remarks at a Wreath-Laying Ceremony at the Lincoln Memorial," 2/12/81.

FOUR
RECOVERY

Michael Grabell and Jennifer LaFleur, "Government Wrongly Labels Some Stimulus Recipients 'Losers,'" ProPublica, 3/8/10; Kate Phillips, "Scuffles over Stimulus Projects," *New York Times*, 6/16/09; White House transcript of Remarks by the President on Financial Reform, 1/21/10; Roberta Rampton,

"Hedge Fund Paid Obama Adviser Summers $5.2 Million," Reuters, 4/6/09; David Cho, "White House Eyes Bailout Funds to Aid Small Firms," *Washington Post*, 7/11/09; Anne Paine, "TVA fined $11.5 Million for Coal Ash Spill," *The Tennessean*, 6/15/10; Shaila Dewan, "EPA's Plan to Regulate Coal Ash Draws Criticism," *New York Times*, 5/4/10; Christina Romer and Jared Bernstein, "The Job Impact of the American Recovery and Reinvestment Plan," 1/9/09; William Douglas and David Lightman, "Earmarks Reform? 2009 Spending Bill Contains 9,000 of Them," McClatchy Newspapers, 2/22/09; J. Taylor Rushing, "Gregg Calls for Re-Vote on Fiscal Panel," *The Hill*, 2/3/10; Joel Achenbach, "NASA Budget for 2011 Eliminates Funds for Manned Lunar Missions," *Washington Post*, 2/1/10; Tony Romm, "Obama to Reboot NASA Budget; Shelby Fires Warning Shot," *The Hill*, 4/14/10; White House transcript of Remarks by the President to House Democratic Caucus, 3/20/10; David Brooks, "McCain and Obama," *New York Times*, 1/8/08; David Brooks, "The Broken Society," *New York Times*, 3/18/10; Christopher Beam, "A Reasonable Man," *New York*, 7/4/10; Carl Hulse, "Senate Approves $15 Billion Jobs Bill," *New York Times*, 2/24/10; Ben Pership, "Reid, Baucus Unveil New $150B Jobs Bill," *Washington Post*, 3/1/10; Brian Montopoli, "Jobs Bill Signed into Law by Obama," CBSNews.com, 3/18/10; White House transcript of Remarks by the President Before Signing the HIRE Act, 3/18/10.

FIVE

SURVIVAL

Deborah Sontag, "Haiti Emerges from Its Shock, and Tears Roll," *New York Times*, 1/14/10; Deborah Sontag, "In Haiti the Displaced Are Left Clinging to the Edge," *New York Times*, 7/10/10; Henry Fountain, "A Deadly Quake in a Seismic Hot Zone," *New York Times*, 1/25/10; MSNBC transcript of interview of President George W. Bush by Brian Williams, 12/12/05; White House transcript of final press conference by President George W. Bush, 1/12/09; Scott

Shane, Mark Mazzetti, and Helene Cooper, "Obama Reverses Key Bush Security Policies," *New York Times*, 1/22/09; Scott Shane, "Detainee's Case Illustrates 'Bind of Prison's Fate," *New York Times*, 10/4/09; David Herszenhorn, "Funds to Close Guantánamo Denied," *New York Times*, 5/20/09; Mark Mazzetti and Scott Shane, "Interrogation Memos Detail Harsh Tactics by the CIA," *New York Times*, 4/16/09; Scott Wilson, "Obama Shifts on Abuse Photos," *Washington Post*, 5/14/09; Statement of Senator Barack Obama on FISA Compromise, Obama campaign e-mail, 6/20/08; Anne E. Kornblut and Dafna Linzer, "White House Regroups on Guantánamo; Counsel Craig Replaced as Point Man on Issue as Deadline for Closing Looms," *Washington Post*, 9/25/09; Peter Baker, "Inside Obama's War on Terrorism," *New York Times*, 1/17/10; Dana Hughes and Kirit Radia, "Underwear Bomber's Alarming Last Phone Call," ABC News, 12/31/09; Eric Lipton, Eric Schmitt, and Mark Mazzetti, "Review of Jet Bomb Plot Shows More Missed Clues," *New York Times*, 1/17/10; White House transcript, Statement by the President on Preliminary Information from His Ongoing Consultations About the Detroit Incident, 12/29/09; White House release, Message from the President to the CIA Workforce, 12/31/09; White House transcript, Remarks by the President on Strengthening Intelligence and Aviation Security, 1/7/10; Peter Bergen and Katherine Tiedemann, "The Year of the Drone," New America Foundation, 2/24/10; Phil Stewart and Robert Birsel, "Analysis: Under Obama, Drone Attacks on the Rise in Pakistan," Reuters, 10/12/09; Mike Allen, "Dick Cheney: Barack Obama 'Trying to Pretend,'" Politico, 12/30/09; Walter Pincus and Carrie Johnson, "Interagency Teams Can Now Question Terror Suspects," *Washington Post*, 2/6/10; John Brennan, "We Need No Lectures," *USA Today*, 2/9/10; Mark Mazzetti and Dexter Filkins, "Secret Joint Raid Captures Taliban's Top Commander," *New York Times*, 2/15/10; Rajiv Chandrasekaran, "U.S. Launches Afghan Surge," *Washington Post*, 2/13/10; C. J. Chivers and Rod Nordland, "Errant Rocket Kills Civilians in Afghanistan," *New York Times*, 2/15/10; Bob Woodward, "McChrystal: More Forces or 'Mission Failure,'" *Washington Post*, 9/21/09; Peter Baker, "How Obama Came to Plan for 'Surge' in Afghanistan,"

New York Times, 12/5/09; John F. Burns, "McChrystal Rejects Scaling Down Afghan Military Aims," *New York Times*, 10/1/09; White House transcript, Remarks of the President on The Way Forward in Afghanistan and Pakistan, 12/1/09; Michael Fletcher, "Obama in Dover as Fallen Troops Arrive Home," *Washington Post*, 10/29/09; Barack Obama, "My Plan for Iraq," *New York Times*, 7/14/08; Peter Baker and Thom Shanker, "Obama Meets with Officials on Iraq, Signaling His Commitment to Ending War," *New York Times*, 1/21/09; Peter Baker, "With Pledges to Troops and Iraqis, Obama Details Pullout," *New York Times*, 2/27/09; Joseph R. Biden and Leslie H. Gelb, "Unity Through Autonomy in Iraq," *New York Times*, 5/1/06; Michael A. Fletcher and Philip P. Pan, "US and Russia to Reduce Arsenals," *Washington Post*, 7/7/09; Nicholas Kulish and Ellen Barry, "Romanians Accept Plan for Basing of Missiles," *New York Times*, 2/4/10; White House transcript, Remarks by President Obama and President Medvedev of Russia at New START Treaty Signing Ceremony and Press Conference, 4/8/10; Michael D. Shear and Andrew Higgins, "Citing Health-care Vote, Obama Delays Trip to Indonesia," *Washington Post*, 3/19/10; Ethan Bronner, "As Biden Visits, Israel Unveils Plan for New Settlements," *New York Times*, 3/9/10; Glenn Kessler, "Clinton Rebukes Israel over East Jerusalem Plans, Cites Damage to Bilateral Ties," *Washington Post*, 3/13/10; White House transcript, Remarks by President Obama and President Préval of the Republic of Haiti, 3/10/10.

SIX

DEADLOCK

Michael Hastings, "The Runaway General," *Rolling Stone*, 6/22/10; Rajiv Chandrasekaran, "'Still a Long Way to Go' for U.S. Operation in Marja, Afghanistan," *Washington Post*, 6/10/10; White House transcript, Remarks by the President on Comprehensive Immigration Reform, 7/1/10.

INDEX

Axelrod, David (*continued*)
  on Obama's relations with aides and
    staff, 5
  Plouffe compared with, 307–308
  presidential campaign of 2008, 54,
    111, 112, 114, 115
  presidential campaign of 2012, 292,
    314, 316
  strategic focus of Obama administra-
    tion, 113–114, 116–117, 295–296
  terrorist threat, Obama's approach to,
    232–233, 236

Bachmann, Michele, 198
Baez, Joan, 48
Baia, Ashley, 24–25
Baker, Howard, 106
Banking system reform, 170–173, 306–307
Banks, Leslie, 136, 138
Baradar, Mullah Abdul Ghani, 237
Barbour, Haley, 285
Barnes, Fred, 58
Barnes, Melody, 91
Barton, Joe, 122–123
Baucus, Max, 67–68, 70–71, 73–74
Bauer, Bob, 226, 278, 306
Beck, Glenn, 193–194
Benenson, Joel, 115, 290
Bennet, Michael, 291–292
Bernstein, Jared, 178
Biden, Joe, 2, 101, 124, 185, 190
  Afghanistan war
    Marja offensive, 281
    McChrystal's replacement, 280–281
    strategy review, 242–244
  Cameron and, 282
  economic stimulus package
    big infrastructure projects and,
      166–167
    Clinton crime bill and, 162–163
    electoral politics and, 284–285
    first anniversary press event,
      153–155
    fraud and stupidity, efforts to
      prevent, 164–166
    White House's communication re-
      garding, 160–161, 162–163

financial regulatory reform, 171
health care reform, 14–16, 17, 22, 86,
  122, 123
Iraq war, 250–253
Israeli-Palestinian peace process,
  265–267, 268
McConnell and, 298–299
presidential campaign of 2008, 15, 163
vice presidential role, 163
Bin Laden, Osama, 317–318
Blackburn, Marsha, 106
Blinken, Tony, 250, 251, 265
Boccieri, John, 140, 141–142, 295
Boehner, John, 91–93, 122, 123, 125, 180,
  310
Bond, Kit, 237
Boren, David, 216
Boucher, Rick, 291
Bowles, Erskine, 185, 186, 187
Boxer, Barbara, 165
BP oil spill disaster, 276–279, 282
Branch, Taylor, 35
Brennan, John, 228–231, 233, 234, 236,
  237, 310
Brooks, David, 194–195
Brown, Scott, 6, 52, 55, 56, 81
Browner, Carol, 277, 278
Burger, Anna, 77
Burr, Richard, 315
Burris, Roland, 11
Bush, George H. W., 257, 276
Bush, George W., 36, 105, 115–116, 159,
  208–209, 214–215, 218, 243, 247,
  257, 263, 287, 319

Cable TV culture, 198–199
Cameron, David, 282–283
Canfield, Natoma, 22, 131–132, 134, 138,
  140, 141–142, 149
Cao, Joseph, 201
Carney, Jay, 308
Carter, Jimmy, 212, 317
Casey, Bob, 136
Central Intelligence Agency (CIA), 216,
  217, 219–220, 230, 231, 232, 236,
  317
Chamber of Commerce, U.S., 306

Dudley, Bob, 278, 279
Dunham, Madelyn, 16, 19
Dunham, Stanley Ann, 18–20, 34, 123–124
Dunn, Anita, 108, 109, 116, 133
Dylan, Bob, 48

Earmark reform, 183–184
Earthquake in Haiti, 203–208, 269–271
Economic stimulus package, 26, 299
    big infrastructure projects and,
        166–167
    clean energy industry and, 156
    crime bill of 1994 and, 162–163
    electoral politics and, 284–285
    first anniversary press event, 153–156
    fraud and stupidity, efforts to prevent,
        164–166
    Obama's collaboration with governors
        on, 190–191
    political pressure to concentrate
        on jobs, 181–183
    public skepticism about, 158–159
    Reagan's experience and, 161–162
    Republican opposition, 157–158,
        180–181
    size of package, 177–179
    TARP and, 159
    unemployment and, 156–157, 159, 177,
        179–180, 182–183
    wealthy Obama supporters and, 161
    White House's communication re-
        garding, 157, 160–161, 162–163,
        178
    White House's sense of urgency, 159
Economic team of Obama administration,
        167–170, 176–177, 310
Edwards, John, 95, 150
Egypt, 311–313
Eikenberry, Karl, 239
Electricity grid upgrade, 166
Electronic surveillance, 221–222
Emancipation Proclamation, 36
Emanuel, Ari, 62
Emanuel, Rahm, 96, 148, 195, 200, 256,
        263, 266, 276, 290
    arms control, 258, 259
    BP oil spill, 279

chief of staff position, 99–100, 101, 103
congressional career, 99, 102
Craig and, 225–226
deficit reduction and spending re-
    form, 283
economic stimulus package, 177–178,
    182
economic team, 168
health care reform
    bipartisanship and, 70–71
    Emanuel's responsibility for prob-
        lems, 55–56
    House passage of Senate bill,
        86–87, 139, 140
    House-Senate reconciliation of
        bills, 55, 80–81
    Obama-Emanuel differences re-
        garding, 103–104
    Obama's meeting with House
        Republicans, 105
    smaller-scale approach, proposals
        for, 82–83, 86
    White House strategy, 61–63
immigration reform, 285–286
insecurity of, 101–102
Massachusetts Senate election, 55
Obama's relationship with, 101–104
personal qualities of, 97–98, 296, 308
on public service, 98, 99
on Republican extremism, 276
strategic focus of Obama administra-
    tion, 113, 114, 116, 117, 299
transition of administrations, 100
Emanuel, Zeke, 10, 61–62, 83
Emerson, Ralph Waldo, 146
Energy policy, 93, 156
Environmental regulation, 175–176
Enzi, Mike, 68, 124

Fattah, Chaka, 136
Favreau, Jon, 38, 40, 42, 43, 46, 72, 150
Financial regulatory reform, 170–173,
    306–307
Finney, Karen, 308
Fiscal commission, 92, 185–188
Foreign policy, Obama's approach to,
    208–213

McCain, John, 28–29, 122, 123, 124,
    126–127, 209, 218, 223, 244,
    262, 301
McCaskill, Claire, 139, 283
McChrystal, Gen. Stanley, 38, 239,
    240–241, 242, 280–281
McConnell, Mike, 216
McConnell, Mitch, 57, 69, 71–72, 92–93,
    122, 123, 124–125, 298–299, 310
McDonnell, Bob, 190
McDonough, Denis, 38, 204–206, 208,
    240, 253, 311, 314
McFaul, Michael, 257, 259, 311
McGinnis, Ross A., 248
Media coverage of politics, 198–199
Medvedev, Dmitri, 257, 259–260
Messina, Jim, 67, 116, 290
Milbank, Dana, 117
Military commissions, 222, 223
Mills, Cheryl, 254–255
Mitchell, George, 265, 266
Mohammed, Khalid Sheikh, 227–228
Moynihan, Daniel Patrick, 66
Mubarak, Hosni, 311–313
Mullen, Adm. Mike, 239
Murphy, Patrick, 295
Muslim world, Obama's outreach to, 211

NASA, 189
National security, Obama's approach to,
    213–215
National Security Council, 244–245
NCAA basketball championship, 142–143
Nelson, Ben, 75, 109
Nesbitt, Marty, 7, 36, 42, 60, 283
Netanyahu, Benjamin, 263, 265, 266–267,
    268
Niebuhr, Reinhold, 40, 41
Nobel Peace Prize, 37–46, 256, 257
Nuclear weapons, 210, 212, 256–260, 264

Obama, Barack, 97
    Abu Ghraib prison photos, 220–221
    Afghanistan war
        Marja offensive, 238, 240, 244,
            248–249, 281
        McChrystal's replacement, 280

Obama's interest in real experi-
    ence of war, 247–249
Obama's Nobel Peace Prize and,
    38, 39, 41
strategy review, 238–242, 243
aides and staff, relations with, 5,
    293–294, 296, 306
ambitions as president, 60–61
American music concerts, 47–49
arms control, 210, 212, 256–260
BP oil spill, 276–277, 278–279, 282
Cameron and, 282–283
childhood obesity program, 90–91
civil rights movement and, 23, 30–37,
    299, 303
Clinton's relationship with, 254–255,
    302
communication of his message,
    108–109, 111, 118
communitarian philosophy, 194–197
community organizing work, 29–30
deficit reduction and spending reform,
    92, 183–187, 188–190, 283
diary of, 145–147
drone attacks in Pakistan, 234
economic stimulus package
    clean energy industry and, 156
    first anniversary press event,
        153–154, 155–156
    fraud and stupidity, efforts to pre-
        vent, 164
    Obama's collaboration with gov-
        ernors on, 190–191
    political pressure to concentrate
        on jobs, 181–182
economic team, 168, 169–170, 177, 310
economic worldview of, 194–197
Egyptian revolution, 311–312
electronic surveillance, 221–222
Emanuel's relationship with, 101–104
Emanuel's selection as chief of staff,
    99–100
emotional displays by, 15–16, 295, 317,
    318
energy policy, 93, 156
ethics reform in Congress, 191–192
faith, reliance on, 34

political character of, 94–96
on political degeneration in America, 197–198
Senate career, 191
"socialist" charge against, 194
space program, 188–89
State of the Union speech, 87
strategic focus of his administration, 111–118
tax credit for small businesses to hire new workers, 173
terrorist detainees, handling of, 217–219, 222–225, 227–228
terrorist threat, approach to, 228–238
torture memos of Bush administration, 219–220
torture policy, 215–217
Veterans Day commemorations, 248
war justification, 44–45
See also Presidential campaign of 2008
Obama, Michelle, 43, 48, 54–55, 63, 129, 150
childhood obesity program, 90–91
Odierno, Gen. Ray, 221
Oil spill of 2010, 276–279, 282
Orszag, Peter, 169, 176, 190, 200, 284
Owens, Marcelas, 22

Pakistan, 208, 234, 242, 246, 317–318
Palestinians, 263–269
Palin, Sarah, 2, 47, 198, 300, 316
Panetta, Leon, 219–220
Parker, Theodore, 37
Patient Protection and Affordable Care Act. *See* Health care reform
Pearl, Danny, 227
Pelosi, Nancy, 17, 21, 77–78, 79, 80, 83, 86, 92, 122, 125–126, 128–129, 143, 148
Pence, Mike, 107
Perriello, Tom, 142, 291, 295
Petraeus, Gen. David, 220, 241–242, 280
Pfeiffer, Dan, 58–59, 87, 105, 109, 116, 132, 133, 147, 150, 161, 187, 198–199, 207, 237, 246–247, 290, 291, 292, 296, 301
Plouffe, David, 101, 108, 111–112, 113, 115,

116, 133, 275, 290, 291, 292, 296, 301
Podesta, John, 100, 101
Political degeneration in America, 197–199
Power, Samantha, 42, 311
Presidential campaign of 2008, 1–2, 4, 31, 133, 206, 273
Afghanistan war and, 242, 247–248
Biden's role, 163
Change theme, 25, 26–27, 114–115, 316, 319
contradictory character, 28–29
conventional politics used in, 109–110
"fierce urgency" theme, 22–23
foreign policy issues, 209, 210, 211
health care reform and, 18–19, 24–25, 27, 150
Iraq war and, 249
Kennedy's endorsement, 13, 286
low points during primaries, 53, 82
national security issues, 215, 221–222
Obama's political character and, 95–96
Obama's toughness for, 15, 54
photo ops, 181
Plouffe's role, 111–112
superdelegates and, 139
Préval, René, 269
Putin, Vladimir, 257

Ralston, Jason, 115
Rasmussen, Scott, 52
Reagan, Ronald, 61, 145, 161–162, 192–193, 257, 276
Recovery Act. *See* Economic stimulus package
Reid, Harry, 17, 74–75, 86, 92, 122, 123, 126, 127, 128, 143–144, 219, 291, 292
Reinstein, Joe, 11–12
Rendell, Ed, 136, 190
Revivalist group, 94–95, 116, 118, 176, 225, 285, 294, 305, 311, 319
Rhodes, Ben, 38, 40, 42–43, 72, 205, 210, 212, 238, 239, 240, 269, 311
Rice, Susan, 311, 312
Road to Serfdom, The (Hayek), 194

ALSO BY
RICHARD WOLFFE

$16.00 PAPERBACK (CANADA: $19.00)
978-0-307-46313-5

Based on Wolffe's unprecedented access to Barack Obama, *Renegade*
reveals the making of a president, both on the campaign trail and before he ran for high office. From a teacher's office in Iowa to the Oval
Office in Washington, we see and hear Barack Obama with an imme-
diacy and honesty never witnessed before. This book is the previously
untold and epic story of how a political newcomer with no money
and an alien name grew into the world's most powerful leader.

**"A thoughtful meditation on Mr. Obama's
life and character."**
—Michiko Kakutani, *New York Times*

**"An insightful, unusually moving,
fully observed portrait . . . Marvelous."**
—Ken Burns

AVAILABLE FROM BROADWAY PAPERBACKS WHEREVER BOOKS ARE SOLD